The Invention of Market Freedom

How did the value of freedom become so closely associated with the institution of the market? Why did the idea of market freedom hold so little appeal before the modern period, and how can we explain its rise to dominance? In *The Invention of Market Freedom*, Eric MacGilvray addresses these questions by contrasting the market conception of freedom with the republican view that it displaced. After analyzing the ethical core and exploring the conceptual complexity of republican freedom, MacGilvray shows how this way of thinking was confronted with, altered in response to, and finally was overcome by the rise of modern market societies. By learning to see market freedom as something that was *invented*, we can become more alert to the ways in which the appeal to freedom shapes and distorts our thinking about politics today.

Eric MacGilvray is Assistant Professor of Political Science at Ohio State University. He is the author of *Reconstructing Public Reason* and of articles in a number of leading journals.

The Invention of Market Freedom

ERIC MACGILVRAY

Ohio State University

CAMBRIDGE UNIVERSITY PRESS
Cambridge, New York, Melbourne, Madrid, Cape Town,
Singapore, São Paulo, Delhi, Tokyo, Mexico City

Cambridge University Press
32 Avenue of the Americas, New York, NY 10013-2473, USA

www.cambridge.org
Information on this title: www.cambridge.org/9780521171892

First published 2011

Printed in the United States of America

A catalog record for this publication is available from the British Library.

Library of Congress Cataloging in Publication data
MacGilvray, Eric, 1971–
    The invention of market freedom / Eric MacGilvray.
      p.   cm.
    Includes bibliographical references and index.
    ISBN 978-1-107-00136-7 (hardback) – ISBN 978-0-521-17189-2 (pb)
    1. Liberty.   2. Republicanism.   3. Liberty – Economic aspects.
    4. Economics – Moral and ethical aspects.   5. Capitalism – Moral
    and ethical aspects.   I. Title.
    JC585.M435   2011
    330.12'2–dc22   2010046721

ISBN 978-1-107-00136-7 Hardback
ISBN 978-0-521-17189-2 Paperback

For Karen

His safety must his liberty restrain:
All join to guard what each desires to gain.
Forc'd into virtue thus by Self-defence,
Ev'n Kings learn'd justice and benevolence:
Self-love forsook the path it first pursued,
And found the private in the public good.

Alexander Pope

You pays your money and you takes your choice.

Punch

Contents

Acknowledgments

This is a very different book from the one that I set out to write, and I am indebted to a large and diverse community of scholars who shared not only their expertise but, more importantly, their confidence and encouragement along the way.

My most immediate debts are to Sonja Amadae, Jennifer Mitzen, and Michael Neblo, my splendid colleagues at Ohio State, who made up an *ad hoc* reading group before which many of the arguments that follow were first aired. Their constructive but candid (or candid but constructive) comments proved crucial at several important points. Special thanks are also due to my former colleague Clarissa Hayward and my new colleague Piers Turner, who offered helpful advice at the early and late stages of writing, respectively.

Bentley Allan, Bruce Baum, Corey Brettschneider, Barbara Buckinx, Doug Dow, Lisa Ellis, Chad Flanders, Michael Frazer, Ted Harpham, Leigh Jenco, Dan Kapust, Steven Kelts, Jessica Kimpell, Stephen Leonard, Jacob Levy, Steven Lukes, Patchen Markell, John McCormick, Russ Muirhead, Cary Nederman, Philip Pettit, Amit Ron, Inés Valdez, and Alex Wendt provided invaluable feedback on points large and small. I accept full responsibility for the errors that remain despite their efforts, and also (though more reluctantly) for any names that I have inadvertently omitted from this list.

Preliminary work on this project was done during a sabbatical year as Sesquicentenary Fellow in the Discipline of Government and International Relations at the University of Sydney, Australia, and I thank my colleagues there once again for helping to make my stay such a pleasant and productive one. Early material was presented both at Sydney and at the

University of Wisconsin–Madison, and I am grateful to the audiences on those occasions, and in particular to Rick Avramenko and Richard Boyd, my former colleagues at Wisconsin, for their thoughtful feedback.

Portions of the book were presented more recently at the annual meetings of the Midwest, Western, and American Political Science Associations; the Association for Political Theory; and the European Consortium for Political Research, and before audiences at the University of British Columbia, the University of Minnesota, the University of Rochester, and Texas A&M University. Thanks are due to the respondents and audiences on those occasions for their comments.

The Department of Political Science at Ohio State has been generous with research support, and I would like to thank Justin Acome, Bentley Allan, Emilie Becault, Erin Graham, Eric Grynaviski, Dennis Johnson, and Amy Ovecka in particular for their assistance, without which this study would have taken much longer to complete. Lew Bateman, Anne Lovering Rounds, and the production team at Cambridge University Press were models of graciousness and efficiency.

The book is dedicated to my wife, Karen, who has been my constant companion through the seven long years that I have been working on it – years that encompassed, among other things, three moves and the birth of our second child. Without her love and support, and that of my beautiful daughters, I never would have made it to the end. Thank you, lucky stars!

Introduction

Republicanism and the Market

> A study of the history of opinion is a necessary preliminary to the emancipation of the mind.
>
> John Maynard Keynes, "The End of Laissez-Faire"

One of the most striking and far-reaching transformations that has taken place in modern political thought concerns the use of the word "freedom." Once used to distinguish the members of a social and political elite from those – women, slaves, serfs, menial laborers, and foreigners – who did not enjoy their privileges or share their ethos, the term is now typically used to refer to the unregulated and unsupervised behavior of individuals, especially, though not exclusively, in the market. So complete is this shift in usage that the phrase "free market" sounds almost redundant to our ears, and the "libertarian," the partisan of liberty, is generally understood to be a person who favors the extension of market norms and practices into nearly all areas of life. Thus the language of freedom, which was once highly moralized and fundamentally inegalitarian, is now fundamentally (if only formally) egalitarian and has been largely drained of moral content: Freedom, in colloquial terms, means doing as one likes and allowing others to do likewise. Moreover, where the enjoyment of freedom was once thought to depend on the existence of a carefully designed and highly fragile set of formal and informal institutions, the uncoordinated actions of free individuals are now said to be capable of generating "spontaneous order" – again, especially, though not exclusively, through the mechanism of the market.[1] These dramatic

---

[1] The claim that complex and efficient social systems can arise spontaneously from the free choices of individuals is most closely associated today with the thought of Friedrich

changes in usage are of more than merely historical interest, because freedom has over the same period of time become one of the most potent words in our political vocabulary, and the effort to expand the use of the market as a means of realizing social outcomes has greatly intensified, especially in recent decades. Indeed, it seems likely that these developments are related; that the widespread and growing influence of market ideology depends in part on its ability to speak in the language and with the authority of freedom.

In this book I seek to explain how the market came to hold such a privileged place in modern thinking about freedom. I do this by contrasting this market-centered way of thinking with the older view, rooted in the tradition of republican political thought, that it largely displaced. Republican freedom makes a natural foil in this inquiry for at least two reasons. First, it is the republican tradition to which the partisan of freedom (or liberty – I will use the terms interchangeably) would necessarily have appealed throughout most of the political history of the West. It follows that any gains that have been made by market freedom in the modern period have come at the expense of the republican view, and that a natural place to begin in trying to account for the state of current debates about freedom is by examining how the republican conception of freedom was confronted with, altered in response to, and finally was overcome by the spread of market norms and practices. Second, there has been an explosion of scholarly interest in republican thought over the last several decades, and as a result its ethical and institutional entailments have now been thoroughly explored in a contemporary idiom. We are therefore in a better position than ever to explore the relationship between republican and market freedom without falling into anachronism.[2]

Hayek; see especially the first volume of his *Law, Legislation and Liberty* (Chicago: University of Chicago Press, 1973). Hayek himself credits the idea that social order can be "the result of human action but not of human design" to Adam Ferguson: ibid., p. 20; cf. Adam Ferguson, *An Essay on the History of Civil Society* (1767), ed. Fania Oz-Salzberger (New York: Cambridge University Press, 1995), p. 119 (part 3, section 2).

[2] The most sophisticated and influential defense of republicanism in recent years is found in Philip Pettit's *Republicanism: A Theory of Freedom and Government* (2nd ed., New York: Oxford University Press, 1999 [1997]), although Pettit expresses some diffidence on the question of whether his analysis is or needs be faithful to the historical republican tradition. Other notable statements include Michael J. Sandel, *Democracy's Discontent: America in Search of a Public Philosophy* (Cambridge, MA: Harvard University Press, 1996); Richard Dagger, *Civic Virtues: Rights, Citizenship, and Republican Liberalism* (New York: Oxford University Press, 1997); Maurizio Viroli, *Republicanism* (New York: Hill & Wang, 1999); Iseult Honohan, *Civic Republicanism* (New York: Routledge, 2002); and John W. Maynor, *Republicanism in the Modern World* (Cambridge, UK: Polity Press, 2003). Highlights

The defenders of republican and market freedom ask us to imagine two ideal worlds: one in which independent and autonomous citizens devote themselves to the good of the community, and one in which the common good is realized through the voluntary exchange of goods and services among individuals, and each person's ability to pursue his or her own ends therefore depends in a very literal sense on the ends of others. A republican politics aims at genuinely collective control over social outcomes; an ideal market society is one in which social outcomes are determined as far as possible by the market itself and are therefore the product of an indefinite number of self-interested decisions by people who are unknown and therefore unaccountable to one another. Each of these ideals has its own attractions and poses its own problems, and the contrast between them raises a number of questions about the meaning of the word freedom, the value that we assign (or should assign) to being free, and the role that the appeal to freedom plays in organizing political thinking and guiding political action. What reasons do we have for valuing freedom, and what are the necessary conditions for its enjoyment? Why did the idea of market freedom hold so little appeal before the modern period, and how can we explain its rise to dominance? What is the relationship between republican and market freedom today: Are they contradictory to, merely compatible with, or in some way dependent on or complementary of one another? Can these kinds of freedom be pursued at the same time, and to the extent that they cannot, why is this? Which of them, or which combination of them, provides the most attractive and feasible model of social and political life?

My aim in raising these questions is not to demonstrate the superiority of one of these kinds of freedom to the other, or to argue that we must somehow choose between them. Rather, I am motivated by a more specific practical concern. To the extent that the defenders of "market solutions" to pressing social and political problems have succeeded in monopolizing the language of freedom – a development that is peculiar to Western, and perhaps more specifically to Anglo-American, political thought – they enjoy a rhetorical advantage in public discourse that

of the now vast historical literature include Bernard Bailyn, *The Ideological Origins of the American Revolution* (Cambridge, MA: Harvard University Press, 1967); Gordon S. Wood, *The Creation of the American Republic, 1776–1787* (New York: W. W. Norton, 1969); J. G. A. Pocock, *The Machiavellian Moment: Florentine Political Thought and the Atlantic Republican Tradition* (Princeton, NJ: Princeton University Press, 1975); Quentin Skinner, *The Foundations of Modern Political Thought* (New York: Cambridge University Press, 1978), vol. 1, and idem, *Liberty before Liberalism* (New York: Cambridge University Press, 1998).

exaggerates the actual merits of their proposals, as great as these may be. By learning to see market freedom as something that was (like republican freedom itself) *invented* – by treating it as the contingent product of a particular set of material and ideological circumstances – I hope that we can become more alert to the various ways in which the appeal to freedom shapes and distorts our thinking about politics today. By paying attention to the various ways in which republican and market freedom can reinforce and undermine each other, I hope that we can become better able to judge the relative merits of allowing a given range of social outcomes to be determined by political or economic means without the heavy thumb of freedom weighing on only one side of the scale. In the broadest sense, then, the aim of this book is a very traditional one: to look to the past in order to see the present more clearly.

I.I. THE PROBLEM OF CONSTRAINT

Any discussion of the meaning and value of freedom has to begin by coming to terms with the bewildering range of meanings that the concept has assumed both in popular and in scholarly discourse. The existence of this kaleidoscope of meanings is due in part to the fact that freedom is one of the most potent words in our political vocabulary: Political actors often begin with the assumption that freedom is, after security, the first public good to be pursued and then go on to define the word in such a way that it can be associated with whatever policies they happen to favor – often ruling out competing definitions as confused or illegitimate in the process. We are therefore faced with the familiar spectacle of different people appealing to the same ideal, or at least the same vocabulary, to defend widely divergent courses of action: Franklin Roosevelt invoking the "four freedoms" to defend the New Deal; Ronald Reagan opposing the Great Society with the warning that "freedom is never more than one generation away from extinction"; Donald Rumsfeld responding to the widespread looting in postwar Iraq with the memorable observation that "stuff happens" in a free society.

Here already there is a fundamental contrast between modern and pre-modern usage. To describe someone as "unfree" in the pre-modern world was simply to state a fact about their position in the social order, most commonly that they were a slave. This usage was similar in many respects to describing someone as "poor" today. Most of us will agree that it is better, all things being equal, to be rich than to be poor, and that many, perhaps most, of the people who are currently poor are not justifiably so – just as Aristotle apparently believed that many of the people who were slaves in 4th-century Athens were not justifiably so.[3] Most of us probably also agree that there could and should be less poverty than there is, and that it would be better, all things being equal, if poverty did not exist at all. However, these moral claims do not follow from the use of the word poor as ineluctably as the analogous claims follow from the use of the word unfree. Freedom today is something that people not only aspire to but feel they are entitled to have; indeed it is, as the sociologist Orlando Patterson observes, "the one value that many people seem prepared to die for."[4] To say that someone is unfree is therefore to perform an act of social criticism, whereas to describe someone as poor is generally not (I am not endorsing this usage, merely reporting it). As the political philosopher David Miller puts it, "[w]hen we describe a person as unfree to do something we imply that an obstacle exists which stands in need of justification, and we are in effect calling on the human race collectively to vindicate its behavior in permitting the obstacle to exist."[5] If such a justification is not forthcoming, then an effort to remove the obstacle is called for.

It is tempting to try to explain this shift in usage by looking to the more general decline of status hierarchies in the modern world, which has made social goods like freedom that were once the exclusive possession of a privileged few available (at least in principle) to a much wider range of people. However, the decline of status hierarchies cannot account by itself for the special potency of the appeal to freedom: After all, the use of other terms that hold a central place in our political vocabulary, such as "equality" and "justice," has changed no less profoundly, and the meanings of these terms are no less contested, and hardly less widely discussed, than that of freedom. It is nevertheless the case that to successfully describe a particular cause as a struggle for *freedom* is to give it a sense of urgency that is not often found in struggles for equality, or even for justice. Nor can the decline of status hierarchies account by itself for the close association between freedom and the market: As I have just pointed out, the social and political significance of differences in *economic* status has been greatly amplified in the modern period, and such differences are widely regarded as being morally acceptable, especially insofar as they

---

[3] *Politics*, book 1, chapter 6.
[4] Orlando Patterson, *Freedom*, vol. 1: *Freedom in the Making of Western Culture* (New York: Basic Books, 1991), p. ix.
[5] David Miller, "Constraints on Freedom," *Ethics* 94 (1983), p. 72. See also S. I. Benn and W. L. Weinstein, "Being Free to Act, and Being a Free Man," *Mind* 80 (1971), p. 199.

can plausibly be attributed to the workings of the market. Indeed, the partisans of freedom on the one hand and of equality and justice on the other disagree most notably over the question of whether markets provide an adequate and morally defensible means of distributing goods to individuals.

Here it is tempting to take a cue from Miller's observation that to describe someone as unfree is not only to call attention to an undesirable state of affairs, but also to point to an identifiable source of constraint, the removal of which would move the person in question from a state of unfreedom to one of at least relative freedom. The constraint may take any number of forms, from the tangible – a set of chains, the four walls of a prison – to the intangible – a pattern of behavior, a social norm. It may lie outside the agent, like an occupying army, or inside, like a desire or compulsion. It may operate individually or collectively, either in its origins or in its effects. It may actually be in force, or it may be only potentially so – as when one is unfree in the sense that one lacks a certain kind of legal standing or protection. Whatever the nature of the constraint, the success of a given appeal to the language of freedom will depend on one's ability to make its presence salient to others, and to persuade them that it can and should be removed. The struggle *for* freedom is thus always a struggle *against* some more or less particular and identifiable thing: We aim for the breaking of chains, the discrediting of a pernicious social norm, the overcoming of a compulsion, the decamping of an occupying army, the repeal or amendment of an oppressive legal code.

The association of freedom with the absence of constraint may seem to account for the special potency of appeals to freedom, because it is always tactically useful when the aims of a cause can be expressed in terms of the removal of an identifiable obstacle. This is especially true when collective action is necessary, because it is usually much easier to get people to agree that something should be eliminated than to get them to agree about what exactly should be put in its place. The latter question is unavoidable in debates about equality and justice: In striving to realize these ends we are necessarily engaged in the difficult work of thinking through the ideals that we share in common and designing policies and institutions to fit them. By contrast, to the extent that the pursuit of freedom can be associated with the mere removal of constraint, it allows us to set these questions aside. It is no accident, according to this line of argument, that freedom is the leading political value in a world that otherwise disagrees fundamentally about moral and political questions. Nor is it an accident that the great popular mobilizations of our time, from Montgomery to Moscow, have aimed at the removal of specific constraints – paradigmatically, oppressive laws and regimes – and that they have tended to lose direction and cohesion once these negative aims have been achieved.

However, we cannot simply equate freedom with the absence of constraint, if only because constraint is such a ubiquitous part of human experience that to do so would rob the word of critical force. We must instead make judgments about what kinds of constraint are salient enough, and salient in the right way, that questions of freedom and unfreedom arise with respect to them. Debates about the meaning and value of freedom therefore tend to center around what we might call the problem of constraining the idea of constraint. Does a constraint have to be imposed by human beings in order to count as freedom reducing, or should "natural" constraints also be included?[6] Do constraints have to be intentionally imposed, or do accidents, negligence, and other kinds of unintended effects also qualify?[7] Should something count as a constraint only if it renders a given course of action impossible, or can the promise of rewards or the threat of penalties also limit freedom?[8] Must a constraint

---

[6] The leading spokesman for the latter view is Thomas Hobbes, who argues that "LIBERTY, or FREEDOME, signifieth (properly) the absence of Opposition...and may be applyed no lesse to Irrationall, and Inanimate creatures, than to Rationall": *Leviathan*, ed. Richard Tuck (New York: Cambridge University Press, 1991 [1651]), p. 145 (chapter 21). Most contemporary scholars follow Isaiah Berlin in drawing a distinction between being unfree and being unable to do something and argue that one is made unfree only when constraints are imposed, directly or indirectly, by human beings: see Berlin, "Two Concepts of Liberty" (1958/1969), in idem, *Liberty*, ed. Henry Hardy (New York: Oxford University Press, 2002), pp. 169–70. For two useful discussions of Hobbes's position, see Skinner, "Thomas Hobbes on the Proper Signification of Liberty," *Transactions of the Royal Historical Society* 40 (1990), pp. 121–51, and Pettit, "Liberty and Leviathan," *Politics, Philosophy and Economics* 4 (2005), pp. 131–51.

[7] For an especially strong version of the former claim, see Hayek, *The Constitution of Liberty* (Chicago: University of Chicago Press, 1960), e.g. pp. 133–4. Berlin holds, on the contrary, that "[t]he criterion of oppression is the part that I believe to be played by other human beings, directly or indirectly, *with or without the intention of doing so*, in frustrating my wishes": "Two Concepts of Liberty," p. 170 (emphasis added). The italicized phrase does not appear, however, in the original version of Berlin's essay: see *Two Concepts of Liberty* (New York: Oxford University Press, 1958), p. 8. Miller, in his "Constraints on Freedom," argues against both of these views that we should focus on responsibility rather than intentionality in thinking about freedom, a position that is defended in more detail by Pettit in his *A Theory of Freedom: From the Psychology to the Politics of Agency* (New York: Oxford University Press, 2001).

[8] One proponent of the view that freedom-reducing constraints must make action impossible is Hillel Steiner; see his "Individual Liberty," *Proceedings of the Aristotelian Society* 75 (1975), pp. 33–50. For a sophisticated treatment of constraints, including threats and inducements, in probabilistic terms, see Felix E. Oppenheim, "Degrees of Power and Freedom," *American Political Science Review* 54 (1960), pp. 437–46. See also Robert Nozick, "Coercion," in Sidney Morgenbesser, Patrick Suppes, and Morton White, eds., *Philosophy, Science, and Method: Essays in Honor of Ernest Nagel* (New York: St. Martin's Press, 1969), pp. 440–72.

be recognized as such, or is feeling free for all practical purposes the same thing as being free?[9] Are some constraints actually freedom enhancing, or does the presence of any constraint entail a reduction in freedom in so far forth?[10] We cannot talk intelligibly about freedom without first responding, at least tacitly, to questions like these, and taken together the various responses that have been offered go a long way toward defining the range of views that have been or could be held.

In other words, the association of freedom with the absence of constraint immediately raises the question of why certain kinds of constraint play a central role in debates about freedom, and other seemingly no less significant kinds of constraint do not. We are therefore led back to the difficult questions that the appeal to constraint was supposed to help us avoid in the first place. Nevertheless, if the effort to explain the salience of freedom by appealing to the salience of constraint is a dead end theoretically speaking, it helps us to see more clearly what is in need of explanation empirically speaking. Specifically, it directs our attention to the question of why the modern language of freedom is so persistently negative in character, despite the fact that the appeal to the removal of constraint necessarily entails – and was once widely understood to entail – an appeal to various positive claims about human beings and the world in which they act. It encourages us to ask in particular why it now seems natural to appeal to the language of freedom in opposing the influence

[9] Maurice Cranston argues that "[n]o one thinks a set of circumstances constraining unless he wants to do something which those circumstances prevent or hinder.... If we have no desire to do things, we should hardly know the meaning of constraint": *Freedom: A New Analysis* (London: Longmans, Green, 1953), p. 4. In the original (1958) version of "Two Concepts of Liberty," Berlin likewise defines negative liberty, following Mill, as "the absence of obstacles to the fulfillment of a man's desires," but he later retracted this formulation on the grounds that it would allow us to "increase freedom as effectively by eliminating desires as by satisfying them": "Introduction" (1969) to *Liberty*, pp. 30–1; cf. "Two Concepts of Liberty," p. 186. However, he seems to slip back into a desire-centered view on at least two occasions, arguing at one point that "all coercion is, in so far as it frustrates human desires, bad as such," and at another that "[a] law which forbids me to do what I could not, as a sane being, conceivably wish to do is not a restraint of my freedom": "Two Concepts of Liberty," pp. 175, 195. For a useful, if inconclusive, discussion of this issue, see Richard J. Arneson, "Freedom and Desire," *Canadian Journal of Philosophy* 15 (1985), pp. 425–48.

[10] Perhaps the most familiar statement of the view that constraints can be freedom enhancing is John Locke's claim, with respect to law, that "that ill deserves the name of confinement which hedges us in only from bogs and precipices": *Second Treatise of Government* §57. Berlin, by contrast, follows Hobbes and Jeremy Bentham in saying that "[l]aw is always a fetter; even if it protects you from being bound in chains that are heavier than those of the law": "Two Concepts of Liberty," p. 170n.

of the state, but difficult or odd to speak of the market as a freedom-reducing institution – especially in light of the fact that, as we will see, the opposite view was once the prevailing one. Inconsistencies like this give us reason to suspect that ideological rather than logical imperatives are at work, and the best way to identify the ideological underpinnings of a given point of view is to bring a different ideological perspective to bear. Thus if we want to make sense of the central role that market freedom plays in modern political discourse, we should start by examining the ideological conflicts in which this way of thinking was forged and through which it rose to dominance.

I.2. TWO CONCEPTS OF LIBERTY?

By framing my discussion in ideological terms, I am departing from the practice of those theorists of freedom who treat ideology, when they treat it at all, as something that distorts our thinking from without rather than animating it from within.[11] These thinkers often begin by proposing a conceptual framework onto which the various first-order views that are held about freedom can be mapped; a typological exercise that paradoxically reminds us that there is more than one thing that we value about freedom while at the same time seeking to persuade us that one of these things is more worthy of being valued than the others. Although the concern to distinguish different kinds of freedom from one another can be traced back at least as far as Aristotle,[12] the prototype for this approach in the modern period is the famous lecture on "ancient" and "modern" liberty that Benjamin Constant delivered in 1819, and the paradigmatic example is Isaiah Berlin's seminal essay on "negative" and "positive" liberty, which provides the conceptual starting point for nearly all post-war theoretical discussions about freedom.[13] The argument that I offer here, focusing as it does on the contrast between republican and market

---

[11] See, for example, G. A. Cohen, "Freedom, Justice, and Capitalism," in idem, *History, Labour, and Freedom: Themes from Marx* (Oxford: Clarendon Press, 1988), esp. pp. 286–91.

[12] With his distinction between freedom understood as "liv[ing] by the rule of the constitution" and as "doing what one likes": *Politics*, book 5, chapter 9 (cf. book 6, chapter 2), quoting R. F. Stalley's revision of the Barker translation (New York: Oxford University Press, 1995 [1946]), pp. 208–9.

[13] Benjamin Constant, "The Liberty of the Ancients Compared with That of the Moderns" (1819), in idem, *Political Writings*, trans. and ed. Biancamaria Fontana (New York: Cambridge University Press, 1988), pp. 307–28; Berlin, "Two Concepts of Liberty," passim.

freedom, follows in this tradition of dichotomous thinking.[14] However, I
believe that Berlin's analysis has outlived its usefulness and that its continued dominance prevents us from addressing some of the most pressing
questions about freedom with which we are now faced. I therefore hope
to persuade the reader that we should set aside the familiar negative-
positive liberty dichotomy and place the contrast between republican and
market freedom directly at the center of attention.

There is some question, of course, as to whether the negative-positive
liberty framework in the form that Berlin defends it is really a dichotomy
at all. As many critics have pointed out, Berlin uses the term positive
liberty in at least three different ways: first, to refer to the idea of self-
government in the ordinary political sense; second, to refer to the idea
of being governed by or (a crucial ambiguity) in the name of a "higher"
aspect or portion of oneself; and third, to refer to the idea of comprehending and accepting the necessities by which one is governed.[15] This
lack of clarity about the meaning of positive liberty gives rise to a corresponding and less widely noted lack of clarity about the meaning of
negative liberty. To the extent that Berlin associates positive liberty with
self-government, he contrasts it with negative liberty understood as the
possession of individual rights against the polity, insisting that "no power,
but only rights, can be regarded as absolute." To the extent that he associates positive liberty with being ruled by one's higher self, he contrasts it

---

[14] Gerald MacCallum famously argues that all statements about freedom involve a "triadic
relation," that freedom is always "*of* something (an agent or agents), *from* something,
to do, not do, become, or not become something," and that positive and negative liberty
are not "genuinely different kinds of freedom" but "serve only to emphasize one or the
other of two features of *every* case of the freedom of agents": "Negative and Positive
Freedom," *Philosophical Review* 76 (1967), pp. 314, 318 (original emphasis). To the
extent that MacCallum concedes that all of the elements of the triadic relation need
not be salient in a given case, and that different ways of conceiving them can give
rise to "vastly different accounts of when persons are free" (ibid., p. 319), his analysis is not inconsistent with the approach that I have adopted here. For Berlin's own
efforts to respond to MacCallum see the "Introduction" to *Liberty*, p. 36n and his
"Final Retrospect" (1998), in *Liberty*, p. 326; for a useful discussion, see Tom Baldwin,
"MacCallum and the Two Concepts of Freedom," *Ratio* 26 (1984), pp. 125–42; for a
more recent defense of MacCallum's position, see Eric Nelson, "Liberty: One Concept
Two Many?" *Political Theory* 33 (2005), pp. 58–78; for doubts about Nelson's view, see
John Christman, "Saving Positive Freedom," ibid., pp. 79–88.

[15] Berlin, "Two Concepts of Liberty," pp. 177–8, 178–81, and 181–91, respectively. For
two influential, if somewhat conflicting, analyses of the varieties of positive liberty to be
found in Berlin's essay, see H. J. McCloskey, "A Critique of the Ideals of Liberty," *Mind*
74 (1965), esp. pp. 494–508, and C. B. Macpherson, "Berlin's Division of Liberty," in
idem, *Democratic Theory: Essays in Retrieval* (Oxford: Clarendon Press, 1973), esp.
pp. 108–19.

with negative liberty understood as the ability to act according to one's preferences whatever they may happen to be, asking simply "how many possibilities are open" to the individual. To the extent that he associates positive liberty with the comprehension and acceptance of the necessities by which we are governed, he associates negative liberty with value pluralism, arguing that we necessarily choose "between ends equally ultimate, and claims equally absolute, the realisation of some of which must inevitably involve the sacrifice of others."[16]

The presence of so many concepts of liberty in Berlin's text has of course made the task of his interpreters and critics more difficult and has led some commentators to conclude that his argument is hopelessly confused.[17] I believe, however, that his rather loose use of terminology does not result from carelessness or lack of acuity, but rather from the fact that, despite the title of his essay, Berlin did not set out to articulate a *conceptual* typology: His aim was to explore the ideological rather than the logical connections between the concepts of liberty that he examines. Considered in the abstract, positive and negative liberty are, in his account, each worthy ideals that are, like all ideals, each prone to abuse. Indeed, he emphasizes that the positive liberty tradition, of which he is mostly critical, has "animate[d] the most powerful and morally just public movements of our time," and that the idea of negative liberty, which he portrays more favorably, "has played its part in generating great and lasting social evils."[18] He defends his own rhetorical slant not by pointing to any deficiency in the idea of positive liberty itself, but rather by appealing to the historical context in which he is writing: "[W]hereas liberal ultra-individualism could scarcely be said to be a rising force *at present*," he writes, "the rhetoric of 'positive' liberty, at least in its distorted form, is in far greater evidence, and continues to play its historic role (in both capitalist and anti-capitalist societies) as a cloak for despotism in the name of a wider freedom."[19]

Needless to say, Berlin's historical context is rather different from ours; indeed, the situation today is a mirror image of the one that he describes: Liberal ultra-individualism has been a "rising force" for some time, and though we are not rid of tyranny (alas), the appeal to freedom does not

---

[16] Berlin, "Two Concepts of Liberty," pp. 211, 177n, and 213–14, respectively.

[17] Arneson concludes, for example, that "[t]he negative and positive contrast as Berlin draws it is not a contrast between two families of ideas about freedom but between one family and a menagerie": "Freedom and Desire," p. 435.

[18] Berlin, "Two Concepts of Liberty," p. 214; "Introduction" to *Liberty*, p. 37.

[19] Berlin, "Introduction" to *Liberty*, p. 39 (emphasis added).

play the prominent role in the rhetorical arsenal of the tyrant that it did during the Soviet period or in the immediate aftermath of colonialism – a development for which Berlin can perhaps claim some credit. There are obvious historical grounds, then, for thinking that it is time for a fresh start in thinking about freedom. It is not, however, simply a matter of inverting Berlin's analysis – of casting positive liberty as the hero and negative liberty as the villain – because this way of framing the discussion is not well suited to addressing the concerns about freedom with which we are now faced. If we want to account for the close association between freedom and the market in modern political discourse, then we need a conceptual framework that makes it possible to see why participation in the market was once seen not as a consequence or expression of but rather as a threat to individual liberty, and why freedom was thought to consist instead in self-government on the part of a social elite. The negative-positive liberty dichotomy does not provide a useful starting point for pursuing either of these lines of inquiry.

Berlin's scattered remarks on the subject of what he calls "economic freedom" suggest that his views on the relationship between freedom and the market were not fully formed. The question is first raised near the beginning of "Two Concepts of Liberty," where he asks whether economic hardship can lead to a loss of negative liberty. The discussion that follows is compressed and inconclusive, but the reader is encouraged to conclude that he is skeptical toward the idea.[20] By contrast, the introduction to *Four Essays on Liberty*, written just over a decade later, includes an extended and spirited attack on the doctrine of laissez-faire that concludes with the claim that "[t]he case for social legislation or planning... can be constructed with as much validity from consideration of the claims of negative liberty as from those of its positive brother." Berlin nevertheless goes on to invoke the laissez-faire-friendly claim that "liberty is one thing, and the conditions for it are another," a claim that is difficult to square in turn with the suggestion in "Two Concepts of Liberty" that the extent of negative liberty should be measured not only by the number of

[20] Specifically, Berlin argues that "this use of the term depends on a particular social and economic theory about the causes of my poverty or weakness," and then names Marxism, Christianity, utilitarianism, and socialism – not a catalog of his favorite views – as possible examples of such a theory: "Two Concepts of Liberty," pp. 169–170 and note. He goes on to argue that "it is a confusion of values to say that although my 'liberal,' individual freedom may go by the board, some other kind of freedom – 'social' or 'economic' – is increased": ibid., pp. 172–3. It is interesting to notice in this connection that immediately after introducing the terms negative and positive liberty, Berlin begins referring to the former as "political" and to the latter as "economic" liberty.

possibilities that are open to the individual, but also by "how easy or difficult each of these possibilities is to actualise."[21] Subsequent discussions have not clarified the issue: In a notable exchange between the political philosophers G. A. Cohen and John Gray, for example, neither party is able by his own admission to decisively answer the question of whether a socialist or a capitalist economy provides more liberty on balance to individuals, despite the fact that they agree – each, it seems, for the sake of argument – to define liberty in strictly negative terms.[22]

Berlin's analysis is even less helpful when it comes to the question of republican freedom. Of the three definitions of positive liberty that he considers, the one that comes closest to the republican view – positive liberty understood as self-government – receives almost no attention, as he shifts almost immediately from the language of self-government to that of self-mastery.[23] Indeed, despite the fact that it is the definition with which Berlin's essay begins, subsequent discussions of positive liberty have typically subordinated the idea of political self-government to the idea of personal self-mastery, no doubt because this is the meaning that the term has carried in Anglo-American political thought since the latter part of the 19th century.[24] As we will see, self-mastery so understood cannot simply be equated with self-government in the republican sense: these two ways of thinking about freedom arise from distinct traditions of thought that are both historically and conceptually opposed to each other.[25] Moreover, there is nothing in the republican conception

---

[21] Berlin, "Introduction" to *Liberty*, pp. 38–9, 45; "Two Concepts of Liberty," p. 177n (cf. "Introduction" to *Liberty*, p. 41).

[22] Cohen argues that the question of whether capitalism or socialism "is better for liberty, all things considered, is a question which may have no answer in the abstract," and Gray agrees that "[t]here is no mechanical way of computing which society has the greater sum of liberties" because "judgments of degrees of freedom on-balance cannot as a rule be made without invoking standards of importance in respect of the liberties being evaluated": Cohen, "Capitalism, Freedom, and the Proletariat" (1979), reprinted in David Miller, ed., *Liberty* (New York: Oxford University Press, 1991), quoted at p. 172; John Gray, "Against Cohen on Proletarian Unfreedom," *Social Philosophy and Policy* 6 (1988), quoted at pp. 104, 105.

[23] Berlin, "Two Concepts of Liberty," pp. 176–8.

[24] See especially T. H. Green, "Liberal Legislation and Freedom of Contract" (1881), in idem, *Lectures on the Principles of Political Obligation and Other Writings*, ed. Paul Harris and John Morrow (New York: Cambridge University Press, 1986), pp. 194–212. On Berlin's debt to Green and the other British idealists see Skinner, "A Third Concept of Liberty," *Proceedings of the British Academy* 117 (2002), pp. 240–3.

[25] For a useful discussion of the origins of the contrast between classical republican freedom and the more subjective (and thus potentially vanguardist) brand of positive liberty with which Berlin is concerned, see Pocock, *Machiavellian Moment*, chapter 14.

of freedom that entails a commitment to positive liberty in either of the stronger senses that Berlin considers: A community can be free in the republican sense without claiming to know what each of its citizens "really" wants, just as it can be free without claiming to know the whole truth about the human condition. To be sure, Berlin concedes that each of the latter positions is a "perversion" of an otherwise worthy ideal, and he insists that his aim is simply to show that they have in fact been derived from it "by steps which, if not logically valid, are historically and psychologically intelligible."[26] Nevertheless, if our aim is to make sense of republican freedom in its own terms, then Berlin's essay does not provide a very helpful starting point.

I therefore believe that it is time to set aside Berlin's typology, not only because it is rather loosely drawn, and not only because it was designed to do a different kind of work in a different historical context, but more importantly because it is poorly suited to addressing the questions about freedom with which we are now faced. I do, however, draw an important point of methodological guidance from Berlin's work: the insight, often overlooked in discussions of his writings on liberty, that no typology and still less any particular concept of liberty exhausts the range of meanings that the word can legitimately carry. Berlin begins "Two Concepts of Liberty" by reminding us that his discussion takes place within a larger tradition of thinking about freedom in which "more than two hundred senses" of the word have been recorded, of which he proposes "to examine no more than two."[27] We are immediately placed, then, on a larger conceptual terrain and told that this terrain will be left largely unexplored. He goes on to define the two concepts on which he will focus by suggesting that they are "involved in the answer" to questions that are "clearly different, even though the answers to them may overlap."[28] Even within the

---

For a contrasting view, see Vivienne Brown, "Self-Government: The Master Trope of Republican Liberty," *The Monist* 84 (2001), pp. 60–76.

[26] Berlin, "Two Concepts of Liberty," p. 198; on the "perversion" of positive liberty see Berlin, "Introduction" to *Liberty*, p. 39.

[27] Berlin, "Two Concepts of Liberty," p. 168. For evidence that Berlin was not exaggerating on this point, see, for example, Ruth Nanda Anshen, ed., *Freedom: Its Meaning* (New York: Harcourt, Brace, 1940) and, more recently, Zbigniew Pelczynski and John Gray, eds., *Conceptions of Liberty in Political Philosophy* (London: Athlone Press, 1984).

[28] The questions are, in the case of negative liberty, "What is the area within which the subject...is or should be left to do or be what he is able to do or be, without interference by other persons?" And in the case of positive liberty, "What, or who, is the source of control or interference that can determine someone to do, or be, this rather than that?": Berlin, "Two Concepts of Liberty," p. 169. Berlin later shortens questions to "How far does government interfere with me?" and "Who governs me?": ibid., p. 177.

relatively narrow terrain that he chooses to explore, we are warned that the two concepts of liberty that we encounter there should not be thought of as aspects of a single underlying phenomenon. Indeed, one of the main goals of the essay is to dispel exactly this kind of confusion.

If all discussions about the meaning and value of freedom are necessarily selective, as Berlin emphasizes, and if the principle of selection that we use reflects the practical concerns that we have, as the shape of his argument suggests, then it follows that the question of which typology we should use to organize our thinking is best answered in practical rather than conceptual terms. This is not to say that conceptual issues do not have an important role to play in this book, as indeed they must in any substantial work of political theory. The question is not whether these issues come into play, but rather how we should go about choosing the conceptual framework around which a given inquiry is framed. I believe that the close association between freedom and the market in contemporary political discourse poses a daunting challenge to recent efforts to revive the republican conception of freedom, and that such a revival is nevertheless desirable, if only because debates about the proper role of markets in modern society could be conducted more intelligently if the language of freedom were not so disproportionately available to one side. I therefore believe that the best way to approach the study of freedom under current circumstances is by examining the ideological struggles in which the market conception of freedom was forged and the republican conception overcome. However, because all theories of freedom are partial (in both senses of the word), and because the struggles in which the language of freedom is implicated change over time, the question of how we might best theorize about freedom is not one that can be answered once and for all. "Everything is what it is," as Berlin famously remarks,[29] but – as he might have added – everything is not what it was, nor will everything always be what it is.

I.3. OVERVIEW

A study that focuses on the republican tradition in political thought must immediately face a complicated and contentious set of issues regarding the meaning of the word republican, the question of whether the aims of republican thought have remained consistent over time, and the extent to which republicanism can be distinguished from other political ideologies,

---

[29] Berlin, "Two Concepts of Liberty," p. 172.

such as liberalism, that also give a central role to the value of freedom. I therefore begin in Chapter 1 by developing and defending a definition of republican freedom. I have already pointed out that freedom in pre-modern political thought consisted on the one hand in the enjoyment of a particular social status – one that protects its bearer from the arbitrary exercise of power – and on the other hand in adherence to certain norms of behavior – certain virtues – that were considered appropriate to someone holding that status. I argue that specifically *republican* thinking about freedom begins at the point where these two aspects of freedom are made to depend on each other, where the practice of virtue is made to depend on the absence of arbitrary power, and vice-versa. This claim – that republicans associate unfreedom not only with servitude but also with servility – distinguishes my definition from other contemporary accounts.[30] The richness and diversity of the republican tradition arises from the fact that the meaning of each of the terms in this relation, and the nature of the relationship itself, are open to more than one interpretation. Indeed, as we will see, the internal complexity of the republican conception of freedom played a crucial role in shaping the response that early modern thinkers offered to the rise of modern commercial societies.

The claim that it is this republican conception of freedom to which the partisan of freedom would necessarily have appealed in the pre-modern period has to be qualified in two ways. First of all, there is a difference between being a republican and holding a republican view about the meaning of freedom. That is, although it is true that not everyone who appealed to freedom as a political value in the pre-modern period is properly described as a republican, it is nevertheless the case – or so I will argue – that anyone who appealed to freedom as a political value would have defined the word in republican terms.[31] Second of all, although republican freedom was the only kind of freedom that was seen as a

---

[30] Pettit and Skinner in particular tend to emphasize the importance of controlling arbitrary power and to downplay the importance of virtue in their treatment of republican (or, as Skinner now prefers to say, "neo-Roman") freedom: see, for example, Pettit, *Republicanism*, pp. 211–12 (but cf. chapter 8) and Skinner, *Liberty before Liberalism*, pp. 22–3.

[31] Skinner argues along similar lines that although it is true that in the early modern period "no one who professed to be a republican (in the strict sense of being an opponent of monarchy) contested the so-called republican theory of liberty...the theory was also espoused by a number of political writers...who would have been shocked to hear themselves described as republican in their political allegiances": *Hobbes and Republican Liberty* (New York: Cambridge University Press, 2008), p. ixn; cf. *Liberty before Liberalism*, p. 55n.

political value in its own right, it is not the only kind of freedom that appears in pre-modern political discourse. According to an equally venerable tradition, rooted in the Roman civil law, freedom consists in "the natural ability to do as one pleases unless prohibited by force or right."[32] As I argue in Chapter 2, this juristic idea of "natural" liberty, unlike the modern concept of negative liberty to which it is otherwise closely related, does not appear in medieval and early modern political thought as a good to be pursued for its own sake. Rather, to the extent that freedom appears as a political value in this tradition – as it does for example in Locke – it is said to consist in obedience to natural law, which therefore appears as the more fundamental political value. Conversely, to the extent that these thinkers equate freedom with the mere absence of constraint – as Hobbes does, for example – they do so in order to argue that it is not a political value at all.

Having cleared the conceptual terrain, I turn in Chapters 3 and 4 to the question of how market freedom emerged out of and ultimately triumphed over these older ways of thinking. I assume for the sake of discussion that the triumph of market *society* over other forms of social organization is not in need of explanation, or more precisely that it can be explained in materialistic terms by looking to technological advances in production, transportation, communication, and so on.[33] The question for our purposes is not why markets came to play such a central role in the modern world, but rather why freedom, understood as the absence of constraint, came to play such a central role in market ideology. My response to this question proceeds in two basic steps. First, as I argue in Chapter 3, the "rise of commerce" posed a fundamental challenge to existing forms of social organization, and the concerns that it raised – that markets are essentially ungovernable, and that participation in a market economy is inimical to the cultivation of civic virtue – were ones that the defenders of republican freedom were in the best position, ideologically speaking, to articulate. However, the rise of commerce also exposed the ambiguities and tensions that had always been contained in the republican conception of freedom, so that by the end of the 18th century republican ideas were being used both to oppose and to defend the emerging social order: Whereas admirers of classical republicanism

---

[32] This formula is found in the Justinian *Digest* 1.5.4, drawing in turn on the *Institutes* of Florentinus, which date from the 2nd century CE – although the view that it expresses is considerably older than that.

[33] This is not to say that the story is not more complicated than this, just that this is not the story that is told in this book.

such as Jean-Jacques Rousseau saw the market as a threat to civic virtue, and thus to freedom itself, defenders of commercial society such as Adam Smith saw it as a means of checking arbitrary power that was more reliable than the classical appeal to virtue, and more flexible than the juristic appeal to natural law.

In Chapter 4 I show how this "commercial" brand of republican thought was woven together over the course of the 18th century with the natural juristic view that human beings are the bearers of certain inalienable rights – the liberal view, as it came to be known. The question of the relative influence of republican and liberal ideas in the 18th century remains one of the most contentious matters of debate among historians of early modern political thought. I argue that the most striking fact about the political thought of this period is not that republican and juristic ideas were in competition with each other, but rather that key elements of both traditions were brought together for the first time into a single political vision, each removing certain ideological weaknesses in the other. In particular, the juristic appeal to the sacred rights of life, liberty, and property made it possible to portray citizenship in a commercial society as something more than a mercenary proposition, and the republican defense of the rise of commerce made it possible to extend the idea that legitimate political rule depends on the consent of the governed from an idealized founding moment into the day-to-day world of market transactions. By placing the potential conflict between government on the one hand and individual and collective prosperity on the other at the center of attention, the defenders of commercial society made it possible to treat freedom, understood in terms of the absence of constraint, not only as a good in itself, but as one that is necessarily in competition with other goods such as self-government, equality, and even justice. With these developments we step outside of the republican and juristic traditions altogether.

In Chapter 5 I take up the question of what became of republican freedom after this triumph of the commercial over the classical republican model of a free society. As it happens, each of the leading developments in 19th-century European history – the rise of mass democracy and of mass production – was influentially portrayed as a threat to republican freedom: Democratization was said to raise the threat of majority tyranny, and industrialization the threat of wage slavery. Here again, a revolution in social and political life gave rise to a corresponding set of disagreements about the meaning and value of freedom. However, it proved difficult to identify a workable alternative to either of these social systems, and so by the turn of the 20th century debates about the meaning and value of freedom centered no longer around the question of how the common good might best be pursued or even around the question of the proper scope and content of individual rights, but rather around the more abstract question of what it means for an individual to have a choice. The republican conception of freedom occupied an uneasy middle ground in these debates between what were now seen as the more straightforward negative and positive liberty views: For proponents of negative liberty, it is the republican commitment to a sphere of autonomous choice that best captures the core meaning of freedom, and for proponents of positive liberty the republican appeal to virtue and the common good anticipates their own rather loftier conception of choice as a matter of individual and collective self-realization. Thus although recognizably republican ideas were invoked on both sides of this debate, the republican conception of freedom itself was all but lost from view.

We might ask ourselves whether the very fact that republican freedom has been eclipsed so thoroughly by market freedom is enough to suggest that any effort to breathe life back into it is doomed to fail. Contemporary republicans can draw some comfort from the fact that the republican conception of freedom has repeatedly shown an ability to adapt to and even flourish in diverse and apparently hostile political environments: It was defunct for more than a millennium after the fall of the Roman republic; recovered as a civic ideal in the late medieval city states; lost from view again with the decline of city-state politics in the 16th century; revived on a national scale in revolutionary England, France, and America; and then overwhelmed by the rise of industrial capitalism. It is perhaps not too much to hope that it can flourish once more in a world that faces the enervating prospect of economic, political, and cultural uniformity. After all, the common thread that runs throughout the rather checkered history of republican thought is the hope that it is possible, at least under certain circumstances, for a people to shape its own political destiny, that we need not embrace the tenets of economic determinism, whether "neo-liberal" or Marxian in form. Insofar as we share this hope, it is possible to begin, as I have here, with the relatively optimistic claim that markets speak with the authority of freedom, rather than insisting, as the economic determinist must, that freedom speaks with the authority of the market.

I

Republican Freedom

There is not a more unintelligible word in the English language than republicanism.

John Adams to Mercy Otis Warren, August 8, 1807

I.I. REPUBLICANISM AND LIBERALISM

Anyone who sets out to study the history of republican thought will immediately be struck by the immense diversity of views to which the label "republican" has been attached. Indeed, among the major political ideologies, republicanism alone cuts across nearly all of the other categories that have been used to organize political thinking. Republicans have been democrats, aristocrats, and even monarchists; liberals and illiberals; imperialists and isolationists; slaveholders and abolitionists; feudalists, capitalists, and socialists; and ancients, medievals, and moderns. They have pursued participatory and representative, bellicose and pacific, and virtue-centered and interest-centered policies. They have been among the staunchest defenders of the status quo and among the most forceful proponents of revolutionary change. Strictly speaking, of course, it is anachronistic to use the word republican outside of the Roman and neo-Roman contexts in which it is etymologically rooted, and so there will always be disagreement about whether and how it should be applied to other cases. Furthermore, it is difficult to define the boundaries of an ideological tradition by appealing to the beliefs and practices with which it has been associated, because beliefs and practices are only loosely constrained by the ideological commitments on which they are said to rest. Nevertheless, any study that seeks to draw on republican ideas must begin by showing that the term republican is not so hopelessly vague that it can mean all things to all people: It must begin, in other words, by showing that there are such things as distinctively (and attractively) republican ideas in the first place.

The usual way of approaching this problem in recent years has been to construct a rough typology of the kinds of views that self-described republicans have held, and then to stake out a position on that spectrum. Thus we find contemporary scholars defending "liberal," "communitarian," "civic humanist," and "populist" brands of republicanism, among others, and dismissing competing strands of republican thought as unappealing or unworkable. This approach has obvious attractions, but it is not the strategy that I will follow here. Instead of laying out a variety of republican positions and picking out the one that is most congenial for my own purposes, I will try to define the aims of republican political thought in such a way that it becomes possible to speak of a republican *tradition* in the broadest sense. I hope to show, in other words, that there is in fact a common thread that runs through the various republicanisms past and present. In saying this, I do not mean to suggest that the internal diversity of the tradition is somehow illusory or unimportant; indeed, we will not be able to come to terms with the relationship between republican and market freedom unless we take this diversity into account. However, the fact that contemporary republicans typically *begin* by taking a fragmented (or, to use republican language, a factional) view of republican thought has prevented them from fully grasping the difficulties involved in pursuing republican ends in a world that is largely governed by and through markets. It is only when we make an effort to see the republican tradition whole that the nature and extent of the conflict between republicanism and the market becomes apparent.

However, we should resist the temptation to reify our terminology, as if every idea and thinker can be placed either inside or outside the republican fold. A given line of argument cannot always be sorted into a single ideological pigeonhole; nor is it always possible to say in definite terms whether a particular thinker does or does not belong to a given ideological tradition, especially when we have access to a different set of ideological categories than the thinker in question. Again, we cannot define the boundaries of the republican tradition, or of any tradition of thought, simply by appealing to the various beliefs and practices with which it has been associated – though such an appeal can of course be used to check the adequacy of a definition that is arrived at by other means. Rather, such boundaries are best drawn by identifying the particular *problem* or *set of problems* with which the tradition in question is concerned. For example, we might define the boundaries of democratic political thought to include everyone concerned with the problem of ensuring that "the people" rule in a given polity, or of liberal political thought to include everyone concerned with the problem of making it possible for all individuals to pursue their own good in their own way.[1] The diversity that we find in each of these traditions can then be attributed not only to the fact that there is disagreement about how to solve each of these problems, but more importantly to the fact that there is disagreement about what should *count* as a solution. We might ask what it means, for example, for the people (or anyone) to "rule," or for individuals to "pursue their own good." This is, after all, why we think of these as *problems* rather than simply as goals, and why it is necessary to "theorize" about democracy and liberalism in the first place. If ideological traditions draw their richness and vitality – and also their contentiousness and instability – from these kinds of disagreements, they are sustained and bound together by a shared belief that the problems in question *matter*.

In this chapter, then, I will define the boundaries of republican political thought in problem-centered terms. In particular, I will argue that republican thought centers around the problem of securing the practice of virtue through the control of arbitrary power, that this is what it means to be committed to the pursuit of republican freedom. Although the exact meaning – or, more precisely, the various possible exact meanings – of this formula will emerge only over the course of the discussion that follows, I believe that it is capacious enough to capture most, if not all, of the thinkers and ideas that have been associated with the republican tradition. To the extent that it is controversial in this respect, this will be because it leads us to find republican ideas espoused by a number of thinkers who are not usually thought of as republicans, or who would have been unlikely to apply the label to themselves. These include not only "pre-republican" thinkers such as Aristotle, but also canonically liberal thinkers such as John Locke and Adam Smith. Of course, the word "liberal" did not take on its present ideological meaning until some time after the turn of the 19th century, and so if there is some doubt as to whether Locke and Smith would have called themselves republicans, it is nevertheless certain that they would not have called themselves liberals. It would be a mistake, however, to put much weight on this line of argument: If the boundaries

---

[1] The latter formulation is of course John Stuart Mill's, as set out in the first chapter of *On Liberty*.

of an ideological tradition are best defined in problem-centered terms, as I have suggested, then there is no reason why republican or liberal ideas could not have been articulated before those particular terms were used to describe them, or why they could not have shaped the thinking of people who did not claim those labels, and who are now more closely (if anachronistically) associated with different ones.[2] We should also keep in mind that political thinkers are typically concerned with more than one set of problems – many today would describe themselves, for example, as democrats, liberals, *and* republicans – and with different problems at different times. It follows that by defining the boundaries of republican thought in problem-centered terms, we do not settle the question of who is or is not a republican; we only make it possible to say whether, when, and to what extent a given thinker's ideas have a republican cast.

The relationship between republican and liberal ideas is of more than historical interest, because the revival of interest in republicanism, like most developments in recent political thought, has been profoundly shaped by the central role that liberal ideas play in contemporary political discourse. This brings us back to the point with which I began: When we are asked to consider which aspects of the republican tradition are living and which are dead, we generally do so, if not from a liberal point of view, then at least from one in which liberalism looms large as the "other" against which competing ideological positions are defined. Thus republican ideas were first invoked in contemporary political theory to call attention to what some saw as the characteristic flaws of liberal polities, such as their commitment to individualism, their tendency to "privatize" social conflicts, their reluctance to admit religious and other "comprehensive" views into the public sphere, and their privileging of rights and interests over duties and responsibilities.[3] In other words,

[2] David Wootton has recently made the striking claim that use of the word "republicanism" to refer to an alternative to monarchy "was invented in later-fifteenth-century Florence," and that "if there is any classical republicanism it postdates what we anachronistically call the 'republics' of Athens and Rome." Wootton focuses on the use of the word republican to refer to a form of government rather than to a conception of freedom, but even if we accept his conclusions we should, as in the case of the word "liberal," distinguish terminological from conceptual anachronism. See David Wootton, "The True Origins of Republicanism: The Disciples of Baron and the Counter-Example of Venturi," in Manuela Albertone, ed., *Il repubblicanesimo moderno: L'idea di repubblica nella riflessione storica di Franco Venturi* (Naples: Bibliopolis, 2006), pp. 271–304, quoted at pp. 271–2.

[3] The most prominent example of this kind of appeal to the republican tradition is found in Michael J. Sandel's *Democracy's Discontent: America in Search of a Public Philosophy* (Cambridge, MA: Harvard University Press, 1996), which elaborates a line of argument that can be traced back to his "The Procedural Republic and the Unencumbered

republicanism so understood provided the historical and conceptual underpinnings of the so-called communitarian critique of liberalism.[4] Even if we grant the descriptive accuracy of this critique – and it is, as a number of liberals have pointed out, partial and misleading in many respects[5] – these communitarian republicans have not been as clear as one might hope in spelling out how the participatory and virtue-centered politics that they envision would actually work in practice, or in explaining how we might go about enacting such a politics in a society that is, by their own account, already deeply committed to liberal ideals.[6] They are therefore vulnerable to the charge that republicanism understood in this communitarian way amounts to little more than an exercise in high-minded nostalgia.[7] Nevertheless, the communitarian-republican critique of liberalism stimulated a number of liberal thinkers to spell out more clearly their own debts to the republican tradition, and to emphasize the central role that self-government, the rule of law, a commitment to deliberative forms of civic engagement, a concern to minimize asymmetries of power among citizens, and an orientation toward the common good play in liberal thought. Indeed, some of these thinkers treat republicanism

Self," *Political Theory* 12 (1984), pp. 81–96. See also Benjamin R. Barber, *Strong Democracy: Participatory Politics for a New Age* (Berkeley: University of California Press, 1984); Robert N. Bellah et al., *Habits of the Heart: Individualism and Commitment in American Life* (Berkeley: University of California Press, 1985); Charles Taylor, "Cross-Purposes: The Liberal-Communitarian Debate," in Nancy L. Rosenblum, ed., *Liberalism and the Moral Life* (Cambridge, MA: Harvard University Press, 1989), pp. 159–82; and from a somewhat different angle, Quentin Skinner, "The Paradoxes of Political Liberty," *Tanner Lectures on Human Values* 7 (1986), pp. 225–50.

4 I use the term "communitarian" with some hesitation, because many of the thinkers to whom this term is commonly applied do not avow it themselves. Alasdair MacIntyre complains, for example, that he has "strenuously disowned [the] label, but to little effect." "The Spectre of Communitarianism," *Radical Philosophy* 70 (1995), p. 34.

5 See, among many possible examples, Amy Gutmann, "Communitarian Critics of Liberalism," *Philosophy and Public Affairs* 14 (1985), pp. 308–22; Charles Larmore, *Patterns of Moral Complexity* (New York: Cambridge University Press, 1987), chapter 5; Will Kymlicka, *Liberalism, Community, and Culture* (Oxford: Clarendon Press, 1989), chapter 4; Ronald Dworkin, *Sovereign Virtue: The Theory and Practice of Equality* (Cambridge, MA: Harvard University Press, 2000), chapter 5.

6 As Don Herzog succinctly puts it, "if liberalism is the problem, how could republicanism be the solution?" "Some Questions for Republicans," *Political Theory* 14 (1986), quoted at p. 484.

7 For three versions of this charge, advanced from very different perspectives, see the essays by Jeremy Waldron, Michael Walzer, and William Connolly in Anita L. Allen and Milton C. Regan, Jr., eds., *Debating Democracy's Discontent: Essays on American Politics, Law, and Public Philosophy* (New York: Oxford University Press, 1998), pp. 32–9, 175–82, and 205–11, respectively. For Sandel's response to this line of criticism see ibid., pp. 325–6, 333–5, and cf. *Democracy's Discontent*, pp. 317–21.

and liberalism not only as compatible but as complementary schools of thought and refer to themselves as "liberal republicans" or "republican liberals."[8] A qualified dissent from this kind of syncretism is found in the work of Philip Pettit, who distinguishes his own neo-Roman brand of republicanism not only from communitarian and populist versions, but also from liberalism itself.[9] However, Pettit, like his communitarian counterparts, is vulnerable to the charge that this distinction can only be maintained if we take a partial and misleading view of the liberal tradition.[10] If we define the boundaries of liberal thought more broadly – as Pettit himself has suggested that we might[11] – then his defense of republicanism can be seen as a refinement of, rather than an alternative to, liberal principles.

---

[8] John Rawls, in a passage that is often quoted by these thinkers, insists that there is "no fundamental opposition" between "classical republicanism," understood as the view that "[t]he safety of democratic liberties requires the active participation of citizens who possess the political virtues needed to maintain a constitutional regime," and his own brand of "political" liberalism, *Political Liberalism* (New York: Columbia University Press, 1993), p. 205. For a defense of "liberal republicanism," see, for example, Cass R. Sunstein, "Beyond the Republican Revival," *Yale Law Journal* 97 (1988), pp. 1539–90; for a defense of "republican liberalism," see, for example, Richard Dagger, *Civic Virtues: Rights, Citizenship, and Republican Liberalism* (New York: Oxford University Press, 1997). For a recent effort to demonstrate the historical interdependence of liberal and republican ideas, see Andreas Kalyvas and Ira Katznelson, *Liberal Beginnings: Making a Republic for the Moderns* (New York: Cambridge University Press, 2008).

[9] Philip Pettit, *Republicanism: A Theory of Freedom and Government* (2nd ed., New York: Oxford University Press, 1999 [1997]), pp. 7–11; for a more extended statement of Pettit's case against communitarian republicanism, see his "Reworking Sandel's Republicanism," *Journal of Philosophy* 95 (1998), pp. 73–96. For another effort to distinguish neo-Roman republicanism from liberalism, one that focuses on the liberal commitment to neutrality rather than to non-interference, see John W. Maynor, *Republicanism in the Modern World* (Cambridge, UK: Polity Press, 2003).

[10] For a version of this argument directed specifically at Pettit, see Charles Larmore, "Liberal and Republican Conceptions of Freedom," in Daniel Weinstock and Christian Nadeau, eds., *Republicanism: History, Theory and Practice* (London: Frank Cass, 2004), pp. 96–119; for one directed at Quentin Skinner, see Alan Patten, "The Republican Critique of Liberalism," *British Journal of Political Science* 26 (1996), pp. 25–44. See also Robert E. Goodin, "Folie Républicaine," *Annual Review of Political Science* 6 (2003), pp. 55–76, and Geoffrey Brennan and Loren Lomasky, "Against Reviving Republicanism," *Politics, Philosophy and Economics* 5 (2006), pp. 221–52.

[11] "[M]any left-of-centre liberals...will see their liberalism as having more in common with the republican position than with the libertarian, and they would probably want to give up the taxonomy of populism, republicanism, and liberalism in favour of an alternative like populism, republicanism/liberalism, and libertarianism," Pettit, *Republicanism*, p. 9. Pettit has since conceded, in response to a suggestion by Richard Dagger, that "there is no good reason" why his position should not be described as "liberal republicanism," "On *Republicanism*: Reply to Carter, Christman and Dagger," *The Good Society* 9 (2000), p. 56.

I do not mean to fault contemporary republicans for their (sometimes tacit) allegiance to liberalism: After all, it would be difficult for a contemporary political thinker of any description to defend a position that was not liberal in the broad sense of being at least formally egalitarian and seeking to show respect for the plurality of beliefs and practices that we find in modern societies. This is, as far as I can see, all for the good. Nor do I not mean to suggest that the use of republican ideas to criticize or refine certain aspects of liberal thought is somehow confused or illegitimate. On the contrary, liberalism raises questions of interpretation and implementation on which the republican tradition can shed considerable light. It is important to keep in mind, however, that these are not the questions that the classical republicans set out to answer; nor are they the questions that were most salient during the period when the crucial confrontation between republicanism and the market took place. If we treat republicanism as a resource for responding to certain problems raised by contemporary liberalism, rather than as a tradition of thought that centers around its own set of problems, our understanding of republican freedom, and thus of the development of the modern language of freedom more generally, will be correspondingly distorted. It follows that if we want to understand why republican freedom was eclipsed by market freedom, we should start by placing at the center of attention the problem on which the republican tradition was founded: the problem of securing the practice of virtue through the control of arbitrary power. This raises the question of what virtue and arbitrary power have to do with freedom, and in order to answer *that* question we have to take a closer look at the origins of Western thinking about freedom.

1.2. THE SOCIAL ORIGINS OF FREEDOM

The word "free" was used in the classical world, by republicans and non-republicans alike, to describe a specific class of people – those men who were not slaves or serfs – as well as the kind of behavior that was associated with or expected from members of that class.[12] Only secondarily was

---

[12] For a useful discussion of the etymological roots of the words "freedom" and "liberty" in the Indo-European languages, see Hanna Fenichel Pitkin, "Are Freedom and Liberty Twins?" *Political Theory* 16 (1988), esp. pp. 528–44; and see also C. S. Lewis, *Studies in Words* (2nd ed., New York: Cambridge University Press, 1960), chapter 5, on which Pitkin draws substantially. My use of gendered language here and elsewhere in my description of classical thinking about freedom is considered, because freedom in this period was an exclusively male privilege.

it used to refer to the absence of constraint, and even here the association may have been derived from the unconstrained movement that was available to free men. Thus Hannah Arendt observes that in the classical world it was "the free man's status which enabled him to move, to get away from home, to go out into the world and meet other people in deed and word."[13] Similarly, the discussion of human status in the Justinian *Digest* of Roman law begins with the observation that "the great divide in the law of persons [*iure personarum*] is this: [that] all men are either free men or slaves." Only then does it go on to define freedom as "the natural ability to do as one pleases unless prohibited by force or right [*iure*]."[14] This status-based usage was of course not without normative implications: To be a free man was to hold a position of privilege, and to accuse a free man of having acted in a slavish or servile manner was to call those privileges into question. Indeed, so strongly were normative expectations attached to the enjoyment of free status that Aristotle was able to build an entire ethics, and the better part of a politics, around the question of what kind of behavior is appropriate for a free man. However, this normative use of the term was unlike our own in that the status distinctions on which it rested were not themselves open to question – at least, not in the name of freedom. A slave in antiquity might have aspired to win his freedom or

---

[13] Hannah Arendt, "What Is Freedom?" in idem, *Between Past and Future: Eight Exercises in Political Thought* (New York: Penguin, 1977), p. 148. Indeed, Richard Mulgan points out that "[t]he construction 'to be free,' with the infinitive, 'to be free to do something,' is not found in standard literary Greek," "Liberty in Ancient Greece," in Zbigniew Pelczynski and John Gray, eds., *Conceptions of Liberty in Political Philosophy* (London: Athlone Press, 1984), p. 12. On the connection in Greek thought between free status and personal liberty see also Mogens Herman Hansen, "The Ancient Athenian and the Modern Liberal View of Liberty as a Democratic Ideal," in Josiah Ober and Charles Hedrick, eds., *Dēmokratia: A Conversation on Democracies, Ancient and Modern* (Princeton, NJ: Princeton University Press, 1996), pp. 93–4.

[14] *Digest* 1.5.3–4. The first formula is drawn from the *Institutes* of Gaius, the second from those of Florentinus; both date from the 2nd century CE, although the views that they express are considerably older than that. I should emphasize from the outset that although it is of course true that questions of social status play a central role in classical republican thought, I do not follow Quentin Skinner in *equating* republican freedom with the enjoyment of free status under law: The Justinian formula is, as J. G. A. Pocock points out, of imperial rather than republican provenance and reflects a much broader classical usage. I should also emphasize that I do not follow Pocock in equating republican freedom with the Aristotelian ideal of participatory self-rule; if Skinner's view is too broad, then Pocock's is too narrow. Compare Skinner, *Liberty before Liberalism* (New York: Cambridge University Press, 1998) and Pocock, *The Machiavellian Moment: Florentine Political Thought and the Atlantic Republican Tradition* (Princeton, NJ: Princeton University Press, 1975). For Pocock's criticism of Skinner on this point, see in particular the afterword to the 2003 edition of *The Machiavellian Moment*, esp. pp. 558–62.

(failing that) to cultivate the kind of character that was considered appropriate for a free man, but it is unlikely that he would have viewed slavery as something that was in need of justification as such, or if he had, that he would have appealed to the language of freedom in criticizing it. When Aristotle offers his qualified defense – and qualified criticism – of the Greek practice of slavery, it is to the language of justice, not freedom, that he appeals.[15]

As salient as the ethical dimensions of the language of freedom ultimately became, it is important to keep the status-based origins of the term firmly in view, not only because they provide the empirical foundation on which the ethical usage was later built, but also because the ways in which these connections were drawn were crucial to the development of a specifically republican conception of freedom. The free man was expected above all to be self-sufficient: As the *Digest* puts it, he is *sui juris*; under his own jurisdiction and not under the power [*potestas*] of another.[16] Indeed, the Romans thought of dependence in more than strictly legal terms. The popular dramatist Pubilius Syrus held, for example, that "to accept a favor is to sell one's liberty," and his contemporary Marcus Tullius Cicero went so far as to argue that "those who think that they are wealthy, honoured and blessed do not want even to be under obligation from a kind service," because for such people "accepting patronage or being labeled as a client is tantamount to death."[17] These remarks convey well the extra-political roots of the classical language of freedom: One is free, in this way of thinking, if one is able to act under one's own initiative instead of merely reacting to the deeds of others, benevolent though they might be. To be free, in other words, is to be free of necessity – even of the moral necessity of repaying a good deed in kind. To depend on another person, whether tyrant or patron, master or benefactor, is to be unfree to that extent.

---

[15] Aristotle, *Politics*, book 1, chapters 4–7. P. A. Brunt observes that the "Greeks and Romans hardly ever embarrassed themselves with the notion that freedom was a natural or divine right, which their acceptance of the institution of slavery denied," "*Libertas* in the Republic," in idem, *The Fall of the Roman Republic and Related Essays* (New York: Oxford University Press, 1988), p. 289. See also Orlando Patterson, *Freedom*, vol. 1: *Freedom in the Making of Western Culture* (New York: Basic Books, 1991), part 2.

[16] *Digest* 1.6.1; here again, the source is Gaius.

[17] Pubilius Syrus, *Sentences* 58; Marcus Tullius Cicero, *On Duties*, trans. Margaret Atkins (New York: Cambridge University Press, 1991), p. 91 (book 2 §69). Ironically, Syrus himself was a freed slave. Cf. also Xenophon, *Memorabilia*, book 1, chapter 2, where Socrates suggests that he is preserving his freedom by refusing payment for his teaching.

It follows, of course, that the free man must be economically independent, so that he does not rely on others for his livelihood and is not obliged either to ask for or to accept favors. As Arendt puts it, paraphrasing Demosthenes, "[p]overty forces the free man to act like a slave."[18] It follows also that the secure ownership of property, and especially of landed property, is essential to the enjoyment of freedom. Thus when Cicero argues that "there is no kind of gainful employment that is better, more fruitful, more pleasant and more worthy of a free man than agriculture," he is not commending the actual practice of agricultural labor, which he describes elsewhere as being menial and therefore beneath a free man's station.[19] Nor is he simply expressing the typically Roman view that rural life, because it is set apart from the factional intrigues of the city, is especially conducive to the cultivation of individual and thus (ironically) of civic virtue, although he certainly shared that view. He is appealing above all to the fact that land is the most secure kind of material possession, and that the wealthy landowner is therefore insulated from economic misfortune in a way that the wealthy merchant, for example, is not. Indeed, Cicero insists that the gains of trade are ephemeral unless and until they have been converted into real property: "[W]e have every right to praise" the successful merchant, he writes, "if ever such men are satiated [*satiata*], or rather satisfied [*contenta*], with what they have gained, and just as they have often left the high seas for the harbour, now leave the harbour itself for land in the country."[20] A similar view is expressed in the opening lines of *The Merchant of Venice*, in which Antonio's friends attribute his unhappiness to anxiety over his commercial ventures: "Your mind," Salarino remarks, "is tossing on the ocean."

As the passage from Shakespeare suggests, the association of commerce with insecurity and of labor with degradation is not peculiar either to Cicero or to the Romans. Aristotle holds, for example, that "it is noble not to practice any sordid craft, since it is the mark of a free man not to live at another's beck and call," and that "[t]he life of money-making" cannot be the best life because it is "undertaken under compulsion." He concludes that in the ideal city only the free citizens would be landowners,

---

[18] Arendt, *The Human Condition* (Chicago: University of Chicago Press, 1958), p. 64; cf. Demosthenes, *Orationes* 57.45. For a broader treatment of Greek sources on this point see K. J. Dover, *Greek Popular Morality in the Time of Plato and Aristotle* (Oxford: Basil Blackwell, 1974), pp. 109–10.

[19] Cicero, *On Duties*, pp. 58–9 (book 1 §151); cf. idem, *De finibus bonorum et malorum*, book 1 §1.

[20] Cicero, *On Duties*, p. 58 (book 1 §151).

and that agricultural labor, like menial labor of any kind, would be reserved for slaves or barbarians. Not only would such an arrangement provide free men with the leisure time necessary for the cultivation and practice of virtue, he argues, but ownership of the land would bind them more closely to the fate of the polity.[21] Nor were such views limited to the realm of the ideal: "[L]ong hair in Sparta," Aristotle reports, "is a mark of a free man, as it is not easy to perform any menial task when one's hair is long"; and "in Thebes there was a law that no one could share in office who had not abstained from selling in the market for a period of ten years."[22] This classical suspicion toward commerce extended from the activities of individuals to those of the polity itself. Plato's Athenian Stranger remarks, for example, that "proximity to the sea...infects a place with commerce and the money-making that comes with retail trade, and engenders shifty and untrustworthy dispositions in souls...thereby tak[ing] away the trust and friendship a city feels for itself and for the rest of humanity." Cicero argues along similar lines that "[m]aritime cities are...subject to corruption and alteration of character," because "the desire for trade and travel" leads citizens to "abandon...the cultivation of fields and of military skill....Nothing did more to weaken gradually, and ultimately to destroy, Carthage and Corinth," he suggests, "than this wandering and dissipation of their citizens."[23]

---

[21] Aristotle, *Rhetoric*, book 1, chapter 9, quoting W. Rhys Roberts's translation in *The Rhetoric and Poetics of Aristotle*, ed. Edward P. J. Corbett (New York: Modern Library, 1984) at p. 59; *Nicomachean Ethics*, book 1, chapter 4, quoting David Ross's translation (New York: Oxford University Press, 1980 [1925]) at p. 7. See also Plato, *Statesman*, 289e–290a and *Laws*, 644a (book 1). On landowning and agricultural labor see Aristotle, *Politics*, book 7, chapters 8–10, and cf. chapter 6 of Xenophon's *Economics*. On the connection between the ownership of private property and a concern for the common good, see also *Politics*, book 2, chapter 5, where Aristotle rejects the argument, advanced by Socrates in Plato's *Republic*, that the ruling class should be barred from owning property. On Greek attitudes regarding economics, see also Dover, *Greek Popular Morality*, pp. 40–1 and, for a more detailed discussion, Paul A. Rahe, *Republics Ancient and Modern: Classical Republicanism and the American Revolution* (Chapel Hill: University of North Carolina Press, 1992), book 1, chapter 3.

[22] Aristotle, *Rhetoric*, p. 59 (book 1, chapter 9); *Politics*, book 3, chapter 5, quoting R. F. Stalley's revision of the Barker translation (New York: Oxford University Press, 1995 [1946]), p. 96.

[23] Plato, *Laws* 705a (book 4), quoting Thomas L. Pangle's translation (Chicago: University of Chicago Press, 1988) at p. 90; Cicero, *De re publica*, book 2 §7, quoting James E. G. Zetzel's translation in idem, ed., *On the Commonwealth and On the Laws* (New York: Cambridge University Press, 1999), p. 35. It is worth pointing out in this connection that Athens and Rome were both naval powers situated at some distance from the sea.

The roots of this way of thinking lie in the fact that the unfree class – composed variously of women, slaves, menial laborers, and foreigners – was responsible for providing the material necessities and comforts that made it possible for free men to devote their time to "higher" pursuits such as politics, warfare, and (somewhat later) the cultivation of the "liberal" ("free") arts. The most straightforward way of defending this arrangement was of course to argue that the subordinate class simply lacked the capacity – in classical terms, the virtue – to participate in these activities, and this argument was indeed often made, especially in the case of women, where it is sometimes made even today.[24] A somewhat more sophisticated version of this line of argument appealed to the corrupting effects of menial labor itself, arguing that members of the unfree class not only lack the opportunity to cultivate their virtue (which is true enough), but that the activities in which they are engaged will be fatal over time to whatever virtue they might originally have possessed. Indeed, for Aristotle the connection between menial labor and the loss of virtue is definitional: "The term 'mechanical' [*banausos*] should properly be applied," he argues, "to any occupation, art, or instruction which is calculated to make the body, or soul, or mind of a freeman unfit for the pursuit and practice of virtue."[25] The implication here is that the unfree class, because it plays a utilitarian role in society, is likely to acquire a utilitarian cast of mind, that they are likely to become self-regarding, calculating, and even duplicitous. Thus Homer has the swineherd Eumaeus remark that "Zeus…takes away one half of the virtue from a man, once the day of slavery closes upon him."[26] As C. S. Lewis observes, and as the passage from Homer suggests, the "servile" character is typically portrayed in literature as being "shrewd, cunning, up to every trick, always with an eye to the main chance, determined to 'look after number one.'" The free man, by contrast, is said to be impartial, ingenuous (a word derived from the Latin *ingenuus*, or free born), and indifferent both to personal comfort and to personal safety – in the former case out of magnanimity rather than asceticism, and in the latter out of courage rather

---

[24] Aristotle famously appeals to the natural incapacity of women, slaves, and "barbarians" to practice virtue in book 1 of his *Politics*, and to that of "mechanics" (*banausoi*) in book 3, chapter 5.

[25] Aristotle, *Politics*, p. 300 (book 8, chapter 2), amended to give "virtue" rather than "goodness" as the translation of *aretē*. Cf. ibid., book 3, chapter 5, Plato, *Republic* 495d and Cicero, *On Duties*, book 1 §§150–1.

[26] Homer, *Odyssey* 17.322–3, quoting Richmond Lattimore's translation (New York: Harper & Row, 1967), p. 261.

than unworldliness.[27] Cicero captures well the paradoxical quality of this
ethos: "[E]xcellence and greatness of spirit," he writes, "shine out both in
increasing influence and in acquiring benefits for oneself and those dear to
one, and also, and much more, in disdaining the very same things."[28]

It is to be expected, of course, that when one group of people enjoys
and seeks to maintain certain privileges with respect to another, it will try
to legitimate its position by drawing invidious distinctions between itself
and the subordinate group. In this sense the ethical use of the language
of freedom was a natural if rather self-serving extension of its more fundamental status-based meaning. Indeed, this weaving together of appeals
to status and virtue gave rise to a coherent ideology of freedom which,
despite its reactionary character, provided the raw material out of which
the republican conception of freedom was ultimately built. The political implications of this "pre-republican" way of thinking are straightforward: If the free man is the autarchic man – one who acts on his own
initiative rather than depending on others – then the free polity is, by
analogy, one that is independent, self-sufficient, and capable of defending itself against its neighbors.[29] Similarly, if the free man is the virtuous
man – one who acts in a way befitting his status – then the free polity
is one that cultivates the virtue of its citizens and provides them with
opportunities to display it, whether in the forum or on the battlefield. The
appeal to freedom so understood was typically made in order to defend
the customary prerogatives of a ruling class – keeping in mind of course
that this class could be "democratic" in the sense of including a fairly
large proportion of the non-slave male population.[30] These prerogatives

[27] Lewis, *Studies in Words*, p. 112; cf. Dover, *Greek Popular Morality*, pp. 114–6.
[28] Cicero, *On Duties*, p. 8 (book 1 §17; cf. §68).
[29] Kurt Raaflaub argues that the language of freedom (*eleutheria*) first acquired political
    salience in the 5th century BCE, when oligarchic Sparta and democratic Athens cooper-
    ated to defend the "freedom" (that is to say, the independence) of the Greeks against the
    Persian invasion, *The Discovery of Freedom in Ancient Greece*, trans. Renate Franciscono
    (revised ed., Chicago: University of Chicago Press, 2004), chapter 3.
[30] Hansen argues that "as a constitutional ideal *eleutheria* was specifically democratic and
    not a value praised in oligarchies or monarchies," that "the oligarchs (and the philos-
    ophers) did not have an alternative interpretation of *eleutheria*" but "simply rejected
    eleutheria as a mistaken ideal," "Liberty as a Democratic Ideal," p. 98. This not only
    overlooks the fact that thinkers such as Xenophon, Plato, and Aristotle appeal to the lan-
    guage of freedom in order to justify the exclusion of the "lower" classes from citizenship;
    it also overlooks Aristotle's distinction between freedom understood as "doing what one
    likes," which he takes to be the "perverted" democratic view, and freedom understood as
    "liv[ing] by the rule of the constitution," that is, in a regime that contains both oligarchic
    and democratic elements: *Politics*, pp. 208–9 (book 5, chapter 9; cf. book 6, chapter 2).
    Raaflaub argues, in contrast to Hansen, that by the end of the 5th century the Greek

could be endangered from without by the threat of invasion and the loss of independence, or from within by the threat of tyranny and the collapse of a public space for the cultivation and display of virtue. Moreover, the internal and external threats to freedom could be traded off against one another: The ruling elites in the smaller Greek *poleis* were sometimes willing and even eager to accept foreign rule if their domestic privileges could thereby be preserved, and the Romans often courted tyranny by empowering dictators to put down rebellions or repel foreign threats.

To the extent that the language of freedom was used to legitimate existing status hierarchies – and *not* to question the way in which power was distributed and exercised within a given polity – the freedom of the ruling class, and of the polity itself, was little more than a background feature of social and political life.[31] However, when a word connoting status is given an ethical meaning, it can then be used for critical as well as for legitimating purposes, and this simple fact created the conceptual space for a more open-ended and contentious understanding of the implications of a commitment to freedom. After all, even the free elite could not entirely overlook the fact that some of the people who were free as a matter of status seemed to lack the expected ethical qualities, and (more troublingly) that some of those who were empirically unfree seemed to possess them. It is telling in this regard that Lewis names Figaro and Odysseus – one a servant by status, the other not – as literary exemplars of the "servile" character type.[32] Although the classical polities were insulated from the radical implications of this insight as long as slavery remained a socially and economically indispensable institution,[33] the disjunction between the empirical and the ethical dimensions of freedom

language of freedom was "intimately connected with the traditional claim of the aristocratic and wealthy upper classes to social eminence and exclusivity" and was indeed "the centerpiece of the oligarchic program and propaganda": "They picked up the politicized typology of the free man propagated by democracy, and declared that it could be valid only for those who by birth, wealth, education, and moral capacity were truly able to live according to the norms expressed in it," "Democracy, Oligarchy, and the Concept of the 'Free Citizen' in Late Fifth-Century Athens," *Political Theory* 11 (1983), pp. 534–5; cf. *Discovery of Freedom*, pp. 243–7.

[31] Thus Raaflaub writes with respect to the early Greeks that "the free – or, more precisely, the noble elite on whom the poet [Homer] focuses – did not ordinarily regard their freedom as a fact worth noting. Freedom was thus either unimportant or taken for granted," *Discovery of Freedom*, p. 30.

[32] Lewis, *Studies in Words*, p. 112.

[33] As Brunt puts it, "Some Greek thinkers had asserted that all men were born free, and that slavery was unjust as an institution, though without demanding its actual abolition: slavery was so deeply rooted in the economic organization and traditions of the Graeco-Roman world that this was never thought of," "*Libertas* in the Republic," p. 289.

nevertheless made it possible to say that even a slave can be free in a met-
aphorical sense, just as a free man can be metaphorically enslaved. This
line of thinking, which is captured well in the fragment of Menander, "live
in slavery with the spirit of a free man, and you will be no slave,"[34] was
most fully developed in Stoic and, somewhat later, in Christian thought.[35]
Indeed, the use of the word "freedom" to refer to the proper ordering of
the soul and the proper orientation of the will is now so well established
in the form of the idea of "positive" liberty that its class origins are all
but forgotten.[36]

More important for our purposes, the perception that there was an
imperfect fit between the empirical and the ethical dimensions of freedom
encouraged some classical thinkers to pay closer attention to the question
of how it is that one comes to acquire or to lose one's virtue in the first
place. As we have seen, Aristotle and Cicero tend to focus on cultivating
the natural virtue of an aristocratic class. Specifically republican thinking
about freedom begins with a more fertile hypothesis: that what makes
it possible for the free man to practice virtue is not his social status as
such, but rather the fact that this status shields him from the influence
of arbitrary power, that is, from power that can be exercised at will (in
Latin, *ad arbitrium*) by those who possess it. According to this way of
thinking, a servile character need not be the result of any personal failing, or even of the fact that one is obliged to perform menial tasks. It can
follow instead from the simple fact that one is not able to display one's
true character as long as one is in the presence and under the thumb of
an arbitrary power: One must instead flatter and grovel before (and, in
private, mock and scheme against) that power.[37] Thus where Aristotle

---

[34] Cited in Lewis, *Studies in Words*, p. 112.

[35] Augustine argues, for example, that "the good man is free, even if he is a slave, whereas
the bad man is a slave even if he reigns: a slave, not to one man, but, what is worse, to as
many masters as he has vices": *The City of God Against the Pagans*, trans. R. W. Dyson
(New York: Cambridge University Press, 1998), p. 147 (book 4, chapter 3; cf. book
19, chapter 15). The scriptural roots of this line of thinking lie in the Gospel of John,
where Jesus says that his true disciples "will know the truth, and the truth will make
[them] free." The Pharisees respond (somewhat puzzlingly) that they "are descendents of
Abraham, and have never been slaves to anyone," to which Jesus responds that they are
nevertheless "slave[s] to sin": John 8:32–34 (NRSV); cf. 2 Peter 2:19. The *locus classicus*
in Stoic thought is book 4, chapter 1 of the *Discourses* of Epictetus.

[36] On this see, for example, Arendt, "What Is Freedom?," esp. pp. 145–8 and, in a more
polemical vein, the first essay of Friedrich Nietzsche's *On the Genealogy of Morals*.

[37] I am indebted here to Pettit's work on republican freedom, though I place more weight
than he does on the role that the cultivation and practice of virtue plays in republican
thought. See especially the first two chapters of his *Republicanism*, as well as Skinner's

argues bluntly that "[t]yrants love to be flattered," and that "nobody with
the soul of a freeman can stoop to that," Tacitus, describing the behavior of the Roman senatorial class under the emperor Tiberius, offers a
more distinctively republican view – that "those times were so tainted
and contaminated by sycophancy" that "brilliancy had to be protected
by compliance" – and suggests that Tiberius himself, "who disliked public freedom, was averse to such prompt and prostrate passivity from the
servile." This vivid depiction of the corrupting effects of absolute rule is
echoed more than 1,500 years later by John Milton, who, writing near
the end of the Interregnum, warns his countrymen that the restoration of
the monarchy would bring with it "the multiplying of a servile crew, not
of servants only, but of nobility and gentry...their minds debased with
court opinions, contrary to all virtue and reformation," and that the freemen of England would again be subject to a king who "pageant[s] himself up and down in progress among the perpetual bowings and cringings
of an abject people."[38]

Thus from a republican point of view a free man's virtue can be threatened not only by vice, but also by the corruption that is wrought by
the presence of arbitrary power. The first step in cultivating virtue must
therefore be to place power under the supervision and control of those
over whom it is exercised. In other words, we must be vigilant against
arbitrary power not only because we do not want to suffer the indignity
of dependence, but also and more importantly because the very fact of
dependence will make us increasingly unable and even unwilling to resist
the power on which we depend, thereby preventing us from cultivating
and displaying our virtue. To be sure, the idea that the absence of virtue can *always* be attributed to the influence of arbitrary power, and that
a commitment to freedom therefore entails a strict egalitarianism, was
not seriously entertained until the 18th century.[39] The more frankly elitist

Liberty before Liberalism, which is, by his own account, "deeply indebted" to Pettit's
ideas (p. 37n; cf. p. xi).

[38] Aristotle, *Politics*, p. 220 (book 5, chapter 11); Tacitus, *Annals*, book 3 §65, quoting A. J.
Woodman's translation (Indianapolis: Hackett, 2004), p. 115; Milton, "The Ready and
Easy Way to Establish a Free Commonwealth" (1660), in idem, *The Major Works*, ed.
Stephen Orgel and Jonathan Goldberg (Oxford: Oxford University Press, 1991), p. 336.

[39] Rousseau is perhaps the earliest candidate for holding such a view, though his
"egalitarianism" is a purely masculine affair. Mary Wollstonecraft may have been the first
to argue (in print) that the servile behavior of women is a product of the arbitrary power
that men have over them: "[T]heir sole ambition is to be fair, to raise emotion instead of
inspiring respect; and this ignoble desire, like the servility in absolute monarchies, destroys
all strength of character....Men have submitted to superior strength to enjoy with impunity the pleasure of the moment – women have only done the same, and therefore till it

view that servile behavior is the sign of a servile character persisted, even among republicans, long after the rise of republican political thought – as it persists, *mutatis mutandis*, even today. Nevertheless, as I suggested at the beginning of this chapter, we can mark the boundaries of specifically *republican* thinking about freedom at the point at which the ability to practice virtue, and thus to live as a free man (or person) should, is associated with the control of arbitrary power. We can attribute the complexity of republican political thought to the wide variety of ways in which this relationship can be understood. It is to these complexities that we now turn.

1.3 REPUBLICAN MEANS

It should already be clear that it would be a mistake, or at least a gross oversimplification, to equate republicanism with direct popular rule, as is suggested by Benjamin Constant's influential claim (itself strongly influenced by the writings of Jean-Jacques Rousseau) that ancient liberty "consisted in exercising collectively, but directly, several parts of the complete sovereignty."[40] It is of course true, as Constant emphasizes, that the enjoyment of republican freedom requires that the rulers of a polity be accountable to those over whom they rule, and that the words "freedom" and "citizenship" were often used interchangeably in the classical republics.[41] However, the republican tradition associates direct popular sovereignty not with freedom, but rather with the arbitrary rule of one social class – the *demos* or *plebs*, the poor majority – over the others.[42]

is proved that the courtier, who servilely resigns the birthright of a man, is not a moral agent; it cannot be demonstrated that woman is essentially inferior to man because she has always been subjected": *A Vindication of the Rights of Woman* (1792), chapter 2.

[40] Benjamin Constant, "The Liberty of the Ancients Compared with That of the Moderns" (1819), in idem, *Political Writings*, ed. Biancamaria Fontana (New York: Cambridge University Press, 1988), p. 311; cf. Rousseau, *On the Social Contract*, book 1, chapters 6–7.

[41] See, for example, Brunt, "*Libertas* in the Republic," p. 296; Lewis, *Studies in Words*, p. 125; and Chaim Wirszubski, *Libertas as a Political Idea at Rome During the Late Republic and Early Principate* (New York: Cambridge University Press, 1950), pp. 3–4.

[42] Thus whereas Claude Nicolet is correct to argue that for the Romans liberty consisted above all in "the certainty that the magistrates' coercive power was not unlimited," he seems to me to err in suggesting that for the Romans a free regime was one "in which the whole people exercises power as directly as possible," and to be closer to the mark in emphasizing that the language of liberty was "invoked by everyone at all levels: by the people as a whole *vis à vis* the dominant oligarchies (patricians and senators), and by the plebs against members of the old *gentes*... by the Senate against pressure from magistrates or the threat of personal power, and by magistrates against the claims of tribunes": *The World of the Citizen in Republican Rome*, trans. P. S. Falla (London: Batsford Academic & Educational, 1980 [1976]), p. 320.

Thus Thucydides reports that the Spartan general Brasidas was able to sway the Acanthians to his side by assuring them that "I do not consider that I should be bringing you freedom in any real sense if I should disregard your constitution, and enslave the many to the few *or the few to the many*." Livy argues along similar lines that "the mob is either a humble slave or a cruel master," unable to observe "the middle way of liberty… with any respect for moderation or law."[43] The classical republicans therefore distinguish between "democracy" understood as the extension of citizenship to previously excluded classes of people and "democracy" understood as a regime that rules in the name and according to the interests of a particular class. The concern to extend citizenship to all who have the capacity for virtue makes it possible (though not strictly necessary) for republicans to be "democrats" in the former sense. The concern to prevent the arbitrary exercise of political power makes it difficult, if not impossible, for them to be "democrats" in the latter.[44]

It follows that the classical republicans were committed not to direct popular sovereignty, as Constant suggests, but rather to a mixture and division of powers that was meant to ensure that no faction in the polity – even, and perhaps especially, a majority faction – was "sovereign" over the others.[45] As Cicero puts it, "if the people has the greatest power and everything is done by its decision, this is called liberty but is in fact license. But when each fears another, both individuals and classes, then because no one is sure of himself, there is a kind of bargain made between the people and the magnates, and out of this arises that combined form of state which Scipio praised."[46] This idea of "combined" or mixed government

---

[43] Thucydides, *The Peloponnesian War*, book 4 §86, quoting T. E. Wick's revision of the Crawley translation (New York: Modern Library, 1982), pp. 268–9 (emphasis added); Livy, *Ab urbe condita*, book 24, chapter 25 §8 (cf. book 3, chapter 65 §11), quoting Aubrey de Sélincourt's translation in idem, *Hannibal's War* (Harmondsworth: Penguin Press, 1965), p. 262.

[44] For the distinction between these two senses of democracy see, for example, Aristotle, *Politics*, book 4, chapter 4 and Cicero, *De re publica*, book 1 §§47–9. The ambiguity on this point in both Greek and Roman political thought arises in part from the fact that, as M. I. Finley points out, the words *demos* and *populus* each carried a double meaning; referring on the one hand to "the citizen-body as a whole," and on the other hand to "the common people, the many, the poor": *Politics in the Ancient World* (New York: Cambridge University Press, 1983), pp. 1–2.

[45] As Finley puts it, "one of the most important privileges of the Greek citizen was the freedom to engage in *stasis*"; that is, to defend the interests of his own class or faction against the encroachments of others: "The Freedom of the Citizen in the Ancient World" (1976), reprinted in idem, *Economy and Society in Ancient Greece* (New York: Viking Press, 1981), quoted at p. 82; cf. *Politics in the Ancient World*, pp. 105–6.

[46] Cicero, *De re publica*, pp. 65–6 (book 3 §23). Josiah Ober argues along similar lines that the Greek *poleis* "can, for the most part, be defined as republics" in the sense that

was most closely associated in antiquity with the Spartan and Roman republics, whose liberty was said to depend on, and even to consist in, the sharing of power by the few and the many – although in the latter case there was (and is) disagreement as to whether this arrangement is best described in consensual terms, as in Cicero, or in conflictual ones, as in Machiavelli.[47] Mixed government was most notably defended in the modern period by Montesquieu, who argues that "[d]emocracy and aristocracy are not free states by their nature," that "[p]olitical liberty is found only in moderate governments...when power is not abused," and that in order to preserve it "power must check power by the arrangement of things."[48] The latter claim, which was famously borrowed by James Madison in *Federalist* 51, aptly summarizes the republican position on popular rule: Political power in a republican polity is exercised by a part acting in the name of, and somehow accountable to, the whole, or by several parts of the whole acting independently of one another, rather than by the collectivity itself. In short, republican freedom, far from consisting in direct popular sovereignty, is invariably the product of careful institutional design.

The concern to balance the interests of different classes against one another has profound, if somewhat equivocal, implications for republican economic policy. On the one hand, citizens enjoy republican freedom only insofar as they are secure against arbitrary interference in their personal affairs, and this requires that their property be respected. As Cicero puts it, "it is the proper function of a citizenship and a city to ensure for everyone a free and unworried guardianship of his possessions." On the

they "existed for a very long time in a state of dynamic social tension, tension that was a direct result of [their] 'failure' to settle into a stable political hierarchy among native-born adult males": *Political Dissent in Democratic Athens: Intellectual Critics of Popular Rule* (Princeton, NJ: Princeton University Press, 1998), p. 4.

[47] The *locus classicus* for the view that Spartan and Roman liberty was due to their "mixed" constitutions is the sixth book of Polybius' *Histories*, dating from the 2nd century BCE. For Cicero's adaptation of the Polybian model, see his *De re publica*, books 1–2, especially book 1 §§41–55; for Machiavelli's, see his *Discourses on Livy*, book 1, chapters 2–6. Polybius credits Lycurgus, the founder of Sparta, with inventing the principle of mixed government, and so it is somewhat puzzling that Constant treats the Spartan constitution as an exemplar of "ancient" liberty in his sense of the term. For a useful discussion of the origins and legacy of this way of thinking, see Wilfried Nippel, "Ancient and Modern Republicanism: 'Mixed Constitution' and 'Ephors,'" in Biancamaria Fontana, ed., *The Invention of the Modern Republic* (New York: Cambridge University Press, 1994), pp. 6–26.

[48] Charles de Montesquieu, *The Spirit of the Laws*, trans. Anne Cohler, Basia Miller, and Harold Stone (New York: Cambridge University Press, 1989 [1748]), p. 155 (book 11, chapter 4).

other hand, a polity is free in the republican sense only if no individual or class is able to enforce its will on the whole, and this requires that the gap between rich and poor not be too great. Otherwise, as Aristotle puts it, "[t]he result is a city, not of freemen, but only of slaves and masters: a state of envy on the one side and of contempt on the other."[49] Needless to say, these two lines of argument point in rather different directions. On the one hand, the most obvious way to check the power of the rich is by regulating the possession and consumption of property, whether through sumptuary laws, legally or socially enforced norms of philanthropy, or as in the case of the modern welfare state, redistributive taxation. A more radical alternative is to redistribute landed property itself, as Lycurgus did in Sparta and as the Gracchi tried to do in Rome. On the other hand, the most obvious reason that property holders have to fear the power of the state is that it might be used to confiscate or otherwise interfere with their property. The challenge of taking both of these insights into account plays a central role in the republican tradition, from the effort to balance the interests of rich and poor that runs through the middle books of Aristotle's *Politics* to the similarly motivated voting schemes that make up the heart of John Stuart Mill's *Considerations on Representative Government*.[50]

Republican political thought in its practical dimension is therefore concerned on the one hand with the design of reliable and (above all) pluralistic forms of political representation, and on the other hand with achieving a durable balance of power among the various classes or factions that exist in a given polity – keeping in mind, of course, that in all classical and most modern republics the largest "faction," made up

---

[49] Cicero, *On Duties*, p. 95 (book 2 §78; cf. §73 and book 1 §§21, 51); Aristotle, *Politics*, p. 158 (book 4, chapter 11; cf. book 2, chapters 5 and 7).

[50] Aristotle, *Politics*, book 4, chapters 8–9, book 5, chapters 1–9, book 6, chapters 1–7; Mill, *Considerations on Representative Government*, chapters 6–8. Eric Nelson traces the careers of the redistributive and property-centered strands of republican thought through the early modern period, although he oversimplifies matters somewhat by labeling the former as the "Greek" and the latter as the "Roman" position. See his *The Greek Tradition in Republican Thought* (New York: Cambridge University Press, 2004). For evidence of a property-centered strand in Greek thought see, for example, Aristotle, *Politics*, book 2, chapters 5 and 7; for evidence of a redistributive strand in Roman thought see, for example, Brunt, "*Libertas* in the Republic," pp. 346–9. On the dangers of reading too much into the "utopian" classical references to the redistribution of property see Finley, *Politics in the Ancient World*, pp. 108–12. Nelson has since argued that the early modern turn from "Roman" to "Greek" theories of property was biblical in inspiration: See his *The Hebrew Republic: Jewish Sources and the Transformation of European Political Thought* (Cambridge, MA: Harvard University Press, 2010), chapter 2.

of women, slaves, and anyone else who was excluded from citizenship, had no legitimate role to play in public life, and thus no freedom at all. However, the existence of institutional safeguards is only one of three conditions that have to be met if arbitrary power is to be checked and republican freedom secured. In order for those safeguards to function properly, the citizens of a republic must be able to agree among themselves about what constitutes an arbitrary exercise of power in the first place; that is, they must be able to distinguish between those political outcomes in which the interests of all citizens have been properly taken into account and those in which the interests of a particular individual or faction have been imposed on the whole. In more traditional language, republican freedom depends on the existence not only of a system of free institutions, but also of a shared conception of the common good. This requirement raises a familiar but nevertheless daunting set of questions: Both republicans and their critics have long recognized that even if the goal of controlling the exercise of political power were to be realized, it is nevertheless likely, and perhaps inevitable, that this power will be exercised in a way that appears arbitrary, and thus freedom-denying, to many people.

If the problem of *checking* arbitrary power accounts for much of the first-order complexity of republican thought, the problem of *recognizing* arbitrary power confronts it with a second-order dilemma that is captured nicely by Rousseau when he writes of the irreducible tension between the general will of the political community and the particular wills of the individuals and groups of which it is composed. We can distinguish between what we might call "supply-side" and "demand-side" strategies for responding to this dilemma. According to the former approach, which is exemplified in Locke's *Second Treatise*, the control of arbitrary power requires that we limit the domain of governmental authority in such a way that it can only be used to pursue the common good. This line of argument takes the definition of arbitrary power as settled and seeks to prevent or minimize the exercise of power so defined. According to the latter approach, which is exemplified in Rousseau's *Social Contract* and in his constitutional writings, a commitment to free government requires that we mold the desires of the citizenry through civic education programs, sumptuary laws, and so on, so that they learn (or are compelled) to place the common good ahead of their own particular interests.[51] This

---

[51] For a detailed appreciation of the central role that the idea of civic education or *paideia* played in Greek political life see Rahe, *Republics Ancient and Modern*, book 1, chapter 4 and passim.

line of argument takes certain ends as settled and tries to ensure that those who are compelled to pursue them will not view the power that compels them as arbitrary. If the former approach makes constant vigilance the price of freedom, the latter associates freedom with something more like constant forbearance. Despite the obvious differences between them, these strategies nevertheless complement and are typically used in conjunction with one another: Republicans have to ensure both that the abuse of political power is resisted and that its legitimate exercise is not. Thus even Locke, the revolutionary, associates liberty with obedience to law, and even Rousseau, the enemy of individual rights, associates the loss of liberty with the failure to resist tyranny.[52]

Not only do republican citizens need to agree about what constitutes an arbitrary use of power and devise ways of checking it, they must also be able to see for themselves where and when such power is exercised. This is perhaps a less familiar claim than the first two, but it is nevertheless reflected in the traditional republican association of a lack of transparency in the conduct of public affairs with the presence or threat of tyranny. Indeed, this concern provides part of the rationale for the classical republicans' allegiance to mixed government: It would seem, after all, that the various classes in a polity need to participate directly in the exercise of political power if they are to be confident that it is being exercised in accordance with their interests. The independent value of transparency was brought out with special clarity, however, at the time of the American Founding, when the authors of the Federal Constitution were faced with the problem of checking a government whose power was derived from a single source: "the people" taken as a whole – or, more precisely, a male and propertied subset of them. Because they could not count on different social classes to check each other, as had been the case in Rome and (on a certain understanding[53]) in Britain, the Federalists devised instead an elaborate system of separated powers, indirect elections, and staggered terms of office that would, they hoped, give the nascent federal government both the ability and the inclination to check itself. As Madison put it in *Federalist* 51, "the separate and distinct exercise of the different powers of government...is admitted on all hands to be essential to the preservation of liberty," and "the great security against a gradual concentration of the several powers in the same department, consists in giving to those

---

[52] Locke, *Second Treatise* §§22, 57; Rousseau, *Social Contract*, book 3, chapter 15.
[53] That is to say, Montesquieu's: see his *Spirit of the Laws*, book 11, chapter 6, and cf. book 19, chapter 27. For Madison's debt to Montesquieu on this point, see especially *Federalist* 47.

who administer each department the necessary constitutional means and personal motives to resist encroachments of the others."

As ingenious as this solution was, opponents of the Constitution saw a threat to liberty in its very complexity. Patrick Henry, for example, argued with some justice that "this government is of such an intricate and complicated nature, that no man on this earth can know its real operation."[54] Bernard Manin captures well the thought behind Henry's complaint: When "each branch [of government] is authorized, but not required, to exercise a part of the function primarily assigned to another ... the people cannot systematically associate each with a certain type of task. Before laying the blame, then, the people must trace *case by case* the particular process which resulted in the decision that they condemn."[55] Such a process is of course both tedious to undertake and highly uncertain in its results, especially when, as Manin points out, the realization of a given outcome may be due in part to the *failure* of a given party to act – as is often the case with respect to judicial review, the presidential veto, or in recent years, the arcane procedures of the Senate. The enjoyment of republican freedom requires not only that governments be prevented from exercising their power in a way that runs contrary to the interests of their citizens, but also that citizens be able to determine where the responsibility for a bad outcome actually lies. As Henry saw, the success of the Founders in achieving the former aim made the achievement of the latter even more difficult.

1.4 REPUBLICAN ENDS

I began this chapter by suggesting that we will only be able to come to terms with the complexity of republican thought, and thus with the complex nature of the relationship between republican and market freedom, if we first make an effort to see the republican tradition whole in its broadest outlines. I have argued that we should mark the boundaries of republican thought at the point where the practice of virtue is associated with the control of arbitrary power, and I have shown how this way of thinking about freedom arose out of an older – though in some ways still influential – and more purely status-based usage. I have argued, finally,

54 Cited in Herbert J. Storing, *What the Anti-Federalists Were For: The Political Thought of the Opponents of the Constitution* (Chicago: University of Chicago Press, 1981), p. 54; cf. chapter 7 passim.
55 Bernard Manin, "Checks, Balances and Boundaries: The Separation of Powers in the Constitutional Debate of 1787," in Fontana, ed., *op. cit.*, pp. 45–6 (original emphasis).

that the enjoyment of republican freedom depends on the satisfaction of three conditions: first, the shared perception of a "common good" that makes it possible for the citizens of a polity to agree about when power has been exercised arbitrarily; second, the existence of institutional safeguards that ensure that those who hold political power are constrained to pursue the common good so defined; and third, the presence of enough transparency in the conduct of public affairs that an attentive citizenry will be able to see where and when power is being abused and to hold those who are responsible accountable for their actions. I have illustrated this line of argument by drawing on thinkers who are as widely separated from one another in time and temperament as Aristotle, Cicero, Machiavelli, Locke, Montesquieu, Rousseau, Madison, and Mill. I hope to have shown, then, that this way of defining the boundaries of the republican tradition is broad enough to capture most if not all of the thinkers and ideas that have been associated with it.

We are now ready to look more carefully at the internal diversity of republican political thought and, in particular, at the variety of ways in which a commitment to republican freedom might be understood. We have already seen that it is possible for republicans to disagree, sometimes rather sharply, over the question of how republican freedom is best preserved: Consider, for example, the disagreements between Cicero and Machiavelli over the relative merits of consensual and conflictual politics, between Locke and Rousseau over the relative importance of limiting the power of the government and limiting the desires of the citizenry itself, and between Madison and Henry over the relative merits of complexity and simplicity in the design of political institutions. These disagreements can be attributed to differences in the challenges with which these thinkers were faced, or to differences in judgment about how best to respond to the challenges that they faced in common. The republican tradition has also been characterized, however, by deep and sometimes fundamental disagreement over the question of what republican freedom itself consists in. This fact may seem to be at odds with my claim to have defined the boundaries of republican thought in terms that are broad enough to transcend these kinds of disagreements. However, even if it is the case, as I have argued, that republican thought centers around the problem of securing the practice of virtue through the control of arbitrary power, there are nevertheless a number of different ways of defining each of the key terms in this expression and of characterizing the relationship between them. These ambiguities create the conceptual space, as we will see, for a variety of "republicanisms," each of which raises its own questions about, and was challenged in its own way by, the rise of modern market societies.

The disagreements among republicans about the nature of arbitrary power arise, as we might expect, from the complex nature of the concerns that lead them to seek to control it in the first place. On the one hand, republicans are guided by the intuition that the absence of regular procedures in public life creates an atmosphere of uncertainty and insecurity that makes it difficult if not impossible for citizens to display whatever virtue they might possess: As Pettit puts it, they will be obliged instead to keep a "weather eye" out for the latest whims of the power to which they are subject.[56] On the other hand, republicans are guided by the intuition that a government that consistently disregards or betrays the interests of its citizens – even if it does so in a procedurally correct and highly predictable manner – fails to show them the respect to which their free status entitles them: They are prevented, if not from displaying, then at least from reaping the benefits of their virtue. There is some question, then, as to whether republicans should be more concerned with the way in which power is exercised or with the ends to which it is put. Chaim Wirszubski observes, for example, that in Roman usage republicanism "signifies not only a *form* of government but also, and primarily, a *purpose* of government," and suggests that the creation of the Augustan Principate – which was, at least at first, "a res publica," if not "the Res Publica" – would have been seen by many Romans as a sacrifice of the former for the sake of the latter.[57] A similar kind of tension can be seen in the contrast between Montesquieu's claim that political liberty "consists in security or in one's opinion of one's security" and therefore requires that individuals enjoy certain legal protections from the state and Rousseau's claim that political liberty consists in obedience to the general will and therefore requires "the total alienation of each associate with all of his rights to the whole community."[58]

The disagreements among republicans are no less substantial when we turn to the question of the meaning of virtue and, in particular, to the question of the relationship between the practice of virtue and the

[56] Pettit, *Republicanism*, pp. 5, 86.
[57] Wirszubski, *Libertas as a Political Idea*, chapter 4, quoted at pp. 121–2 (emphasis added).
[58] Montesquieu, *Spirit of the Laws*, p. 187 (book 12, chapter 1), cf. p. 157 (book 11, chapter 6); Rousseau, *Social Contract*, book 1, chapter 6, quoting idem, *The Social Contract and Other Later Political Writings*, trans. and ed. Victor Gourevitch (New York: Cambridge University Press, 1997), p. 50.

control of arbitrary power. In one sense, this relationship is a straightforward one: It is virtue that makes republican citizens willing to place the common good ahead of their own personal interests and thus to obey the laws and the properly constituted political authorities, just as it is virtue that leads them to be vigilant in resisting the abuse of power and in guarding against those forces from inside or outside the polity that might pose a threat to its freedom. It is virtue, too, that enables the founders of a republic to design, and its rulers to preserve, free institutions in the first place. However, as long as the value of virtue is defined in purely instrumental terms, republican thought would seem to run in a rather tight circle: We are free only insofar as the institutions by which we are governed function in a certain way, and we should therefore shape our desires and actions in such a way that this end can be achieved. Virtue so understood requires that citizens subordinate their personal interests to the common good without giving them a clear motivation for doing so.

One straightforward way of responding to this dilemma would be to say that we display our virtue in public life so that we can do as we please in our private lives. Indeed, Quentin Skinner has suggested in a series of articles[59] that the republican defense of freedom rests on exactly this line of argument, which he associates most closely with Machiavelli, but which, he argues, "represents the heart and nerve of all classical republican theories of citizenship."[60] According to Skinner, the freedom that republicans seek in devoting themselves to the common good is, paradoxically, nothing more or less than the freedom to pursue their own ends in their own way: "The prudent citizen," he argues, in contrast to the myopically self-interested citizen of the modern liberal state, "recognizes that, whatever the extent of negative liberty he may enjoy, it can only be the outcome of – and if you like the reward of – a steady recognition and

---

[59] See, in addition to "The Paradoxes of Political Liberty," cited earlier, his "Machiavelli on the Maintenance of Liberty," *Australian Journal of Political Science* 18 (1983), pp. 3–15; "The Idea of Negative Liberty," in Richard Rorty, Jerome B. Schneewind, and Quentin Skinner, eds., *Philosophy in History: Essays on the Historiography of Philosophy* (New York: Cambridge University Press, 1984), pp. 193–221; "The Republican Ideal of Political Liberty," in Gisela Bock, Quentin Skinner, and Maurizio Viroli, eds., *Machiavelli and Republicanism* (New York: Cambridge University Press, 1990), pp. 293–309; and "Two Views on the Maintenance of Liberty," in Philip Pettit, ed., *Contemporary Political Theory* (New York: Macmillan, 1991), pp. 35–58.

[60] Skinner, "Idea of Negative Liberty," p. 208. Skinner has since amended this claim to refer to "all neo-Roman theories of freedom and citizenship": See the revised version of the essay reprinted in his *Visions of Politics*, vol. 2: *Renaissance Virtues* (New York: Cambridge University Press, 2002), at p. 199. This terminological adjustment does not affect the point that I am making here.

pursuit of the public good at the expense of all purely individual and private ends."[61] By contrast, "whenever we corruptly permit or pursue...policies hostile to the common good, we begin to subvert the free institutions of our community, and hence our own personal liberty at the same time."[62] Republicanism so understood simply defines the necessary conditions under which we can enjoy freedom in "the ordinary negative sense of being free from constraint to act according to [our] own will."[63] Skinner is rather quick to dismiss the (Machiavellian?) thought that it might be rational for the republican citizen to free ride on the civic virtue of others, but this is in other respects an ingenious reading of the republican tradition, not least because it provides a motive for practicing republican virtue that, the current dominance of rights-based liberalism notwithstanding, is likely to be intelligible and attractive to the contemporary reader.

However, there is reason to think that there is both more and less to republican virtue than this. There can be no doubt, of course, that Machiavelli thought of virtue in fundamentally instrumental terms. This is, after all, the view that has always been most closely associated with his name. It is less clear that either he or the classical republicans saw virtue as being instrumental to the enjoyment of negative liberty. To begin with, although he expresses a qualified preference for popular republics such as Rome, in which power is shared between the "great" (*grandi*) and the "people" (*popolo*), over oligarchic republics such as Sparta and Venice, in which the people are excluded from public life, he does not hesitate to describe Sparta and Venice as free cities. It is clear, then, that a polity can be free in Machiavelli's sense even if it does not allow the people to live as they please. Indeed, his preference for the Roman model is not based on its popular character per se – he says that the Spartan model, if only it could be made to last, "would be the true political way of life and the true quiet of a city" – but rather on the fact that when power is shared between the great and the people the republic will be able to expand as the demands of ambition or necessity dictate. In republics in which the great are not able to arm the people or to count on their support in wartime, by contrast, the freedom of the city will depend on its remaining small and poor so that it does not pose a threat to or make a tempting target for its neighbors.[64] Moreover, Machiavelli endorses the Roman view that

---

[61] Skinner, "Idea of Negative Liberty," p. 218.

[62] Skinner, "Two Views on the Maintenance of Liberty," p. 210.

[63] Skinner, "Idea of Negative Liberty," p. 213.

[64] Machiavelli, *Discourses on Livy*, book 1, chapters 4–6, quoting Harvey C. Mansfield and Nathan Tarcov's translation (Chicago: University of Chicago Press, 1996) at p. 23; cf.

the freedom of *any* republic is best preserved through enforced poverty and military discipline, which makes it difficult to see how he could be said to associate freedom with an expanded sphere of choice even on the part of the ruling class: "[K]eeping the public rich and the private poor, and maintaining military exercises with the highest seriousness," he argues, "is the true way to make a republic great." Indeed, he echoes his classical predecessors in associating (what is now called) negative liberty with license and republican liberty with self-discipline: "[W]here choice abounds," he insists, "at once everything is full of confusion and disorder. Therefore it is said that hunger and poverty make men industrious, and the laws make them good."[65]

We can conclude, as we might have expected in light of our discussion so far, that Machiavelli does not associate freedom with the absence of constraint, but rather with the absence of dependence,[66] and above all with the political independence of a city. Indeed, the word *libertà* and its cognates appear in his writings more often as predicates of cities or peoples than of individuals. The aim of practicing virtue in a Machiavellian republic is to ensure that the polity remains free in the sense of not being subject to a prince or foreign power, and to live as a free citizen is to value the freedom of one's city above all else – to love one's country, as Machiavelli famously put it, more than one's soul.[67] It follows that the challenge facing anyone who hopes to establish and maintain a popular republic is to persuade the people, who after all just want to be left

book 2, chapters 3 and 19 and Polybius, *Histories*, book 6 §50. For Skinner's summary of this discussion, which ignores the Spartan and Venetian alternatives to Roman imperialism, see especially "Idea of Negative Liberty," pp. 204–12.

[65] Machiavelli, *Discourses on Livy*, pp. 173, 15 (book 2, chapter 19; book 1, chapter 3). On poverty see also ibid., p. 79 (book 1, chapter 37) and book 3, chapter 25 passim; on military discipline see also ibid., p. 190 (book 2, chapter 25) and book 3, chapter 16 passim.

[66] Skinner seems to conflate constraint and dependence at "Idea of Negative Liberty," pp. 205–7, though he has more recently followed Pettit in distinguishing between them: See, for example, *Liberty before Liberalism*, e.g., p. 70n, and "A Third Concept of Liberty," *Proceedings of the British Academy* 117 (2002), pp. 237–68. Pettit and Skinner continue to disagree over the question of whether the absence of constraint (what Pettit calls non-interference) should be treated as a value that is coequal with the absence of dependence (what Pettit calls non-domination), or whether non-interference is, as Pettit believes, at best a subordinate value: See Pettit, "Keeping Republican Freedom Simple: On a Difference with Quentin Skinner," *Political Theory* 30 (2002), pp. 339–56, and cf. Skinner, *Liberty before Liberalism*, pp. 82–5.

[67] The remark paraphrased here is found in a letter from Machiavelli to Francesco Vettori dated April 16, 1527. Maurizio Viroli suggests that it expresses an anti-clericalism that was widely shared among the Florentine republicans of the day: See his *Machiavelli* (New York: Oxford University Press, 1998), p. 152.

alone, to adopt this set of priorities. Clearly their motivation for doing so cannot come simply from self-interest, enlightened or not, because the aim is to persuade them to adopt a particular conception of what their interests are. Machiavelli appeals, then, not to self-interest but rather to self-respect – the kind of self-respect that will make someone see dependence on another (especially a foreign "other") as a fate worse than death – although, this being Machiavelli, the appeal is supplemented with a healthy dose of fear: fear of the gods and (what may, in a Machiavellian republic, amount to the same thing) the laws.[68] In other words, the greatest threat to republican freedom comes not from a myopic failure on the part of the people to grasp the connection between the practice of virtue and the enjoyment of their own personal (negative) liberty, but rather from the fact that they are so easily corrupted into preferring a comfortable but servile life of dependence to a strenuous but free life of independence.[69]

Machiavelli's instrumental defense of virtue rests, then, on the classical association of freedom with the absence of dependence, and the motivation for practicing virtue comes in his account not from a desire to live as one pleases, but rather from a desire to avoid the humiliation that comes (or that should come) from being subject to the will of another – a humiliation that he, as a *Cinquecento* Florentine, felt keenly. To be sure, he does make the traditional republican observation, most closely associated with Sallust, that free states are more prosperous than servile ones. However, like Sallust, he sees this prosperity as the by-product rather than as the aim of republican freedom: The free man, in Machiavelli's view, does not want to be free (of constraint) so that he can be prosperous; rather, he is willing to become prosperous because he is free (of dependence). "[A] free way of life," he writes, "is being able to enjoy one's things freely, without any suspicion, not fearing for the honor of wives and that of

---

[68] See especially *Discourses on Livy*, book 1, chapters 10–15.

[69] Machiavelli argues in particular that "a people into which corruption has entered in everything cannot live free" because "it is used to living under the government of others" and likens such a people to "a brute animal that, although of a ferocious and feral nature, has always been nourished in prison and in servitude": ibid., p. 44 (book 1, chapter 16). The metaphor is echoed and amplified by Rousseau – also no friend of "negative" liberty – who argues that "[a]s an untamed Steed bristles its mane, stamps the ground with its hoof, and struggles impetuously at the very sight of the bit while a trained horse patiently suffers whip and spur, so barbarous man will not bend his head to the yoke which civilized man bears without a murmur, and he prefers the most tempestuous freedom to a tranquil subjection": *Discourse on the Origins of Inequality*, part 2, quoting idem, *The Discourses and Other Early Political Writings*, trans. and ed. Victor Gourevitch (New York: Cambridge University Press, 1997), p. 177.

children, not to be afraid for oneself," and so the free man "does not fear
that his patrimony will be taken away, and he knows not only that [his
children] are born free and not slaves, but that they can, through their
virtue, become princes."[70]

This Machiavellian way of connecting the enjoyment of freedom
with the practice of virtue can be contrasted – as indeed it is, *mutatis
mutandis*, in Skinner's analysis[71] – with a second, non-instrumental view
that has an equally distinguished republican pedigree. According to this
line of argument, it is only by playing an active role in public life that we
are able to develop our "higher" faculties and realize our true nature as
human beings. Here the emphasis is not placed on the qualities of character that enable us to check arbitrary power and thus to avoid dependence, but rather on the qualities of character that we are able to display
once the corrupting influence of arbitrary power has been removed. The
line between these two positions is blurred, of course, by the fact that
participation in politics has often been seen, in a tradition of thought
that stretches back at least as far as Aristotle's claim that man is *zōon
politikon*, as a central part of human flourishing more generally speaking.
Nevertheless, the immediate appeal of Machiavelli's instrumental defense
of civic virtue should not cause us to lose sight of the fact that republican
thought begins with the problem of creating the conditions under which
a free man can display the character befitting his station, and that this has
often – even usually – been thought to entail a commitment to a "thicker"
and more substantive understanding of what virtue consists in.

1.5 AMBIGUITY AND RESILIENCE

We have seen that the language of freedom in the West has its roots in
the existence of status distinctions that separate the ruling class in a given

---

[70] *Discourses on Livy*, pp. 45, 132 (book 1, chapter 16; book 2, chapter 2). The latter
passage is cited, to rather different effect, by Skinner at "Idea of Negative Liberty,"
pp. 206–7 and "Paradoxes of Political Liberty," p. 240. The *locus classicus* for this line of
argument is chapter 7 of Sallust's *Bellum Catilinae*; for a parallel claim about Athenian
liberty see Herodotus, *Histories*, book 5, chapter 78.

[71] See especially "Paradoxes of Political Liberty," pp. 230–5. Skinner has since amended
his reading of Machiavelli to say, correctly, that he aims at the avoidance of servitude
rather than the maximization of negative liberty, while maintaining the contrast with the
more traditional Aristotelian view: See, for example, his "Surveying *The Foundations*: A
Retrospect and Reassessment," in Annabel Brett and James Tully, eds., *Rethinking the
Foundations of Modern Political Thought* (New York: Cambridge University Press,
2006), pp. 256–60, esp. p. 258, and cf. *Liberty before Liberalism*, pp. 37–8, 46–7.

society from those who do not enjoy their privileges or share their ethos, and we have traced the origins of republican freedom to the point at which the ability to practice the virtue befitting a free man is seen to depend on the circumstance of not being subject to the corrupting influence of arbitrary power. I have argued that we should call an idea or line of argument "republican" if and insofar as it is concerned with this problem – the problem of securing the practice of virtue through the control of arbitrary power – whether or not the thinker in question would (or even could) have owned the label. I have also identified three conditions that have to be met in order for republican freedom so understood to be enjoyed: First, there must be agreement on a shared conception of the common good, so that the citizens of a given polity are able to agree about when power has been exercised arbitrarily; second, there must be institutional mechanisms in place that prevent any individual or faction from acquiring arbitrary power so defined; and third, there must enough transparency in the conduct of public affairs that citizens have not only the tools but also the information that they need to hold their leaders accountable. By defining the boundaries of republican thought this broadly, I hope to have shown that it is possible to speak of a republican *tradition*, despite the wide variety of seemingly incommensurable policies that have been pursued under the republican banner.

The complexity of the republican tradition arises, I have argued, from the fact that republican freedom consists both in the enjoyment of a certain social status and in a kind of activity befitting those who enjoy this status: One is free in the first sense if and to the extent that one is not subject to arbitrary power, and in the second sense if and to the extent that one displays or practices virtue. As we have seen, the exact meaning of each of these terms and the nature of the relationship between them is open to dispute, and so too is the question of what the practical implications of a commitment to republican freedom actually are. With respect to arbitrary power, there is the question of whether power becomes non-arbitrary if it is exercised in a regular and predictable way – if it is forced to obey a rule – or whether non-arbitrariness requires instead or in addition that the exercise of power serve the interests of those over whom it is exercised. There are, in other words, *procedural* and *substantive* understandings of what the non-arbitrary exercise of power consists in. Similarly, with respect to virtue, there is the question of whether we should practice virtue in order to prevent power from becoming arbitrary, or whether on the contrary we wish to be free from arbitrary power so that we can practice virtue. There are, in other words, *instrumental* and *intrinsic* ways of understanding the value of virtue.

These positions are not mutually exclusive – we might believe that power should be governed by a rule *and* that it should be forced to serve our interests, and we might practice virtue in order to check arbitrary power *and* for its own sake. Indeed, for the classical republicans any power that could be exercised at will without checks or controls was seen as arbitrary, no matter how benevolent the intentions of those who held such power might have been. Any power that failed to take into account the interests of those who were subject to it was likewise seen as arbitrary, no matter how regularly or predictably it was exercised. Similarly, no republican citizen could be considered virtuous who was completely indifferent to the need to prevent the arbitrary exercise of power, just as no citizen could be considered virtuous who treated the control of arbitrary power as an end in itself. These positions are nevertheless analytically distinct, and the durability and resilience of the republican tradition can be credited in large part to its ability to hold them in fruitful tension with one another, thus maintaining a certain degree of ambiguity on the question of which among the logically possible positions republicans were ultimately committed to.

Indeed, the most striking thing about classical republican thought when seen from this standpoint is not the presence of disagreement over these issues, but rather the fact that the substance of these disagreements was so rarely articulated. This lack of clarity (as it seems to us) was made possible by certain empirical features of the social world in which republican thought developed – or, more precisely, by certain beliefs that republican thinkers held about that world. Thus, for example, the question of whether arbitrary power is objectionable because it is not rule-governed or because it harms those over whom it is exercised did not need to be raised as long as these were seen as two sides of the same coin, that is, as long as republicans could not conceive of a power (save God's) that was inscrutable in its intentions, ungovernable in its actions, and yet reliably beneficial in its effects. Instead, the lack of external checks on the exercise of power was thought to lead inevitably to its abuse. Similarly, the question of whether virtue is intrinsically or only instrumentally valuable did not need to be raised as long as republicans could not conceive of a way to prevent the arbitrary exercise of power that did not depend on the conscious efforts of virtuous individuals. Instead, the capacity and willingness to be active in public affairs – to rule and be ruled, in Aristotle's terms – was seen both as a necessary condition for the enjoyment of freedom and as an essential part of human excellence more generally.

The most striking point of contrast between classical and modern republicanism lies in the fact that these ambiguities have now been made explicit. This fact cannot be credited, I think, simply to the superior insight of modern republican thinkers. Rather, it is a consequence of the fact that the social world in which we live and the beliefs that we hold about that world have changed in fundamental ways since the heyday of classical republicanism. Among the most fundamental of these changes was, of course, the rise of modern market societies – the rise of commerce, as it was called – in the early modern period. This development led, as we will see, to a fundamental rethinking of the republican conception of freedom. Here was a decision-making mechanism that promised to yield unprecedented levels of material well-being precisely insofar as little or no effort was made to regulate it. Here was a model of society that promised to keep arbitrary power in check not through the conscious efforts of a virtuous citizenry, but rather as an unintended by-product of the self-regarding actions of a disorganized multitude. In short, here was an institution that put the pluralism, and thus the resilience, of the republican conception of freedom to the test – a test that it ultimately failed. We can therefore trace the dissolution of the republican tradition to the same period – roughly speaking, the second half of the 18th century – during which the appeal to the value of freedom first came to occupy the central place in political discourse that it still occupies today. Before we try to make sense of this seemingly paradoxical outcome, however, we must first come to terms with the development over the course of the preceding centuries of a more purely individualistic conception of freedom, one that centered around the protection of rights rather than the cultivation of virtue.

2

Liberalism before Liberty

> To obey his just commands is perfect freedom.
>
> Boethius, *The Consolation of Philosophy* 1.5 (Walsh trans.)

2.1. EGALITARIANISM AND INDIVIDUALISM

We have seen that the republican conception of freedom is ambiguous with regard to the question of whether arbitrary power should be defined in procedural or substantive terms, and that it is similarly ambiguous with regard to the question of whether virtue is of intrinsic or only of instrumental value. We have given less sustained attention to a second pair of ambiguities having to do with the scope rather than the content of republican freedom. The first of these concerns the relationship between *egalitarian* and *inegalitarian* conceptions of republican citizenship. Classical republican thought, emerging as it did at a time when the existence of fundamental differences in status between women and men and between slaves and free men were taken for granted, was of course not remotely egalitarian by current standards. However, the classical republicans were committed to extending the privileges and responsibilities of citizenship to all and only those who could benefit the polity by possessing them, and this commitment was sometimes used to justify an expansion of the existing boundaries of citizenship, whether on epistemic grounds, as in Aristotle's view that the "many" have a kind of wisdom that exceeds that of even the wisest person, or on military grounds, as in Machiavelli's claim that a republic that refuses to arm the people must remain small and poor if it is to maintain its freedom.[1] To be sure, Aristotle and Machiavelli, like many republican thinkers, were each tempted by the attractions of a more purely aristocratic (or oligarchic) politics.[2] It is nevertheless the case that the classical republican debates about the proper boundaries of citizenship took place on a continuum between relatively egalitarian and relatively inegalitarian views in which the poles – the enfranchisement of all adult persons on the one hand and absolute rule by the "best" on the other – lay outside the boundaries of discussion.

There is a similar ambiguity in classical republican thought between *individualistic* and *collective* conceptions of freedom: The word "free" could be used to refer not only to the status of a given class of people, but also to that of the polity to which they belonged. Indeed, as we saw in the case of Machiavelli, the former usage was sometimes derived almost entirely from the latter. This raises the question – paradigmatically captured in the contrast between Athens and Sparta – of whether republican freedom is a predicate of individuals or collectivities: Are the citizens of a republic free because of the freedom of the polity to which they belong? Or, as Pericles famously suggested, should a polity be called free because of the freedoms that its citizens enjoy? On one side of the issue are thinkers like Aristotle and Madison who, though they disagree on many fundamental questions, each hold that the proper aim of political society is to further the interests of individuals. On the other side are thinkers like Machiavelli and Rousseau who do not distinguish clearly between the freedom of the individual and the freedom of the polity of which he is a citizen – and who argue that in cases of conflict the former should be strictly subordinated to the latter. Here again we have a continuum of views in which the poles – complete neglect of individual concerns by the collective and complete neglect of collective concerns by the individual – lie outside the boundaries of discussion.

---

[1] Aristotle, *Politics*, book 3, chapter 11; Machiavelli, *Discourses on Livy*, book 1, chapters 5–6.

[2] Aristotle argues that the best form of rule is that of "a single man, or a whole family, or a number of people, surpassing all others in virtue": *Politics*, book 3, chapter 18, quoting R. F. Stalley's revision of the Barker translation (New York: Oxford University Press, 1995 [1946]) at p. 132, amended to give "virtue" rather than "goodness" as the translation of *aretē*. Similarly, Machiavelli argues that an oligarchic republicanism such as that found in Sparta and Venice, "if the thing could be balanced in this mode...would be the true political way of life and the true quiet of a city": *Discourses on Livy*, book 1, chapter 6, quoting Harvey C. Mansfield and Nathan Tarcov's translation (Chicago: University of Chicago Press, 1996), p. 23.

It is not surprising that questions about the limits of egalitarianism and individualism play an important role in classical republican political thought: These questions arise in some form in all ideological traditions. What makes the republican tradition unique in this respect is the fact that the language of freedom was deployed on both sides of these debates. A strictly egalitarian conception of republican freedom could not plausibly be defended as long as it was taken for granted that a free polity could only function properly if a significant proportion of its population was unfree, just as a strictly individualistic conception could not plausibly be defended as long as individual death or slavery was the usual result of the loss of collective freedom.[3] Classical republican thinkers therefore could, and often did, invoke the distinction between liberty and license in order to limit the boundaries of citizenship, just as they could, and often did, invoke this distinction in order to limit the sphere of individual discretion. By the end of the 18th century, however, these disagreements had been all but decisively resolved in favor of the egalitarian and individualistic views: claims that were treated as manifestly absurd in Greek and Roman political thought are treated as first principles by thinkers otherwise as different from one another as Rousseau and Adam Smith, and as self-evident truths by the American and French Revolutionaries. To be sure, the existence of *actual* differences in status – of hereditary privileges, for example – remained a central fact of social and political life in the West until well into the 19th century, and legalized gender hierarchies remained in place for considerably longer than that. However, to be committed to the cause of freedom was by this time to be committed either to eradicating these privileges (as in the case of John Stuart Mill) or to giving them at best an instrumental role to play in checking the power of the democratic state (as in the case of Alexis de Tocqueville).

As we saw in the previous chapter, contemporary republicans – who, like their classical forebears, disagree among themselves about the meaning of arbitrary power and the value of virtue – nevertheless agree in thinking that any revival of republican ideas should begin from egalitarian

---

[3] P. A. Brunt points out that in antiquity "it was more manifest than it has often been in the modern era that the defence of the community in war…conduced to the safety of the citizen," because "the consequences of defeat might be massacre or enslavement": "*Libertas* in the Republic," in idem, *The Fall of the Roman Republic and Related Essays* (New York: Oxford University Press, 1988), p. 299. Similarly, Orlando Patterson reminds us that in traditional societies individual freedom "amounted to social suicide and, very likely, physical death": *Freedom*, vol. 1: *Freedom in the Making of Western Culture* (New York: Basic Books, 1991), p. 23.

and individualistic premises.[4] To this extent, at least, they are defending a position whose practical implications are similar to those of modern liberalism. Indeed, some of the thinkers to whom I have attributed republican views – most notably Locke and Montesquieu – are often thought of today as liberals rather than republicans, despite the fact that the word liberal did not take on its present ideological meaning until some time after the turn of the 19th century. Given that liberals, unlike republicans, treat individual liberty (understood as the ability to pursue one's own good in one's own way) as the first and highest political end to be pursued, and that they have therefore typically been receptive to the idea of turning a wide range of social decisions over to the market, it is tempting to conclude that the invention of market freedom was a by-product of the broader triumph of liberal ideals in the modern period.[5] According to this line of argument, we should not ask why republican freedom was supplanted by market freedom, but rather why republicanism was supplanted by liberalism more generally speaking. The question of why the language of freedom is now so closely associated with the market would then simply be a version of the larger question of why liberalism is the reigning political ideology in the modern world. In other words, we would find ourselves on familiar (if nevertheless puzzling and contentious) conceptual and ideological terrain.

The problem with this line of argument is that it asks the wrong historical question. The question for our purposes is not how republicanism could have been overcome by a competing ideology; after all, securing a practical commitment to republican ideals has, by the testimony of republicans themselves, always been a fragile and temporary

---

[4] It may seem odd to say that the so-called communitarian republicans begin from "individualistic" premises. I mean not that they adhere to an atomistic social ontology, but rather that they treat the good of individuals as the proper aim of the community, rather than the reverse.

[5] I do not mean to minimize the disagreements among liberals regarding the implications of a commitment to individual liberty and the role that markets have to play in realizing it. Such disagreements exist, as I have emphasized, in all ideological traditions. Nevertheless, I think that Ronald Dworkin is right to say that for the liberal "there are no better mechanisms available, as general political institutions, than the two main institutions of our own political economy: the economic market, for decisions about what goods shall be produced and how they shall be distributed, and representative democracy, for collective decisions about what conduct shall be prohibited or regulated so that other conduct might be made possible or convenient": "Liberalism," in idem, *A Matter of Principle* (Cambridge, MA: Harvard University Press, 1985), pp. 193–4. For my own understanding of the practical implications of liberal ideals, see my *Reconstructing Public Reason* (Cambridge, MA: Harvard University Press, 2004).

achievement.[6] Rather, the question is how the language of freedom – the one political value to which republicans had privileged rhetorical access – was not only appropriated by another ideological tradition, but appropriated so completely that it now requires some effort to grasp its original meaning. I will argue that this development was made possible by a weaving together of republican and (what are now thought of as) liberal ideas about freedom, and that the historical relationship between these two schools of thought is therefore one not of conflict and super-session, but rather of cross-fertilization and synthesis.[7] This synthesis was slow to develop, in part because these two schools of thought formed in response to very different practical challenges and drew on distinct and even opposing sets of ideas in addressing them. Nevertheless, the fact that each tradition had its own long and rather complicated history of appealing to the language of freedom for political purposes proved to be instrumental in bringing about a *rapprochement* between them, and the resulting ideological alliance gave rise, as we will see, to an altogether new and predominantly market-centered view.

This line of argument rests on two further claims about the role that the language of freedom played in early modern political thought. The first, which I defend in this chapter, is that the early modern defenders of the idea that human beings are the bearers of natural rights – the liberals, as they came to be known – were not defenders of individual liberty in any politically meaningful sense. To the extent that freedom is treated as a political value in this tradition, it is said to consist in – rather than being limited by – obedience to natural law. It follows that natural law, rather than liberty, is the more fundamental political value. Conversely, to the extent that these thinkers equate freedom with the mere absence of constraint, they do so in order to argue that it is not properly speaking a political value at all. The second claim, which I defend in the next chap-ter, is that the early modern debates about the political implications of the rise of modern commercial societies were motivated not by a "liberal" concern for individual freedom, but rather by a traditional republican concern for the common good – that is, for the security of the polity and the well-being of its citizens. They therefore centered around a series of

---

[6] For an extended meditation on this theme, see J. G. A. Pocock, *The Machiavellian Moment: Florentine Political Thought and the Atlantic Republican Tradition* (Princeton, NJ: Princeton University Press, 1975).

[7] For a recent argument to this effect see Andreas Kalyvas and Ira Katznelson, *Liberal Beginnings: Making a Republic for the Moderns* (New York: Cambridge University Press, 2008).

equally traditional republican questions having to do with the control of arbitrary power, the compatibility of wealth and virtue, and the harmonization of individual and collective purposes. As we will see, the answers that were given to these questions in the early modern period had a profound impact on the subsequent development of republican thought.

If modern republicanism has its roots in the early modern debates about the rise of commerce, liberalism has its roots in the other formative experience in modern European history: the long and bloody religious conflicts that were set into motion by the Protestant Reformation. The wars of religion brought to the foreground more vividly than ever the two problems that had always been at the bottom of Christian political thought: the problem of defining the proper boundaries of sacred and secular authority and the related and more fundamental problem of determining why and under what conditions Christian subjects are obligated to obey the political authorities under which they happen to find themselves. The thinkers who set out to respond to these problems therefore had to confront a series of questions, not about the nature of political freedom, but rather about the nature and extent of political authority itself: questions of legitimacy, obligation, and resistance. These questions differ sharply in scope and content from the largely prudential kinds of questions that were posed by the rise of commerce, and the vocabulary that was used to respond to them – that of natural law, individual rights, and social contract; of reason, justice, and consent – had its roots in the tradition of natural jurisprudence, a tradition that is conceptually distant from and in some ways diametrically opposed to the republican one. Indeed, as I have suggested and as I will now argue, there is some question as to whether this school of thought treats freedom as a political value at all.

2.2. THE JURISTIC TURN

We saw in the previous chapter that according to the classical republicans freedom can only be maintained through the careful design of political institutions and the vigilance of virtuous citizens. Nevertheless, the absence of freedom is felt most keenly in the day-to-day experience of degradation and humiliation that it brings, rather than in the fact of political exclusion as such. The word "freedom" was therefore also used in the classical world, as it is today, to refer to the legal privileges and immunities that are enjoyed by free men in private life, such as the right to own property and to move about without hindrance, and the immunity from arbitrary arrest and from certain forms of punishment. This is of course why the distinction of status between free men and slaves stands at the head of the Roman law. Just as the association of freedom with legal status predates the rise of republican political thought, so too did it persist after the institutional forms of republican government had withered away. For example, when the Apostle Paul escapes a flogging by invoking his (imperial) Roman citizenship, the centurion responds, in the King James translation, by saying that he had purchased his own freedom "with a great sum."[8] Similarly, in medieval usage the appeal to political liberty typically refered not to the absence of arbitrary power, but rather to membership in a larger entity – such as a guild, a city, or the clergy – that enjoyed certain legal exemptions from the feudal authority of the king or local nobility. Thus in a development that had profound implications for modern ideas about market society, we have "bourgeois" – civic or urban – freedom.[9]

From a republican standpoint this purely juristic understanding of freedom is plainly inadequate: As long as we enjoy our freedoms at the pleasure of a power that can take them away at will (*ad arbitrium*), we are not, in republican terms, really free at all – a lesson that both Paul and the nascent Church were soon to learn by hard experience.[10] Nevertheless, the definition of freedom that passed from the Roman law into the mainstream of juristic thought in the High Middle Ages – "the natural ability to do as one pleases unless prohibited by force or right" – was, as J. G. A. Pocock has emphasized, of imperial rather than republican provenance, in that it was rooted in the language of law rather than of citizenship.[11]

---

[8] *Acts of the Apostles* 22:28, cited (in slightly different form and with the verse misattributed) in J. G. A. Pocock, "Virtue, Rights, and Manners: A Model for Historians of Political Thought" (1981), in idem, *Virtue, Commerce, and History: Essays on Political Thought and History, Chiefly in the Eighteenth Century* (New York: Cambridge University Press, 1985), p. 44.

[9] For a useful overview, see Alan Harding, "Political Liberty in the Middle Ages," *Speculum* 55 (1980), pp. 423–43.

[10] As Chaim Wirzsubski puts it, "[w]hat was wrong in the [Roman] Principate from the point of view of libertas was the absence of effective safeguards against the abuse of power by the emperor. Not that the Princeps was exempted from all existing checks; in theory some checks existed as before...but when a concentrated and permanently overwhelming power emerged, those checks were of little, if any, use. They were not abolished, but they became shams": *Libertas as a Political Idea at Rome During the Late Republic and Early Principate* (New York: Cambridge University Press, 1950), p. 132. For a more recent discussion of this theme, see Philip Pettit, *Republicanism: A Theory of Freedom and Government* (2nd ed., New York: Oxford University Press, 1999 [1997]), and Quentin Skinner, *Liberty before Liberalism* (New York: Cambridge University Press, 1998).

[11] See especially Pocock, "Virtue, Rights, and Manners," as well as the afterword to the 2003 edition of *The Machiavellian Moment*. The juristic definition of freedom is taken from the Justinian *Digest* 1.5.4.

The practical implications of this definition, as of Roman civil law more generally, were worked out most fully within the intellectual framework of the Christianized Aristotelianism (or Aristotelianized Christianity) that was characteristic of the time, and that is now most closely associated, especially in its ethical and political dimensions, with the writings of Thomas Aquinas. Needless to say, the philosophical underpinnings of Thomistic thought are no less distant from those of the republican tradition than are the imperial and monarchical underpinnings of the Roman law itself. Nevertheless, as the discussion of natural law, natural right, and natural liberty that is found in Aquinas was disassembled and reassembled over the course of the following centuries, the juristic and republican appeals to the language of liberty became intertwined in a way that proved decisive for the further development of each tradition.

At the heart of the political thought of the natural jurists is the claim that political authority was created by human beings to realize certain definite moral purposes, and (here some jurists hesitate) that it can be resisted or remade if it fails to serve those purposes. They rejected two lines of argument in particular that could be advanced against this view: the Augustinian (and Filmerian) claim that government was instituted among human beings directly by the will of God and must therefore be obeyed unquestioningly, and the humanistic claim that the legitimacy of political authority depends on local customs and practices and cannot be criticized from any "higher" standpoint than that. For the natural jurists, the proper aims of political life are defined by the dictates of practical reason and therefore transcend the circumstances of any particular time and place while remaining accessible to human understanding. From this point of view, the salient question is not how political power should be checked and controlled, but rather what the content of the laws governing its authority should be. Thus if the genius of republican political thought is sociological and institutional in nature, that of juristic political thought is moral and casuistic; it is primarily concerned with the ends to which the exercise of political power can legitimately be put, rather than the means by which it can be constrained to pursue them.

When the natural jurists appeal to the language of liberty, it is not to political liberty – the kind of liberty that is enjoyed by the citizens of a free polity – but rather to "natural" liberty – the kind of liberty that human beings enjoy insofar as they are not subject to constraint.[12]

---

[12] As we will see in the next chapter, Aquinas sometimes appeals to the republican conception of freedom when writing about matters of governance. He defines a "free community," for example, as one "which may make its own laws": *Summa Theologiae* 1a2ae q 97 art

Natural liberty is, as its name implies, a kind of freedom that all agents can be said to possess as long as they are able to exercise the faculty of choice in a given domain. Thus where the republican conception of freedom is rooted in the distinctions of status and character that set one class of people over another, the appeal to natural liberty is fundamentally egalitarian. It is also morally and politically vacuous taken in itself: Any value that the natural jurists attach to the faculty of free choice is contingent on its being put to the proper ends, in more traditional terms, on its being exercised in accordance with the demands of natural law. To be sure, they view liberty itself as a good thing. Indeed, Aquinas describes it as "one of the foremost blessings" of human life.[13] Its value arises, however, not from the fact that it provides individuals with a space within which they can do as they please, but rather from the fact that it lends a special moral character to right actions: "a deed is rendered virtuous and praiseworthy and meritorious," he argues, "chiefly by the way in which it proceeds from the will." In other words, human freedom is to be valued primarily because right actions become moral actions only if and insofar as they are done freely – that is to say, willingly or, as we would now say, autonomously. Aquinas emphasizes that actions can be done freely in this sense "even where there is a duty of obedience," that is, even when the threat of legal coercion is present.[14]

Aquinas goes on to argue that although the enjoyment of "one liberty for all men" is "consistent" with the demands of natural law, it is not an *entailment* of natural law properly speaking. Rather, the practice of slavery and relationships of authority more generally speaking were "added" to natural law "by human reason for the advantage of human life" in order to remove the practical disadvantages of the natural condition of equality – just as the custom of wearing clothing was "added" to natural law in order to remove the practical disadvantages of the natural condition of nakedness.[15] Thus even if it is the case that human beings naturally find themselves in a state of liberty, they do not have a natural right to *remain* in such a state: There are obvious goods to be gained by giving up our liberty, just as there are obvious goods to be gained by wearing clothing. To the extent that Aquinas allows for the existence of

---

3 ad 3, in idem, *Political Writings*, trans. R. W. Dyson (New York: Cambridge University Press, 2002), p. 155.

[13] Ibid., 1a q 96 art 4 obj 3 (*Political Writings*, p. 3).

[14] Ibid., 2a2ae q 104 art 1 ad 3 (*Political Writings*, p. 58); cf. 1a2ae q 96 art 5 resp (*Political Writings*, p. 146).

[15] Ibid., 1a2ae q 94 art 5 ad 3 (*Political Writings*, pp. 124–5).

a sphere of individual action that is not governed by human law, it is not because he believes that the government has no right to interfere in such matters. Such forbearance depends instead on the contingent fact that certain areas of human behavior cannot practicably be governed by coercive means, either as a matter of principle, as in the case of sinful thoughts and desires, or of prudence, as in the broad range of cases in which the effort to impose "perfect virtue" would be likely to do more harm than good.[16]

The political aims of the natural jurists might seem at first to complement those of the classical republicans: If natural law defines the proper ends of human association, then republican institutions provide the necessary means for ensuring that those ends are pursued. As we will see, this division of labor played an important role in the political thought of the 18th century, and it is possible to find medieval thinkers such as Ptolemy of Lucca, Marsilius of Padua, John of Paris, and even Aquinas himself thinking along these lines as well.[17] However, the effort to harmonize republican and juristic ideas was hindered by the fact that most natural jurists harbored grave doubts about the idea of placing political power in the hands of the people, and of making freedom rather than justice the end of political life. Aquinas writes, for example, that "provinces or cities which are not ruled by one man toil under dissensions and are tossed about without peace," whereas "provinces and cities governed by a single king rejoice in peace, flourish in justice and are gladdened by an abundance of things."[18] Elsewhere he argues, in an especially influential formulation, that although the prince is bound by the "directive" force of natural law, he cannot be bound coercively and "is indeed above the law inasmuch as he can change the law, and dispense from it in whatever way is expedient to time and place."[19] Although he concedes that government by the many is the "most tolerable" form of rule "if the government should fall away into injustice," he insists that this is only because it is "weaker" and thus

[16] On the practical limitations of human law, see especially ibid., 1a2ae q 91 art 4 resp, and cf. q 96 art 2 passim (*Political Writings*, pp. 90 and 139–41, respectively).

[17] For a useful overview, see James M. Blythe, "'Civic Humanism' and Medieval Political Thought," in James Hankins, ed., *Renaissance Civic Humanism: Reappraisals and Reflections* (New York: Cambridge University Press, 2000), pp. 30–74.

[18] Aquinas, *De Regimine Principum* (c. 1267), book 1, chapter 3 (*Political Writings*, p. 11). The authorship of this treatise is disputed, and the latter part, which was completed c. 1300 by Aquinas's disciple, Ptolemy of Lucca, is considerably more favorable toward republican rule and more hostile toward monarchy than the portions attributed to Thomas. It is worth keeping in mind that Aquinas himself is said to have intended to dedicate the treatise to the king of Cyprus.

[19] Aquinas, *Summa Theologiae* 1a2ae q 96 art 5 ad 3 (*Political Writings*, p. 147).

less able to do lasting harm, and he warns, following much classical precedent, that the rule of the many is more likely to devolve into "extreme"
tyranny than the rule of a king. "It is fitting," Aquinas concludes, "that
just government should be exercised by one man alone."[20] The distance
between this juristic defense of just kingship and the republican concern
to prevent the arbitrary exercise of power is captured nicely in the parting
words of Virgil to Dante in the *Purgatorio*: "Free, upright and healthy is
your will [*arbitrio*] / And not to do its bidding would be wrong / Thus
o'er yourself I give you crown and miter."[21]

2.3. NATURAL LIBERTY AND ABSOLUTE
GOVERNMENT: FROM AQUINAS TO HOBBES

It is only with the emergence of a school of thought that focused on the
protection of personal or "subjective" rights rather than the pursuit of
"objective" right that it became possible to bring juristic and republican
ideas together into a single political vision. This development was made
possible by an ambiguity in the original juristic definition of liberty as
"the natural ability to do as one pleases unless prohibited by force or
right." As we have seen, Aquinas associates liberty so defined with the
human capacity to make morally correct choices and thus to realize their
proper end as rational creatures. His was, in short, what would now be
called a "positive" conception of liberty: Liberty is not limited but rather
guaranteed by the laws of the political community as long as those laws
are consistent with natural law, as all genuine laws are in the Thomistic
view.[22] Here the emphasis falls on the appeal to "right" in the juristic
formula, because to act wrongly is in this view not to act freely at all.
According to a second point of view, however, the relationship between
liberty and the law is contingent and potentially adversarial: Liberty is
defined in "negative" terms as the ability to choose as one wishes within
a given sphere, and the purpose of human law is to constrain or shape

---

[20] Aquinas, *De Regimine Principum*, book 1, chapters 4 and 6 (*Political Writings*,
pp. 11–15, 16–17, quoting p. 13). Aquinas goes on to endorse the standard republican
criticism of tyrannical rule – that "men who are nourished in a climate of fear…degener-
ate into a servile condition of soul and become fearful of every manly and strenuous act,"
even as he dismisses the classical republican hostility to monarchical rule as such: ibid.,
p. 14. For a more favorable assessment of mixed government see *Summa Theologiae*
1a2ae q 95 art 4 resp and q 105 art 1 passim (*Political Writings*, pp. 136, 52–6).
[21] Dante Alighieri, *Purgatorio* 27.140–2. I have attempted my own translation.
[22] On the derivation of human law from natural law, see especially *Summa Theologiae*
1a2ae q 95 art 2 passim (*Political Writings*, pp. 129–31).

those choices in such a way that they conform to the demands of natural law. Here the emphasis falls on the "force" side of the juristic formula, because it is assumed that the demands of right alone are not enough to keep free human action within its proper bounds.

As we might expect, the modern language of natural rights emerged out of this second school of thought, which represented a substantial break from the original Thomistic view. Aquinas and his immediate successors do not distinguish clearly between the demands of natural law and natural right: The proper function of law (*lex*) is to instantiate the principles of right (*ius*), and so when the content of law is consistent with the dictates of practical reason the two terms collapse into one another.[23] As we have seen, this objective conception of natural right leaves no room for an appeal to natural liberty as an independent value in political life. The political activation of the language of freedom within the juristic tradition begins instead with the development over the course of the following two centuries of a conception of personal or "subjective" rights and the resulting differentiation of the category of natural right from that of natural law. Thus in the early 15th century the French theologian Jean Gerson offered a pioneering definition of right as "a *facultas* [capability] or power appropriate to someone and in accordance with the dictates of right reason," of liberty as "a *facultas* of the reason and will towards whatever possibility is selected," and of law as "a practical and right reason according to which the movements and workings of things are directed towards their ordained ends."[24] In the Gersonian tradition, the language of right no longer stands, as it had for Aquinas, simply for "that which is right," but rather for something more like "right of way," that is, for the rightful ability of an agent to act without opposition in a

---

[23] See especially ibid., 2a2ae q 57 passim, and cf. 1a2ae q 94 art 4 sed contra (*Political Writings*, p. 121), where *ius naturale* is used as an equivalent for *lex naturalis*.

[24] Jean Gerson, *Definitiones Terminorum Theologiae Moralis* (1400–1415), in idem, *Oeuvres Complètes*, ed. Palémon Glorieux (Paris: Desclée, 1973), vol. 9, p. 134, cited and translated in Richard Tuck, *Natural Rights Theories: Their Origin and Development* (New York: Cambridge University Press, 1979), pp. 26–7. I am indebted to Tuck's account of the development of subjective-rights theories here and in the following paragraphs. For some doubts about the central role that Gerson plays in Tuck's analysis, see Brian Tierney, "Tuck on Rights: Some Medieval Problems," *History of Political Thought* 4 (1983), pp. 429–41; his "Origins of Natural Rights Language: Texts and Contexts, 1150–1250," *History of Political Thought* 10 (1989), pp. 615–46; and, more generally, his *The Idea of Natural Rights: Studies on Natural Rights, Natural Law, and Church Law, 1150–1625* (Atlanta: Scholars Press, 1997). The chronological and genealogical issues that are raised by this dispute do not, as far as I can see, affect the underlying point that I am making about the role that the language of freedom played in this tradition.

given domain. Because claims of right were now associated not with the existence of a specific moral duty on the part of the agent in question, but rather with the existence of a duty of forbearance on the part of other agents, there was a close conceptual relationship in this way of thinking between natural right and natural liberty, both of which are limited (or, as Gerson says, "directed" [*regulantur*]) by the law.

The purpose of subjective-right theories is to define the legitimate claims that an individual has on the world. Thus for Gerson and his followers, a claim of right – even over ourselves – is equivalent to a claim of property in the relevant sphere. It is a short step from this premise to the conclusion that rights can, like property, be alienated at the discretion of the individual who holds them and that, because the presence of a right implies the presence of the liberty to exercise it, liberty itself is alienable.[25] This line of argument was soon brought to bear on the problem of defining the limits of political authority. The natural jurists were already accustomed to thinking of political rule as something that is (or was) "added" to a prior condition of natural liberty, and this development was now described as a surrender of natural right, and thus of natural liberty, on the part of political subjects for the sake of certain goods that they receive in return – most notably peace and security. It follows, according to this way of thinking, that the legitimacy of political rule depends on the voluntary or rightful character of the transaction in which natural rights are surrendered, and that the proper boundaries of political authority can be determined by defining the conditions under which such a transaction would have taken place. For these thinkers, the political salience of human freedom lies not in the question of how it is preserved, as it does for republicans, but rather in the question of how it is given up – and of whether, when, and for what purposes it might be reclaimed.

---

[25] Annabel Brett points out that for Gerson the language of right (*ius*), unlike the language of liberty, can be predicated not simply of rational agents, as was the case for the Thomists, but also of irrational creatures. Thus a horse can be said to have a right to the hay that it eats. She argues that the 16th-century Thomists of the Salamanca school – Francisco de Vitoria and Domingo de Soto in particular – should be credited with combining the Gersonian definition of *ius* as a *facultas* with the Thomistic conception of liberty as the distinguishing feature of a rational agent into a conception of natural right as a sphere of alienable liberty. See Annabel S. Brett, *Liberty, Right and Nature: Individual Rights in Later Scholastic Thought* (New York: Cambridge University Press, 1997), esp. pp. 76–87 and chapter 4 passim. Again, the chronological and genealogical issues that are raised by her account do not affect the underlying point that I am making about the political implications of the juristic language of liberty.

Here, as in Aquinas, an appeal is made to natural right in order to define the proper ends of political life. However, the Thomistic view has now been turned on its head: Instead of suggesting, as Aquinas had, that political rule is a useful *addition* to (objective) natural right, the subjective-rights theorists defend the proto-contractarian view that political authority is founded on the voluntary *surrender* of (subjective) natural right. Implicit in this possessive and transactional theory of rights is the assumption that the liberty of an agent is something that he or she has reason to value *ceteris paribus*. Thus with the emergence of this way of thinking it became possible for the first time for natural liberty to appear as a distinct value in juristic thought and not, as it had in the original Thomistic formulation, simply as a logically necessary and morally salient, but politically inconsequential, corollary of rational agency. However, even for the subjective-right theorists the value of freedom is strictly subordinated to the demands of natural law: The idea of natural liberty is used as a starting point for an analysis of the limits of political authority and as a way of describing the position in which political subjects may or may not find themselves with respect to a given range of actions, but it is not treated as an end that a political community might pursue for its own sake. This conception of the relationship between freedom and politics is therefore no less distant from the republican position than from the Thomistic one.

Indeed, the most striking political consequence of the emergence of subjective-right theories was not to advance what is now thought of as the contractarian case for limited government, but rather to provide a new and powerful secular defense of the legitimacy of absolute rule. The origins of this line of argument lie in the late medieval and early modern debates over the legitimacy of slavery – debates that, with the advent of European colonialism, were of more immediate practical concern in the 16th century than they had been to the early Scholastic thinkers. According to the orthodox Thomistic view, which is rooted in the thought of Aristotle, the subjection and enslavement of human beings can only be justified by the presence of some rational or moral deficiency in them – a line of argument that 16th-century Spanish Thomists such as Francisco de Vitoria and Domingo de Soto were able to draw on, albeit with some difficulty, both to justify and to call into question the practices of the *conquistadores*.[26] The development of a subjective conception of

---

[26] For a useful analysis of the Thomistic defense of colonial expropriation, see Anthony Pagden, "Dispossessing the Barbarian: The Language of Spanish Thomism and the Debate Over the Property Rights of the American Indians," in idem, ed., *The Languages of*

natural rights made it possible, however, to advance the more radical claim not only that slavery is permitted by natural law under certain objectively defined conditions, but that individuals can voluntarily contract themselves into slavery by alienating their liberty – and that they can do so, as Richard Tuck sardonically puts it, "for any sort of return, ranging from their lives to a string of beads."[27] By setting aside the rather cumbersome Thomistic appeal to the natural capacities of the people concerned, this line of argument provided a defense of slavery that was more easily tailored to the practices of the European colonists in Africa and the Americas.

The Spanish Jesuit Francisco Suárez was among the first to argue, toward the end of the 16th century, that this line of argument could be used to justify the collective alienation of natural right on the part of political subjects, and thus to legitimize the absolute authority of a ruler with whom such a transaction has been performed. The analogy between "voluntary" enslavement and absolute political rule was notably endorsed by the Dutch jurist Hugo Grotius, who argued in his seminal treatise *De Jure Belli ac Pacis* (1625) that if "[i]t is lawful for any Man to engage himself as a Slave to whom he pleases," then it should "therefore be as lawful for a People that are at their own Disposal, to deliver up themselves to any one or more Persons, and transfer the Right of governing them upon him or them, without recovering any Share of that Right to themselves."[28] It was not long before Thomas Hobbes argued even more provocatively that "*children* are no less subject to those who look after them and bring them up than *slaves* [*servi*] are to *Masters*, or *subjects* to the holder of *sovereign power* in the commonwealth," and that "the difference…between a *free citizen* and a *slave*" is that "the FREE MAN…serves only the commonwealth, while the SLAVE serves also his fellow citizen."[29] Indeed, whereas Grotius had written of the

Political Theory in Early-Modern Europe (New York: Cambridge University Press, 1987), pp. 79–98; see also Tierney, *Idea of Natural Rights*, chapter 11. For Aristotle's defense of "natural" slavery, see *Politics*, book 1, chapters 4–7; for Aquinas's views on slavery, see for example *Summa Theologiae* 2a2ae q 57 art 3 (*Political Writings*, pp. 163–4).

[27] Tuck, *Natural Rights Theories*, p. 54.

[28] Hugo Grotius, *De Jure Belli ac Pacis*, book 1, chapter 3, section 8, quoting the 1738 translation by John Morrice et al., reprinted in Hugo Grotius, *The Rights of War and Peace*, ed. Richard Tuck (Indianapolis: Liberty Fund, 2005), p. 261. On the use of this line of argument by Suárez, see Tuck, *Natural Rights Theories*, pp. 56–7, and Quentin Skinner, *The Foundations of Modern Political Thought* (New York: Cambridge University Press, 1978), vol. 2, pp. 182–4.

[29] Thomas Hobbes, *On the Citizen* (1642), trans. Richard Tuck and Michael Silverthorne (New York: Cambridge University Press, 1998), pp. 110, 111–12 (chapter 9; original

collective alienation of natural liberty in de facto terms – as a possibility that may or may not have been realized in the history of a given people – Hobbes argued de jure that natural law, whose content is defined for him, as for Grotius, by the overriding concern for self-preservation, requires the complete and nearly unconditional surrender of the natural liberty of subjects to a sovereign power that (or who) will represent their interests and act on their behalf.

For Hobbes and Grotius, natural liberty is something that is enjoyed not *through* but rather *outside* the law. Right and law are therefore not equivalent concepts, as they are in Aquinas, but rather opposing ones. As Hobbes puts it, "Law, and Right, differ as much, as Obligation, and Liberty."[30] However, they use this distinction not to argue that the state is obliged to respect the natural rights of its citizens, but rather to neutralize the appeal to the language of rights, and thus of liberty, on the part of political subjects. The law of nature obliges us to surrender our natural rights in order to secure our own preservation, and the liberty that is left to subjects under this arrangement does not arise from any claim of right on their part – although Hobbes, unlike Grotius, grants them the right to defend their own lives *in extremis*.[31] Rather, it arises from the contingent fact that the sovereign has chosen not to impose a rule of conduct in a certain range of cases. It follows for Hobbes that the "Greatest Liberty" of subjects "depend[s] on the Silence of the Law" and "is in some places more, and in some lesse; and in some times more, in other times lesse, according as they that have the Soveraignty shall think most convenient."[32] In other words, the extent of the liberty of subjects depends almost entirely on the will of the sovereign, and because the sovereign judges and acts on behalf of the commonwealth as a whole, it is literally unthinkable that it (or he) could judge or act in a way that runs contrary to the subjects' interests. In a revealing passage

---

emphasis). This is a rare case in which Hobbes follows Aristotle, who argues that the difference between slaves and other menial laborers lies in the fact that although both do "necessary tasks" in the city, "slaves do them for individuals," whereas "mechanics and laborers…do them for the community": *Politics*, p. 95 (book 3, chapter 5). Aristotle concludes, of course, that both classes are unfit for citizenship in the ideal city.

[30] Thomas Hobbes, *Leviathan* (1651), ed. Richard Tuck (New York: Cambridge University Press, 1991), p. 91 (chapter 14). Cf. ibid., p. 200 (chapter 26): "*Right* is *Liberty*, namely that Liberty which the Civil Law leaves us: But *Civill Law* is an *Obligation*; and takes from us the Liberty which the Law of Nature gave us" (original emphasis).

[31] See, for example, ibid., pp. 93–4, 150–2 (chapters 14 and 21), and cf. Grotius, *De Jure Belli*, book 1, chapter 4, section 2.

[32] Hobbes, *Leviathan*, p. 152 (chapter 21).

from the Latin edition of *Leviathan*, Hobbes argues that "[w]hat the law imposes is imposed for the good of the one who commands, i.e., for the public good."[33]

Hobbes was of course well aware, writing as he was during the time of the English Commonwealth, that his analysis of the liberty of subjects was at odds with the republican view. Indeed, one of his chief aims was to expose what he saw as the incoherence and perniciousness of that view.[34] He attacks the classical republicans in particular – mentioning Aristotle and Cicero by name – for giving men "a habit (under a falseshew of Liberty,) of favouring tumults, and of licentious controlling the actions of the Soveraigns; and again of controlling those controllers, with the effusion of so much blood; as I think I may truly say, there was never anything so deerly bought, as these Western parts have bought the learning of the Greek and Latine tongues." His notorious conclusion that "[w]hether a Common-wealth be Monarchicall, or Popular, the Freedome is still the same," and that it is therefore "very absurd for men to clamor as they doe, for the Liberty they so manifestly enjoy," was of course as jarring to the ears of republicans at the time as it is to those of liberals today.[35] Nevertheless, this line of argument is firmly rooted, as we have seen, in the juristic tradition of thinking of liberty in terms of a sphere of unhindered choice – as is the characterization of "popular" rule as tumultuous and licentious. It remains to be seen how the language of subjective natural right could be used to advance the more traditional juristic aim of limiting the scope of political authority – and, more importantly for our purposes, how it could be tied to the traditional republican ideal of virtuous citizenship and limited government.

2.4. NATURAL LIBERTY AND LIMITED GOVERNMENT: FROM AQUINAS TO LOCKE

We have seen that the classical republicans saw the existence of a sphere of personal independence as a necessary (though not sufficient) condition

---

[33] Thomas Hobbes, *Leviathan, with selected variants from the Latin edition of 1668*, trans. and ed. Edwin Curley (Indianapolis: Hackett, 1994), p. 383n (chapter 42).
[34] For a detailed discussion, see Quentin Skinner, *Hobbes and Republican Liberty* (New York: Cambridge University Press, 2008).
[35] Hobbes, *Leviathan*, ed. Tuck, pp. 150, 149, 147 (chapter 21). Elsewhere Hobbes remarks that "if a man should talk to me…of *A free Subject*; *A free-will*; or any *Free*, but free from being hindred by opposition, I should not say that he were in an Errour, but that his words were without meaning; that is to say, Absurd": ibid., p. 34 (chapter 5; original emphasis).

for the enjoyment of freedom. By associating freedom with the possession of individual rights – that is, with the ability to act without hindrance in a legally defined area – the subjective-rights thinkers provided a powerful tool for identifying cases in which this condition has been violated. The conflict between the republican and juristic traditions arises not from the appeal to subjective rights itself, but from the further claim that these rights have to be surrendered if we are to enjoy the benefits of political society, and that there is therefore no difference in principle between political subjection and slavery. From a republican point of view this claim is not only objectionable but incoherent: If individuals can cultivate and display their virtue only if they are secure against the depredations of arbitrary power, then it follows that the existence of a sphere of personal independence is a necessary condition for the existence of meaningful human agency. To surrender this kind of freedom is to step outside the realm not only of republican freedom, but of humanity itself. As Rousseau puts it in his response to Grotius, "[t]o renounce one's freedom is to renounce one's quality as a man, the rights of humanity, and even its duties," and thus to "deprive one's actions of all morality" – an outcome that is, he argues, "incompatible with the nature of man."[36]

For republicans it is not enough to say that political power should be exercised in accordance with the demands of natural law; we must also ensure that it is not exercised arbitrarily, that is, at the discretion of the ruler or ruling class. As long as we find ourselves under a power that is arbitrary in this sense – as long as we enjoy our freedom at the pleasure of our rulers rather than as the reward of our virtue – then we are not, in republican terms, free at all. Among the first thinkers to respond to Hobbes in these terms was his countryman James Harrington, whose *Commonwealth of Oceana* (1656) is one of the leading statements of 17th-century English republicanism. After quoting the passage from *Leviathan* in which Hobbes equates "Monarchicall" with "Popular" liberty, Harrington invokes the traditional republican distinction between being free "from" and being free "by" the laws to argue that "the liberty of a commonwealth consisteth in the empire of her laws, the absence whereof would betray her unto the lusts of tyrants." "The greatest bashaw" under a despotic government, he reminds us, "is a tenant, as well of his head as of his estate, at the will of his lord," whereas the citizen

---

[36] Jean-Jacques Rousseau, *On the Social Contract* (1762), book 1, chapter 4, in idem, *The Social Contract and Other Later Political Writings*, trans. and ed. Victor Gourevitch (New York: Cambridge University Press, 1997), p. 45.

of a republic "is a freeholder of both, and not to be controlled but by the law."[37] Harrington's response to Hobbes captures well the great distance, verging on mutual incomprehension, between the republican conception of freedom and one that equates it, as Hobbes does, with unhindered choice. However, by associating "the liberty of the commonwealth" with "the empire of the laws," Harrington also calls attention to an obvious point of contact between republican and juristic thought, one that was developed more fully by natural jurists of a less authoritarian stripe.

In fact, as Rousseau's appeal to the "rights of humanity" suggests, the mainstream of natural jurisprudence did not follow Suárez and Grotius in finding a foundation for absolute rule in the surrender of natural right. The more orthodox view was that the demands of natural law place substantial limits on the form that this surrender can take. As we have seen, even Hobbes insists that subjects cannot alienate their right to self-preservation in the last resort. He therefore grants them the right not only to resist the sovereign when their lives are directly threatened, but also to refuse to give self-incriminating testimony or even to perform "any dangerous, or dishonourable Office" – a potentially expansive loophole in an otherwise tightly woven theory of sovereignty.[38] This line of argument rests on the contractarian claim that if legitimate government is based on consent, then its authority must be limited to what rational people, comparing the benefits of natural liberty with those of living in political society, *would* have consented to in alienating their natural right. Hobbes, with his dim view of the condition of natural liberty and his rather narrow conception of human interests, takes a correspondingly limited view of the liberties that political subjects can claim as a matter of right. However, his reasoning on this point has its origins in an older tradition of thought that places the question of the proper limits of political authority within a moral and theological framework that is more favorable toward the idea that subjects retain certain rights against their rulers.

---

[37] James Harrington, *The Commonwealth of Oceana* (1656), in idem, *The Commonwealth of Oceana and A System of Politics*, ed. J. G. A. Pocock (New York: Cambridge University Press, 1992), pp. 19–20. Interestingly, Hobbes seems to endorse this line of argument in *De Cive*, arguing that "[a] major part of the *liberty* which is harmless to the commonwealth and essential to happy lives for the citizens, is that they have nothing to fear but penalties which they can anticipate or expect": *On the Citizen*, p. 151 (chapter 13; original emphasis). Hobbes does not address the apparent conflict between this claim and his view that the sovereign can make and dispense with the law as he sees fit.

[38] Hobbes, *Leviathan*, p. 151 (chapter 21). Tuck points out that even Grotius expresses some reservations about the idea that natural right can be unconditionally alienated: *Natural Rights Theories*, pp. 70–1, 79–80.

The claim that certain rights are inalienable rests on two separate but related lines of argument, each of which is firmly rooted in natural law principles: First, individuals cannot rightfully give up the means to their own preservation, and second, those who hold positions of authority have an obligation to pursue the good of those over whom they rule. The first line of argument is the narrower of the two, and so it not surprising that it is the one on which Hobbes relies in defining the natural rights of subjects. The claim that rulers are obliged to pursue the common good would seem to have more far-reaching implications, suggesting as it does that political authority can be resisted or even overthrown if it harms those over whom it is exercised, even if those harms are not substantial enough to pose a threat to the survival of the community or its members. However, Aquinas himself is cautious on this point, arguing like Hobbes that the good of the political community consists not in its liberty, but rather in "the preservation of its unity." He concludes that even tyrannical rulers should be obeyed "unless the tyranny is so excessive that it ravages the entire community" – that is, unless the demands of self-preservation are also in play. Opposition to a tyrant, he suggests, will only make the tyranny more extreme, and even a successful revolution is likely to lead to the rise of a new tyrant who is even worse than the old.[39]

Here again it is instructive to contrast the premises of juristic with those of republican political thought. Machiavelli agrees with Aquinas in thinking that a people that overthrows a tyrannical prince is likely to "quickly return...beneath a yoke that is most often heavier than the one it had removed from its neck a little before." However, he makes an exception for those peoples – such as the Romans after the expulsion of the Tarquins – who have not yet been "corrupted" by princely rule, arguing that they "could easily be brought to live free and ordered."[40] Machiavelli's dissent from the juristic tradition on this point provides

---

[39] Aquinas, *De Regimine Principum*, book 1, chapters 3–7 (quoting *Political Writings*, pp. 10, 16). David Hume echoes this line of argument some 500 years later, arguing that "the *tyrannicide* or assassination, approved of by ancient maxims, instead of keeping tyrants and usurpers in awe, made them ten times more fierce and unrelenting": "Of Passive Obedience" (1748), in idem, *Political Essays*, ed. Knud Haakonssen (New York: Cambridge University Press, 1994), p. 203 (original emphasis).

[40] Niccolò Machiavelli, *Discourses on Livy*, pp. 44–5 (book 1, chapters 16–17). Ptolemy of Lucca argues along similar lines that "political government was better for wise and virtuous persons, such as the ancient Romans," but that "in corrupt nature regal government is more fruitful": *De Regimine Principum*, book 2, chapter 9, quoting James M. Blythe's translation (Philadelphia: University of Pennsylvania Press, 1997), p. 124. On the disputed authorship of this treatise, see note 18.

an especially clear illustration of the role that the appeal to civic virtue plays in distinguishing republican from juristic thought. Whereas Aquinas insists that the most just and peaceful rule is that of a single man and calls attention to the "dissensions" that are associated with the "popular" alternative, Machiavelli argues that "where the matter is not corrupt, tumults and scandals do not hurt," and that "where it is corrupt, well-ordered laws do not help." Princely rule may be a necessary fallback when the corruption of the people – a corruption that is fostered by princely rule itself – makes a "free way of life" impossible, but the "tumultuous" rule of a virtuous people over itself is nevertheless to be preferred to the peaceful rule of even a just prince. As Rousseau later put it, "a little agitation energizes souls, and what causes the species truly to prosper is not so much peace as freedom."[41]

The absolutist tone of juristic political thought began to soften with the rise of the Conciliar movement in the 14th century, and still more dramatically with the Protestant Reformation and the onset of the wars of religion in the 16th century. A number of natural jurists now began to defend the potentially radical claim that political subjects have not alienated but rather only delegated their natural right to govern themselves, that rulers hold their authority as a trust from the community, and that this authority can be reclaimed, by force if necessary, when that trust is violated. Needless to say, this line of argument raises the question of who gets to decide when the necessary conditions for resistance have been met and where political authority is then to be placed, and the apparent intractability of these questions led Hobbes and like-minded thinkers to dismiss the idea of delegated authority as being hopelessly confused in its premises and dangerously anarchic in its implications. Aquinas himself had been careful to emphasize that in the rare cases when resistance to a tyrannical ruler becomes necessary "steps are to be taken…not by the private presumption of any persons, but through public authority."[42] Even thinkers who were more receptive toward the view that it may be legitimate in some cases to overthrow an unjust government were reluctant to place the right to revolution in the hands of the people themselves, arguing instead that the decision must be taken, and political authority reconstituted, by duly authorized subordinate powers such as the lesser nobility or the people's elected representatives, or by a commonly recognized superior power such as the emperor. When direct popular resistance

---

[41] Rousseau, *Social Contract*, p. 106n (book 3, chapter 9).
[42] Aquinas, *De Regimine Principum*, pp. 19–20 (book 1, chapter 7).

was enjoined it was not through an appeal to the common good, but rather to the more fundamental and immediately pressing duty of self-preservation.[43]

It was not until the second half of the 16th century that the appeal to natural rights was explicitly attached, not only to the view that rulers have an obligation to pursue the common good of the community, but also to a full-blown theory of popular sovereignty that gave the people as a whole – and even, in some accounts, any individual citizen – the right to resist and even to overthrow a tyrannical government.[44] The canonical statement of this line of argument is found in John Locke's *Second Treatise of Government*, but we can now see that Locke makes his case by drawing on a series of traditional juristic claims about the nature and limits of political authority, many of which can be traced back to the writings of Aquinas himself.[45] In particular, he argues that human beings are "naturally" free, in the sense that they do not naturally, and did not originally, recognize or live under "any Superior Power on Earth," and that "whatever superiority some politicians now would place in [the first men], they themselves claimed it not; but by consent were all *equal*, till by the same consent they set Rulers over themselves." He famously concludes that the "Superior Power" that is created through this act of consent is "to be directed to no other *end*, but the *Peace, Safety*, and *publick good* of the People," and that "whenever the *Legislators endeavour to take away, and destroy the Property of the People*, or to reduce them to Slavery under Arbitrary Power, they put themselves in a state of War with the People" and thereby *"forfeit the Power*, the People had put into their hands, for quite contrary ends." This power then "devolves to the People, who have a Right to resume their original Liberty, and, by the Establishment of a new Legislative (such as they shall think fit) provide for their own Safety and Security, which is the end for which they are in Society."[46]

---

[43] For a useful discussion of the development of theories of resistance in the late medieval and early modern periods, see Skinner, *Foundations of Modern Political Thought*, vol. 2, esp. chapters 7–9.

[44] Among the earliest exponents of this view was the Scottish humanist and jurist George Buchanan in his *De Jure Regni apud Scotos* (1579). See the discussion in Skinner, *Foundations of Modern Political Thought*, vol. 2, pp. 340–5.

[45] The proximate sources of Locke's natural jurisprudence are found of course in the writings of 17th-century Protestant jurists such as Grotius and Samuel Pufendorf. Nevertheless, as Mark Goldie has pointed out, the use by Locke and other radical Whigs of a theory of resistance that was ultimately derived from the Scholastic tradition exposed them to charges of "papism" from their royalist contemporaries: "John Locke and Anglican Royalism," *Political Studies* 31 (1983), pp. 61–85.

[46] John Locke, *Second Treatise of Government* §§22, 102, 131, 222 (original emphasis).

The originality of Locke's position does not lie in the fact that he defines the proper limits of political authority by appealing to a condition of natural liberty – that line of argument would have been familiar enough to his audience.[47] Nor does it lie in the fact that he is more bold than many of his predecessors in drawing out the radical implications of this premise. It lies instead in the fact that the definition of freedom that he appeals to is verbally identical to the republican one: "Freedom is not," he argues, "*A Liberty for every Man to do what he lists*: (For who could be free, when every other Man's Humour might domineer over him?) But a *Liberty* to dispose, and order, as he lists, his Person, Actions, Possessions, and his whole Property, within the Allowance of those laws under which he is; *and therein not to be subject to the arbitrary Will of another*, but freely follow his own." In other words, natural liberty does not consist for Locke, as it does for the earlier subjective-right thinkers, in being able to do as one pleases; nor does it consist simply, as it does for the objective-right thinkers, in obedience to natural law. It is defined instead as a condition in which people are able to "order their Actions, and dispose of their Possessions, and Persons as they think fit, within the bounds of the Law of Nature, *without asking leave, or depending upon the Will of any other Man*."[48] Here Locke weaves together the juristic view that freedom consists in obedience to the law of nature and the republican view that freedom consists in the absence of arbitrary power, thus opening the door, at least verbally speaking, to a reconciliation of the two positions. However, as I will now argue, Locke's appeal to republican language falls substantially short of a genuinely republican conception of freedom. It was therefore left to his 18th-century successors to work out a genuine synthesis of republican and juristic ideas.

2.5. LOCKE ON LIBERTY

Although he uses recognizably republican language in associating unfreedom with dependence on the arbitrary will of another person, Locke's

---

[47] Indeed, Robert Filmer himself, writing some fifty years earlier, held that "[the] desperate assertion, whereby kings are made subject to the censures and deprivations of their subjects, follows (as the authors of it conceive) as a necessary consequence of that former position of the supposed natural equality and freedom of mankind, and liberty to choose what form of government it please," and he notes that this view has been "common opinion…[s]ince the time that school divinity [i.e., Scholasticism] began to flourish": *Patriarcha*, in idem, *Patriarcha and Other Writings*, ed. Johann P. Sommerville (New York: Cambridge University Press, 1991), quoted at pp. 2–3 (chapter 1 §1).
[48] Locke, *Second Treatise* §§57, 4 (emphasis added); cf. §22.

theory of freedom departs from classical republican usage in two important ways. First of all, he endorses the traditional juristic view that
disobedience to the law of nature, like disobedience to the laws of the
commonwealth, is not an expression but rather a forfeiture of one's
freedom.[49] It follows, as we have seen, that only those liberties that we
have independent reason to value – that is, those liberties that make it
possible to fulfill the demands of natural law – are morally and politically
salient. Thus individual liberty taken by itself has no independent value
for Locke, or at least none that rulers are obliged to recognize. Indeed,
because the exercise of natural liberty gives rise to the very "inconve-
niencies" that lead human beings to enter into political society in the first
place, he requires that each citizen "part...with as much of his natural
liberty in providing for himself, as the good, prosperity, and safety of the
Society shall require."[50] Even in its radical Lockean form, then, the appeal
to natural rights does not treat freedom, understood as the absence of
constraint, as a value for the sake of which a people might legitimately
resist or rebel against its rulers. Rather, Locke follows the mainstream of
natural jurisprudence in arguing that we are free only insofar as we obey
the demands of natural law, and that the purpose of political rule is to
ensure that human behavior is kept within those bounds.

It is therefore not surprising to find that Locke also makes the non-
arbitrariness of political rule depend on its conformity to natural law:
"[T]he *Municipal Laws* of Countries," he argues, "are only so far right, as
they are founded on the Law of Nature, by which they are to be regulated
and interpreted."[51] Even consent, the defining feature of political rule and
the linchpin of his theory of political obligation, does not provide an
independent check on political authority: The question is not, as it is for
Grotius, what we have *actually* consented to, but rather, as for Hobbes,
what we *should* have consented to in the establishment of political rule.[52]
Salus populi, and not *vox populi*, is the watchword of Locke's political

---

[49] See especially ibid. §§54–63, and cf. the discussion of freedom in the *Essay Concerning
Human Understanding*, book 2, chapter 21, esp. §§47–52. On the juristic roots of Locke's
theory of liberty, see, for example, James Tully, *An Approach to Political Philosophy: Locke
in Contexts* (New York: Cambridge University Press, 1993), chapter 8.

[50] Locke, *Second Treatise* §130.

[51] Ibid., §§136, 12 (original emphasis); cf. §135.

[52] For a recent argument to this effect see Lena Halldenius, "Locke and the Non-Arbitrary,"
European Journal of Political Theory 2 (2003), pp. 261–79; for a classic statement see
John Dunn, "Consent in the Political Theory of John Locke," *Historical Journal* 10
(1967), pp. 153–82, and cf. also Hanna Pitkin, "Obligation and Consent – I," *American
Political Science Review* 59 (1965), pp. 994–7.

thought.[53] It follows that although consent can be withdrawn if the government subverts the ends for the sake of which it was established, the withdrawal of consent is illegitimate if the government has succeeded in fulfilling those ends. Locke holds that "*whoever*, either Ruler or Subject, by force goes about to invade the Rights of either Prince or People, and lays the foundation for *overturning* the Constitution and Frame of *any Just Government*, is guilty of the greatest Crime, I think, a Man is capable of," that "those, *whoever* they be…are truly and properly *Rebels*."[54] The famous Lockean right of revolution is therefore rather timid when compared to the more radical – and genuinely republican – view espoused by John Milton, who, writing in the immediate aftermath of the execution of Charles I, argues that "since the king or magistrate holds his authority of the people…then may the people, as oft as they shall judge it for the best, either choose him or reject him, retain him or depose him, *though no tyrant*, merely by the liberty and right of free-born men to be governed as seems to them best."[55]

Even Locke's theory of property, which has often been seen as a pioneering defense of market freedom,[56] is grounded in natural law principles in such a way that it cannot easily be made to support such a view. Locke rests his defense of property rights on the fundamental juristic right of self-preservation, which is not for him, as it is for Hobbes, simply an interest that we happen to have, but rather a duty that we owe to God as our creator. In particular, he insists that we have a natural right to acquire property through the use of our labor in order to avoid the paradoxical and possibly blasphemous conclusion that God gave us a bountiful earth without giving us the means, moral as well as material, to

[53] Locke cites the traditional formula "*salus populi suprema lex esto*" approvingly at *Second Treatise* §158, and in the 1764 edition of the *Two Treatises* it is used as an epigraph for the work as a whole. In an earlier work, Locke remarks of the saying "*vox populi, vox Dei*" that "we have been taught a most unhappy lesson how doubtful, how fallacious this maxim is, how productive of evils, and with how much party spirit and with what cruel intent this ill-omened proverb has been flung wide lately among the common people": *Essays on the Law of Nature* (1663–4), trans. W. von Leyden, in idem, *Political Essays*, ed. Mark Goldie (New York: Cambridge University Press, 1997), p. 106. Significantly, this comment is made at the beginning of a section titled "Can the Law of Nature Be Known from the General Consent of Men? No."

[54] Locke, *Second Treatise* §§230, 226 (emphasis added).

[55] John Milton, "The Tenure of Kings and Magistrates" (1649), in idem, *The Major Works*, ed. Stephen Orgel and Jonathan Goldberg (Oxford: Oxford University Press, 1991), quoted at p. 281 (emphasis added).

[56] The view that Locke offers a proto-capitalist defense of unlimited acquisition is most influentially set out in chapter 5 of C. B. Macpherson's *The Political Theory of Possessive Individualism: Hobbes to Locke* (New York: Oxford University Press, 1962).

enjoy it. As James Tully puts it, property rights define "man's privilege to use a world which is not essentially his own and which is to be used, and not abused, for purposes not his own."[57] Here again Locke follows the Scholastic tradition, which treats private property as a useful "addition" to natural law on the grounds that it makes possible the peaceful, orderly, and productive use of natural resources.[58] Because property rights arise from the divine imperative "to enjoy" the world that God has given us, they are limited by the requirement that we take no more than we can use before it spoils, and (more mysteriously) that we leave "enough and as good" behind for others.[59] It follows for Locke not only that we have a duty to refrain from harming the persons and property of others, but that "no Body has an absolute Arbitrary Power over *himself*... to destroy his own Life" or to misuse his own property, because "[n]othing was made by God for Man to spoil or destroy."[60] We are very far here from the market conception of freedom as the right to do as one pleases with what one owns.[61]

The second important difference between Locke's theory of freedom and the classical republican view lies in the fact that he shows a notable lack of interest in the traditional republican project of designing free political

[57] James Tully, *A Discourse on Property: John Locke and His Adversaries* (New York: Cambridge University Press, 1980), p. 72. A similar view is expressed by Jeremy Waldron, who points out that for Locke "being permitted to help oneself [to natural resources] is not a divine indulgence of the self-interested inclination of an acquisitive being. It is the naturally requisite next step following our creation once we accept that we were created subservient to God's design": *God, Locke, and Equality* (New York: Cambridge University Press, 2002), p. 160. The theological foundations of Locke's theory of property are laid out at *Second Treatise* §§25–30.

[58] Aquinas, *Summa Theologiae* 2a2ae q 66, borrowing a line of argument from Aristotle's *Politics*, book 2, chapter 5.

[59] Locke, *Second Treatise* §§31–3; cf. §§27, 38, 46. For two contrasting efforts to make sense of the "enough and as good" proviso, see Robert Nozick, *Anarchy, State, and Utopia* (New York: Basic Books, 1974), pp. 175–82, and Jeremy Waldron, *The Right to Private Property* (Oxford: Clarendon Press, 1988), pp. 209–18, 280–3.

[60] Locke, *Second Treatise* §§135, 31 (emphasis added).

[61] Locke does argue, in an unpublished note dated 1695, that "what anyone has he may value at what rate he will, and transgresses not against justice if he sells at any price, provided he makes no distinction of buyers." However, he supports this claim not through an appeal to natural right, but rather to the material benefits of trade: Any effort to impose a more stringent doctrine of just pricing would, he argues, "quickly put an end to merchandizing," so that "mankind would be deprived of the supply of foreign mutual conveniences of life." Moreover, he goes on to emphasize that any right to set prices on the part of the seller is trumped by the more fundamental right to self-preservation on the part of the buyer: "He is so far from being permitted to gain to that degree, that he is bound to be at some loss, and impart of his own to save another from perishing": "Venditio," in *Political Essays*, pp. 341, 342–3.

institutions and cultivating virtue in the citizenry: "By *Common-wealth*," he writes, "I must be understood all along to mean, not a Democracy, or any Form of Government, but *any Independent Community* which the *Latines* signified by the word *Civitas*."[62] His subordination of the republican concern for institutional design to the juristic concern for substantively correct outcomes is brought out especially clearly in his discussion of prerogative power, in which he makes the striking claim that "a good prince...cannot have too much *Prerogative*."[63] This claim, with its echoes of the Thomistic view that the prince is bound by the directive but not the coercive force of the law, is directly at odds with the republican view that unchecked power is destructive of liberty regardless of the ends to which it is put. Locke's contemporary, Algernon Sidney, takes a stricter republican line in his *Discourses Concerning Government* (written in the early 1680s and published posthumously in 1698), arguing that "we in *England* know no other King than he who is so by Law, nor any power in that king except that which he has by Law." Locke, by contrast, treats positive law as a "determination" and "definition" of the prerogative power of kings to pursue the public good and insists that the mere presence of unchecked power does not give subjects reason to withdraw their consent from government. Indeed, he observes that "Prerogative was always *largest* in the hands of our wisest and best Princes" – princes who, he concedes, "had some Title to Arbitrary Power, by that Argument, that would prove Absolute Monarchy the best Government."[64]

This willingness to grant, if only in principle, that absolute monarchy might be the best form of government when placed in the right hands puts Locke closer to the mainstream of juristic than of republican political thought. To be sure, he hastens to add that "the Reigns of good Princes have been always most dangerous to the Liberties of their

---

[62] Locke, *Second Treatise* §133 (original emphasis); cf. Hobbes, *Leviathan*, p. 120 (chapter 17).

[63] Locke, *Second Treatise* §164 (original emphasis).

[64] Algernon Sidney, *Discourses Concerning Government* (1683/1698), chapter 3 §21; Locke, *Second Treatise* §§162–3 (cf. 110–11), 165–6 (original emphasis). Sidney concedes that Aristotle (whom Filmer cites on this point) is correct to say that virtuous kingship is the best form of government. However, where Locke is willing to speak of "our" princes in considering this line of argument, Sidney treats the existence of a truly virtuous king as little more than a theoretical possibility, going so far as to defend Aristotle against the charge that he is "a trifler, for speaking of such a man as can never be found": ibid., chapter 3 §23; cf. chapter 2 §1. For a useful discussion of the debates about prerogative power in late 17th-century England, see Alan Houston, "Republicanism, the Politics of Necessity, and the Rule of Law," in Alan Houston and Steve Pincus, eds., *A Nation Transformed: England After the Restoration* (New York: Cambridge University Press, 2001), pp. 241–71.

People" precisely because of the bad precedent that their "God-like" rule sets,[65] and he endorses, though only in passing, the traditional republican view that the executive and legislative powers should not be placed in the same hands.[66] In the final chapter of the *Second Treatise* he defends what might be thought of as the ultimate check on arbitrary power, arguing that "the properest way to prevent the evil, is to shew them the danger and injustice of it, who are under the greatest temptation to run into it" – that is, to remind would-be tyrants that consent can be withdrawn and revolution undertaken if they fail to perform their duties.[67] Nevertheless, his rather perfunctory treatment of the question of how just political rule can be secured falls considerably short, both in scope and in depth, of what we find in a genuinely republican thinker such as Harrington, whose *Commonwealth of Oceana* centers around this question, or Sidney, who devotes the later chapters of his *Discourses* to a detailed defense of popular government and limited monarchy.

Why, then, does Locke use the republican language of arbitrary power and dependence in stating his definition of liberty? The answer lies, I think, in the fact that he places the responsibility for seeing that the demands of natural law are met by the government on the shoulders of the people themselves – indeed, on each individual person[68] – thereby giving the juristic conception of freedom a radically egalitarian and participatory dimension that it had previously lacked. In this respect, the argument of the *Second Treatise* is precisely analogous to that of Locke's *Letter Concerning Toleration*: Just as it would be irrational to give the government the arbitrary power to dictate the means to one's own salvation, so too would it be irrational to give it the arbitrary power

---

[65] Locke, *Second Treatise* §166; cf. §92, where Locke observes that "he that thinks *absolute Power purifies Mens Bloods*, and corrects the baseness of Humane Nature, need read but the History of this, or any other Age to be convinced of the contrary" (original emphasis).

[66] Ibid., §143, 159; but cf. §§151–2 and 213ff, where Locke alludes, apparently without disapproval, to the English practice of giving the executive a "share" in the legislative power, and §153, where he considers, again without expressing disapproval, the possibility that the legislative power might be placed in "a single Person," who would thus "naturally have the Supream Executive Power, together with the Legislative."

[67] Ibid., §226.

[68] "And where the Body of the People, *or any single Man*, is deprived of their Right, or is under the Exercise of a power without right, and have no Appeal on Earth, there they have a liberty to appeal to Heaven, whenever they judge the Cause of sufficient moment.... And this Judgment they cannot part with, it being out of a Man's power so to submit himself to another, as to give him a liberty to destroy him; God and Nature never allowing a Man so to abandon himself, as to neglect his own preservation": ibid., §168 (emphasis added); cf. §241.

to dictate how the law of nature should be applied more generally. In each case we would be renouncing a duty that we owe to ourselves as rational agents and to God as our creator. Thus if Locke defends a traditional juristic position in associating freedom with obedience to natural law, he innovates in arguing that each of us has a natural and inalienable right to decide for ourselves whether the trust that we have placed in government to execute that law on our behalf has been violated. Moreover, we have the further right to resist or even "dissolve" the government if it infringes on our freedom so defined, that is, if it does us an injustice. It is this "very strange Doctrine"[69] – that the responsibility for ensuring that just rule is maintained lies on each and every citizen – that leads Locke to invoke the republican language of arbitrary power in his otherwise juristic treatment of natural liberty, and it is the extreme egalitarianism and individualism of this line of argument, and not the appeal that it makes to natural rights, that gives him a claim to be the first liberal thinker.

Locke therefore categorically rejects the traditional republican view that differences in status and virtue provide a basis for differential claims to political authority: Although he grants that "*Age* or *Virtue* may give a Men a just Precedency," and that "*Excellency of Parts and Merit* may place others above the Common Level," he insists that "all this consists with the *Equality*, which all Men are in, in respect of Jurisdiction or Dominion one over another," that is, with the "*equal Right* that every Man hath, *to his Natural Freedom*, without being subjected to the Will or Authority of another Man."[70] To be sure, the appeal to right reason as the proper criterion for citizenship leaves room for substantial forms of exclusion: Some people – children, most obviously, but also "*Lunaticks* and *Ideots*," "*Innocents*" and "*Madmen*" – lack the capacity for reason and so properly fall under the care of others. Others – criminals of various kinds – reveal themselves by their actions to have "quitted Reason" and may therefore be treated like "wild beast[s], or noxious brute[s], with whom Mankind can have neither Society nor Security."[71] Indeed, although Locke does not pursue this line of argument himself, the appeal to right reason has been used to justify many of the same exclusions on which republican societies, and indeed almost all human societies, have traditionally rested. Not only children but also women, slaves, the poor, the working class,

---

[69] Ibid., §9.
[70] Ibid., §54 (original emphasis). By my count, this passage contains one of only three passing references to virtue in the *Second Treatise*.
[71] Ibid., §§60, 172 (original emphasis).

and colonized peoples have simply been said to lack reason in the relevant sense.[72] Nevertheless, the shift from a republican to a juristic theory of citizenship brings with it a fundamental shift in the terms of exclusion: It is no longer based, as it had been at least since the time of Aristotle, on the claim that the excluded classes have no contribution to make *as citizens* to the common good of the political community, but rather on the claim that they are incapable *as human beings* of understanding and acting in accordance with the law of nature.

I began this chapter by pointing out that the classical republicans disagreed not only about the meaning of arbitrary power and the value of virtue, but also about the extent to which republican citizenship is an egalitarian ideal, and the extent to which republican freedom is a property of individuals or of collectivities. In these latter respects, classical republicanism is sharply and, morally speaking, somewhat awkwardly at odds with the egalitarian and individualistic premises of modern liberalism. We have seen that the origins of this "liberal" conception of politics – which, needless to say, contains its own ambiguities – can be traced back to the political writings of John Locke, and through him to the natural-right theories of the late medieval and early modern natural jurists. This is, of course, hardly a surprising finding. However, I also hope to have shown that the origins of what is now thought of as the liberal conception of *freedom* – of freedom understood as the ability to pursue one's own good in one's own way, a kind of freedom that is paradigmatically enjoyed in and through the market – cannot be located here. Rather, Locke remains faithful to his juristic forebears in arguing that freedom in the sense of unhindered action has no independent moral or political value. The claim that freedom is an end that political societies might pursue for its own sake was a product instead of the debates over the political implications of the rise of modern commercial societies that took place over the course of the following century. These debates were initially framed, as I will now argue, in republican rather than juristic terms.

---

[72] On the use of the appeal to reason to exclude women, see, for example, Carole Pateman, *The Sexual Contract* (Stanford, CA: Stanford University Press, 1988); on its use to exclude the poor and laboring classes, see Macpherson, *Political Theory of Possessive Individualism*, chapter 5; on its use to exclude colonized peoples, see, for example, Uday Singh Mehta, *Liberalism and Empire: A Study in Nineteenth-Century British Liberal Thought* (Chicago: University of Chicago Press, 1999). For doubts about the validity of Pateman's and Macpherson's arguments as applied to Locke himself, see Waldron, *God, Locke, and Equality*, chapters 2 and 4, respectively.

3

The Rise of Commerce

> What else makes a Common-wealth, but the private wealth, if I may so say,
> of the members thereof in the exercise of Commerce amongst themselves,
> and with forraine Nations?
>
> Edward Misselden, *The Circle of Commerce*

3.1. COMMERCE AND CHRISTIANITY

I have argued that despite the sometimes bewildering variety of views
that republican thinkers have held, it is possible to identify a common
core of republican thought that is concerned with the problem of controlling arbitrary power in order to secure the practice of virtue. However, to
put the point this way is to begin rather than end a discussion about the
nature of republican freedom. Indeed, it is precisely the indeterminacy of
this way of thinking that gives the republican tradition its uniquely pluralistic character. I now wish to argue that a decisive turning point in the
political use of the language of freedom came with the emergence of the
commercial republics of the Renaissance and early modern periods, and
then more emphatically with the debates about the political implications
of the so-called rise of commerce over the course of the 18th century.
As we will see, the ideological challenge that was posed by these developments brought the various ambiguities in the republican conception
of freedom to the surface, giving rise to a distinctively modern way of
thinking that treated commerce not as a threat, but rather as a means to
the enjoyment of republican freedom. However, if the development of a
"commercial" republicanism was a necessary step, it was nevertheless not
a sufficient step toward the invention of market freedom. That further

development was the result, as I have suggested and as I will argue in the next chapter, of a synthesis of commercial republican and Lockean liberal ideas.

Commerce is, of course, not a modern invention, nor were modern political thinkers the first to discover that the pursuit of commerce has implications for the enjoyment of freedom. For the classical republicans these implications were, as we have seen, largely negative. To be sure, the right to own property and to use and dispose of it as one pleases was seen both as a privilege of and as a precondition for the enjoyment of free status, and interference with this right was therefore counted among the paradigmatic examples of the arbitrary exercise of power. Nevertheless, these thinkers saw the economic realm as a realm not of freedom but of necessity, in the Aristotelian sense that it was concerned with the goods – such as food, shelter, and clothing – that make life possible, not the goods – above all the virtues – that make it worth living. The acquisition and consumption of material goods is obligatory for all people – there can be no particular honor or dignity in that – and so freedom is associated in this way of thinking with the activities that one is able to engage in once these material needs have been satisfied. In short, although the secure ownership of property was seen in classical republican thought as one of the essential marks of free status, active participation in the realm of production and trade was thought to be incompatible with the cultivation of virtue, and thus beneath a free man's station.

This classical prejudice against commerce was in some ways amplified in the political thought of the High Middle Ages, as the disdain for commercial activity that was found in the newly recovered Aristotelian corpus was integrated into a Christian worldview that already regarded the pursuit of material goods as a necessary evil at best. Thus we find Thomas Aquinas, the most profound and influential of the Christian Aristotelians, drawing on traditional republican language to portray commercial societies in unflattering terms: "[G]reed is introduced into the citizens' hearts by commerce," he writes, "and so it comes to pass that all things in the city are made venal...the public good is despised, everyone pursues his own advantage, zeal for virtue ceases, and everyone puts profit before the honour of virtue. Hence in such a city civic life will necessarily be corrupted." Indeed, the classical dimensions of the medieval critique of commerce threaten at times to obscure its Christian roots altogether. Aquinas goes beyond what we might think of as a properly Christian concern with the cultivation of virtue to advance the traditional republican view that commerce is politically suspect because it encourages "association with foreigners" and because it is "more at odds with military prowess than are most other occupations."[1] In these, as in many other respects, it is possible to draw a direct line from the political thought of antiquity to that of the medieval period.

However, the Christian orientation of medieval thought entailed a rejection of certain essential features of the classical worldview, and so it is not surprising to find that medieval writings about commerce often differ substantially in tone and content from their classical forebears. It is of course difficult to overstate, and even more difficult to summarize, the influence of Christianity on the development of Western thought, and I will touch only briefly on the three aspects that speak most directly to the question of the relationship between freedom and the market. First and most obviously, the Christian belief, which is firmly rooted in Hebrew scripture, that all people are created equal in the eyes of God called the existence of fundamental status distinctions radically into question. Freedom is therefore associated in Christian thought, as it is in some of the prominent strands of secular moral philosophy that informed it (most notably Stoicism), not with the enjoyment of a particular social status, but rather with an orientation of the will that is available, at least in principle, to all human beings.[2] The reception of this Christian brand of egalitarianism, like the reception of all radical ideas, was of course diffuse, gradual, and imperfect in many respects. Nevertheless, it is fair to say that the rise of Christianity was instrumental in helping to bring about a resolution of the longstanding ambiguity about the proper scope of republican citizenship in an egalitarian direction, thus making room for a more favorable assessment of the mundane practices of production and trade in which the "many" are typically engaged.

This new regard for the dignity of labor brings us to the specifically economic dimensions of Christian thought. Here the teachings of Jesus,

---

[1] Thomas Aquinas, *De regimine principum* (c. 1267), book 2, chapter 3, in idem, *Political Writings*, trans. R. W. Dyson (New York: Cambridge University Press, 2002), p. 50.

[2] As Augustine puts it, "[t]he choice of the will…is truly free only when it is not the slave of vices and sins. God gave to the will such freedom, and…it cannot be restored save by Him who could bestow it": *The City of God Against the Pagans*, trans. R. W. Dyson (New York: Cambridge University Press, 1998), p. 605 (book 14, chapter 11; cf. book 22, chapter 30). Epictetus argues along similar lines that "the road that leads to freedom, the only release from slavery, is this, to be able to say with your whole soul: 'Lead me, O Zeus, and lead me, Destiny / Whither ordainèd is by your decree'": *Discourses*, book 4, chapter 1, quoting P. E. Matheson's translation in Whitney J. Oates, ed., *The Stoic and Epicurean Philosophers* (New York: Modern Library, 1957), p. 418. The concluding couplet is from a prayer by the Stoic philosopher Cleanthes.

which are again rooted in Hebrew scripture, advance the interconnected and distinctly non-classical views that it is the poor and humble rather than the rich and noble who enjoy God's favor, that the rich have a moral obligation to provide for the poor, and that the possession of wealth, the enjoyment of luxury, and the pursuit of material gain are therefore not only properly subordinated to the practice of virtue, but morally suspect in and of themselves. Needless to say, this concern for the welfare of the needy strongly colored the Christian reception of classical economic thought. For example, many late medieval thinkers drew on the Aristotelian distinction between use value and exchange value to defend the claim that there is such as thing as a "just" price for commodities against which the legitimacy of even consensual market transactions should be measured, especially in times of hardship. The same distinction was used to reinforce the traditional Christian suspicion toward the practice of lending money at interest.[3] Each of these developments raised significant ideological barriers to the development of a commercial economy, and the temporal influence of the Church – exerted, for example, in its repeated (if sporadic) efforts to enforce "just" pricing and to ban the practice of usury – ensured that these barriers were not merely ideological in nature.

The most complicated and contentious question in late medieval economic thought concerned the nature and extent of the right to private property, the secure possession of which stood at the heart of the classical republican conception of freedom, just as it now stands at the heart of market ideology. The orthodox Christian position on this question was articulated in the 7th century by the Archbishop Isidore of Seville, who held that natural law prescribes "the common possession of everything," and that rights to private ownership are therefore only positive and not natural in character. This raises the question of how and under what conditions positive rights to property can be justified, a question that took on a new urgency in the 13th century as the emerging mendicant orders – the Franciscans most notably among them – appealed to the Christian ethic of poverty in calling for the faithful to renounce worldly goods and thus, *a fortiori*, the ownership of property altogether. Indeed, the renunciation of property was associated in Franciscan thought not simply with the renunciation of material wealth, but more broadly with the renunciation

[3] Aristotle's discussion of the difference between use and exchange value and his criticism of usury is found at *Politics*, book 1, chapters 9–10; cf. *Nicomachean Ethics*, book 5, chapter 5; Aquinas takes up these issues at *Summa Theologiae* 2a2ae qq 77–8. For a useful discussion of Scholastic thinking on these questions, see Odd Langholm, "Economic Freedom in Scholastic Thought," *History of Political Economy* 14 (1982), pp. 260–83.

of social status and a voluntary assumption of the social role of the servant or slave [*servus*], in imitation of the perfect servitude to others that was exemplified by the life of Christ. In other words, the Franciscan ethic of poverty was opposed not only to the ideal of security and independence that lies at the center of the republican conception of freedom, but more broadly to the relationships of *dominium* – of mastery over things and social "inferiors" – on which the free man's status was built.[4]

As we have seen, the Dominican response to the doctrine of apostolic poverty, which was borrowed from Aristotle by Aquinas and was to become the official Roman Catholic position, defends property rights as a useful "addition" to natural law on the grounds that the existence of well-defined spheres of ownership tends to promote diligence, order, and peace.[5] Aquinas affirms, however, that the earth was given to humankind in common and emphasizes that property rights can be overridden in cases of individual or communal need, and that confiscation and even theft can therefore be justified under certain conditions, most notably in times of famine.[6] This line of argument proved to be highly influential and extremely durable: Even as uncompromising a defender of property rights as John Locke can be found arguing, some four centuries later, that "God the Lord and Father of all, has given no one of his Children such a Property, in his peculiar Portion of the things of this World, but that he has given his needy Brother a Right to the Surplusage of his Goods, so that it cannot justly be denied him, when his pressing Wants call for it."[7]

---

[4] For a useful discussion, see Annabel S. Brett, *Liberty, Right and Nature: Individual Rights in Later Scholastic Thought* (New York: Cambridge University Press, 1997), chapter 1, and see also Brian Tierney, *The Idea of Natural Rights: Studies on Natural Rights, Natural Law, and Church Law, 1150–1625* (Atlanta: Scholars Press, 1997), part 2.

[5] Aquinas, *Summa Theologiae* 2a2ae q 66 art 2 resp (*Political Writings*, p. 208). Aquinas draws here on Aristotle's *Politics*, book 2, chapter 5.

[6] Aquinas, *Summa Theologiae* 2a2ae q 66 art 7 passim (*Political Writings*, pp. 216–7). Indeed, Aquinas denies that the taking of property under conditions of need can properly be called theft.

[7] John Locke, *First Treatise of Government* §42. Locke applies this line of argument to the realm of commerce and states it even more strongly in an unpublished note dated 1695: "though he that sells his corn in a town pressed with famine at the utmost rate he can get for it does no unjustice against the common rule of traffic, yet if he carry it away unless they will give him more than they are able, or extorts so much from their present necessity as not to leave them the means of subsistence afterwards, he offends against the common rule of charity as a man and if they perish any of them by reason of his extortion is no doubt guilty of murder": "Venditio," in *Political Essays*, ed. Mark Goldie (New York: Cambridge University Press, 1997), p. 342. For a discussion of the role that this line of argument plays in Locke's political thought, see John Dunn, "Justice and the Interpretation of Locke's Political Theory," *Political Studies* 16 (1968), pp. 68–87, where "Venditio" was first reprinted. For a detailed examination of its medieval roots, see Scott G.

Needless to say, this contingent defense of property rights, like the related defense of "just" pricing and the prohibition of usury, calls into question one of the pillars of market ideology – just as, by giving the poor a claim of right against the resources of the rich, it calls into question one of the pillars of classical republican thought. Nevertheless, by combining an appreciation of the instrumental benefits of private ownership with a concern for the well-being of all people, the Thomistic defense of property rights opened the door to a line of inquiry that proved central to the defense of modern commercial society. It was now possible to argue not only that the laboring and trading classes have an integral role to play in the life of the polity, as Christian egalitarianism would seem to imply, and that the individual pursuit of material gain can promote the common good, as Aristotle had suggested, but that the common good of the political community *consists*, at least in part, in the material well-being of its members. In other words, it became possible to argue that rulers should respect the property rights of their subjects for the simple reason that to do otherwise would be to undermine the basis of collective prosperity, and thus to harm the interests not only of the subjects, but of the ruler himself. We can therefore find in late medieval thinkers such as Marsilius of Padua, Brunetto Latini, and John of Paris some of the first efforts to detach questions of political economy from the moral and theological framework in which they had traditionally been embedded in order to focus more exclusively on the question of how the material well-being of the polity might best be advanced.[8] Their efforts helped to prepare

---

Swanson, "The Medieval Foundations of John Locke's Theory of Natural Rights: Rights of Subsistence and the Principle of Extreme Necessity," *History of Political Thought* 18 (1997), pp. 399–459. On the legacy of the Thomist provision for famine in early modern thought more generally, see Istvan Hont and Michael Ignatieff, "Needs and Justice in the *Wealth of Nations*: An Introductory Essay," in idem, eds., *Wealth and Virtue: The Shaping of Political Economy in the Scottish Enlightenment* (New York: Cambridge University Press, 1983), esp. pp. 26–44.

[8] These early efforts to detach economic analysis from traditional moral and theological categories have been explored in the recent work of Cary J. Nederman: see, for example, his "Confronting Market Freedom: Economic Foundations of Liberty at the end of the Middle Ages," in Robert J. Bast and Andrew C. Gow, eds., *Continuity and Change: The Harvest of Late Medieval and Reformation History* (Boston: Brill Academic, 2000), pp. 3–19; "Community and Self-Interest: Marsiglio of Padua on Civil Life and Private Advantage," *Review of Politics* 65 (2003), pp. 395–416; and "Commercial Society and Republican Government in the Latin Middle Ages: The Economic Dimensions of Brunetto Latini's Republicanism," *Political Theory* 31 (2003), pp. 644–63, as well as the essays collected in part 4 of his *Lineages of European Political Thought: Explorations along the Medieval/Modern Divide from John of Salisbury to Hegel* (Washington, DC: Catholic University of America Press, 2009). The first and third essays cited here appear in revised form as chapters 9 and 14 of that volume, respectively.

the way, as we will see, for a fundamental rethinking of the relationship between freedom and the market.

3.2. FROM THEOLOGY TO HISTORY

If the influence of Christian egalitarianism and the Scholastic defense of property rights cleared away some of the ideological obstacles that stood in the way of the invention of market freedom, the most important positive step came with the advancement of the more purely secular claim that the pursuit of commerce is essential to the security and independence, and thus to the freedom, of the polity itself. This line of argument, which was first stated in its fully developed form by the Italian civic humanists of the 15th and 16th centuries,[9] and which played an equally important role in the political thought of the 17th-century English republicans,[10] raised the question of whether the pursuit of commerce, and thus of wealth, might replace or at least stand alongside the cultivation of virtue as an essential means to the enjoyment of freedom – and, if so, of what kind of government is most conducive to this end. Despite the novelty and efficacy of the arguments that were advanced in favor of commerce in this debate, it is essential to keep in mind that it was a *debate*. As we will see, the "republican" defense of commercial society was hotly contested by thinkers who held more traditional views about the nature of republican citizenship, and many thinkers – and, we can suppose, many ordinary citizens – had mixed or ambivalent feelings on the subject. Again, I do not intend to argue that

---

[9] For a recent argument to this effect, see Mark Jurdjevic, "Virtue, Commerce, and the Enduring Florentine Republican Moment: Reintegrating Italy into the Atlantic Republican Debate," *Journal of the History of Ideas* 62 (2001), pp. 721–43; for a classic statement, see Hans Baron, "Franciscan Poverty and Civic Wealth as Factors in the Rise of Humanistic Thought," *Speculum* 13 (1938), pp. 1–37, revised, expanded, and reprinted as chapters 7–9 of idem, *In Search of Florentine Civic Humanism: Essays on the Transition from Medieval to Modern Thought* (Princeton, NJ: Princeton University Press, 1988). Jurdjevic is reacting against J. G. A. Pocock's claim that the Florentine republicans were uniformly opposed to the "corrupting" effects of commerce on civic virtue; for Pocock's defense of that claim, see especially part 2 of his *The Machiavellian Moment: Florentine Political Thought and the Atlantic Republican Tradition* (Princeton, NJ: Princeton University Press, 1975).

[10] On this, see, for example, Steve Pincus, "Neither Machiavellian Moment nor Possessive Individualism: Commercial Society and the Defenders of the English Commonwealth," *American Historical Review* 103 (1998), pp. 705–36, as well as Joyce Oldham Appleby, *Economic Thought and Ideology in Seventeenth-Century England* (Princeton, NJ: Princeton University Press, 1978). As his title suggests, Pincus too is reacting against Pocock's view – in this case to part 3 of *The Machiavellian Moment* – though he concedes that Pocock provides an accurate portrait of a "conservative" faction of 17th-century English republicans, composed most notably of James Harrington and John Milton.

any of these positions is the authentically republican one. Rather, I hope to show that the debate itself was conducted in republican terms, in the sense that each side had recognizably republican ends in view.[11]

The debate took on an additional dimension as commerce, instead of being seen as a background feature of social and political life, was associated with a particular level of civilizational development, so that it became possible to speak not just of commerce, but of the "rise" of commerce. This shift from a moralized to an historicized point of view is reflected in the so-called stadial theories of history that enjoyed wide currency during the second half of the 18th century.[12] According to this way of thinking, human societies naturally progress over time through hunter-gatherer, pastoral, agricultural, and commercial stages of development, each stage arising from the preceding one for a distinct set of material reasons, and each making a distinct set of material and ideational demands on those who live under it. It follows, as is usually the case with materialist theories of history, that we cannot properly evaluate the norms and institutions that govern a particular society unless we first take into account the level of economic development that it has reached. This line of argument called into question the contemporary relevance of classical political thought: If the modern age is a commercial age – or, more precisely, an age in which the transition from an agricultural to a commercial economy is taking place in Europe – then it follows that the appeal to classical ideas is misguided insofar as they can be shown to have arisen under a different set of economic conditions.

The 18th-century debates about the political implications of the rise of commerce were largely preoccupied with negotiating this newly

---

[11] Thus although I agree with Jurdjevic, Pincus, and others who find Pocock's to be a rather selective reading of what he calls the "Atlantic republican tradition," I find equally misleading Jurdjevic's claim that "*nowhere* in humanist language was commerce condemned as antithetical to the common good or republican virtue": "Virtue, Commerce, and the Enduring Florentine Republican Moment," p. 732 (emphasis added). Maurizio Viroli advances a similarly one-sided view, arguing that "[i]n *no* classical republican work can we find a criticism of commercial society" – a claim that is difficult to square with the fact that Viroli himself attributes to his beloved Francesco Guicciardini the view that "[c]ommerce and finance ha[d] extinguished the love of liberty and glory" in Medicean Florence: Viroli, *Republicanism* (New York: Hill & Wang, 2002), p. 32 (emphasis added); *From Politics to Reason of State: The Acquisition and Transformation of the Language of Politics, 1250–1600* (New York: Cambridge University Press, 1992), pp. 211–12.

[12] Although they are most closely associated with the thinkers of the Scottish Enlightenment – with Adam Smith in particular – stadial theories had a substantial impact on Continental, and especially on French, thought as well. For a useful discussion, see Ronald L. Meek, *Social Science and the Ignoble Savage* (New York: Cambridge University Press, 1976).

historicized terrain. On one side were thinkers such as François Fénelon, Jean-Jacques Rousseau, the Abbé de Mably, Adam Ferguson, and Thomas Jefferson, who looked to classical history – most notably to the turbulent history of the late Roman republic – for clues about how the loss of liberty and the rise of despotism could be avoided, or at least forestalled, under modern conditions. According to this way of thinking, the classical ideal of freedom and virtuous citizenship was still within reach if only political institutions could be redesigned, property redistributed, educational practices reformed, and consumption regulated in the right way. On the other side were thinkers such as Bernard Mandeville, Charles de Montesquieu, David Hume, Adam Smith, and Alexander Hamilton, who held that the challenges facing modern commercial societies were qualitatively different from those that faced the classical republics, and that the appeal to the lessons of Greek and Roman antiquity was therefore anachronistic and foolhardy. Rather than looking to classical models, these thinkers saw in the rise of commerce itself a new set of resources for realizing freedom in the modern world. Again, I do not mean to suggest that all of the participants in this debate are best described as republicans – still less that they would have applied the label to themselves. It is nevertheless the case that the problems with which they were wrestling are recognizably republican problems, and that the effort to claim the mantle of freedom for modern commercial societies hinged, at least at first, on the question of whether they could be defended in republican terms.

Some additional words of caution are in order before we turn to a more detailed examination of this debate. The early modern period was of course a time of great ideological ferment, in which republican and quasi-republican ideas were deployed in dramatically different ways in different social and political contexts. During the 18th century, for example, the opposition "Country" party in England – the party that is now most commonly described as having been "republican" in its aims – drew ideological inspiration from sources as various as Cicero's conception of civic virtue, Locke's doctrine of natural rights, James Harrington's schemes for the redistribution of landed property, the English common law tradition, and the mythology of the ancient Saxon constitution. The governing "Court" party laid claim to much of the same ideological terrain. The ideological forces that were unleashed by the French Revolution found expression in appeals to half-forgotten feudal traditions of corporatist or mixed government, to neo-Spartan conceptions of civic virtue and collective self-rule, and to the expansively cosmopolitan language of the Declaration of the Rights of Man. The aims of American republicanism – which were most famously expressed in Lockean terms – shifted over the course of a single decade from a straightforward effort to harness the natural virtue of the people to a governing philosophy that was described by its proponents as the "policy of supplying, by opposite and rival interests, the defect of better motives." It is difficult in the face of this kind of diversity to say with any confidence which of these ways of thinking was the authentically "republican" one.[13]

The political concerns that early modern thinkers raised about the rise of commerce were equally diverse. Some drew on classical republican thought to associate commerce directly with corruption and vice, either because it is frankly oriented toward the pursuit of material gain[14] or because the luxuries with which it is often (and perhaps necessarily) concerned are inimical to the cultivation of virtue.[15] For others, the connection between the rise of commerce and the loss of freedom was less direct: Some suggested that the interests of the emerging commercial class are necessarily at odds with those of the polity as a whole,[16] whereas others pointed out that the liquid capital to which this class has

---

[13] The quoted passage is from James Madison, *The Federalist* 51 (1788). For an overview of the development of English, French, and American republicanism in the 18th century, see Mark Goldie, "The English System of Liberty," Keith Michael Baker, "Political Languages of the French Revolution," and Gordon S. Wood, "The American Revolution," in Mark Goldie and Robert Wokler, eds., *The Cambridge History of Eighteenth-Century Political Thought* (New York: Cambridge University Press, 2006), pp. 40–78, 628–59, and 601–25, respectively.

[14] Montesquieu observes, for example, that "in countries where one is affected only by the spirit of commerce, there is traffic in all human activities and all moral virtues; the smallest things, those required by humanity, are done or given for money": *The Spirit of the Laws* (1748), trans. Anne Cohler, Basia Miller, and Harold Stone (New York: Cambridge University Press, 1989), pp. 338–9 (book 20, chapter 2).

[15] Thus Rousseau argues that "luxury is either the effect of riches, or makes them necessary; it corrupts rich and poor alike, the one by possession, the other by covetousness; it sells out the fatherland to laxity, to vanity; it deprives the State of all its Citizens by making them slaves to one another, and all of them slaves to opinion": *On the Social Contract*, book 3, chapter 4, quoting idem, *The Social Contract and Other Later Political Writings*, trans. and ed. Victor Gourevitch (New York: Cambridge University Press, 1997), p. 91. This line of argument was closely associated in the 18th century with François Fénelon's *Les aventures de Télémaque* (1699); on the relationship between Rousseau and Fénelon, see Patrick Riley, "Rousseau, Fénelon, and the Quarrel Between the Ancients and the Moderns," in idem, ed., *The Cambridge Companion to Rousseau* (New York: Cambridge University Press, 2001), pp. 78–93.

[16] Smith, for example, describes the trading and manufacturing class as "an order of men, whose interest is never exactly the same with that of the public, who have generally an interest to deceive and even to oppress the public, and who accordingly have, upon many occasions, both deceived and oppressed it": *An Inquiry into the Nature and Causes of the Wealth of Nations* (Oxford: Clarendon Press, 1979 [1776]), I.xi.p.10.

access – and the dependence of governments on this capital in an era of deficit spending – created unprecedented opportunities for political corruption.[17] It is difficult, to say the least, to sort out which of these lines of argument – each of which is still salient today – was most influential in a given time and place, and for what reasons. Thus even if it were possible to determine which of the various ideological factions that were influential during the early modern period can properly be called "republican," we would still face the challenge of determining which of the concerns that they raised about the rise of commerce had the greatest impact on the development of republican thinking about freedom. Nevertheless, if we define the boundaries of the republican tradition in problem-centered terms, as I have suggested, then it becomes clear that the debates about the political implications of the rise of commerce were to a large extent debates about the practical implications of a commitment to republican freedom under modern conditions. It is to this argument that we now turn.

3.3. *PAX COMMERCIALIS?*

The classical republicans associated freedom with autarchy: The free man, like the free state, is secure not only from the corrupting influence of tyrants and masters, but also from dependence on the arbitrary will of other people (or peoples) for the material necessities that make the good life possible. Unfreedom is therefore associated in this way of thinking not only with poverty, a condition that places the practice of

---

[17] The corruption of government through the sale of public debt to private investors was of particular concern in Hanoverian England; the *locus classicus* is John Trenchard and Thomas Gordon's response to the South Sea Bubble in *Cato's Letters* (1720–1723); see also Hume's essay "Of Public Credit" (1752, revised 1764), in idem, *Political Essays*, ed. Knud Haakonssen (New York: Cambridge University Press, 1994), pp. 166–78, and, for an influential discussion, chapters 13–14 of Pocock's *The Machiavellian Moment*. For a consideration of the extent to which Hume's own views about the nature of the threat posed by the public debt evolved over time, see Istvan Hont, "The Rhapsody of Public Debt: David Hume and Voluntary State Bankruptcy," in idem, *Jealousy of Trade: International Competition and the Nation-State in Historical Perspective* (Cambridge, MA: Harvard University Press, 2005), pp. 325–53. As Hont observes, it is ironic that the malign political consequences of public debt were most fully realized not in Britain but in France – and that they led to the downfall not of a republic but of an absolute monarchy. For a discussion of the role that the public debt played in 18th-century French political discourse, see Michael Sonenscher, *After the Deluge: Public Debt, Inequality, and the Intellectual Origins of the French Revolution* (Princeton, NJ: Princeton University Press, 2007).

virtue beyond the reach of even the naturally virtuous man, but also with labor, which entails dependence on an employer and on the availability of remunerative work, and with trade, which highlights by its very existence the fact of dependence. Although trade, labor, and poverty were of course irreducible features of social life in the pre-modern world, just as they are today, entanglement in any one of them was thought to render a person presumptively unfit for the privileges and responsibilities of citizenship in a free state. The rise of the commercial republics of the Renaissance and early modern periods, coupled with the distinctively 18th-century claim that the modern age is an age of commerce, placed this traditional republican suspicion toward the economic realm under significant ideological pressure, and with this pressure came a new willingness to rethink traditional ideas about the nature and aims of republican citizenship. Indeed, as we will see, even those who were reluctant to retreat from the tenets of classical republicanism nevertheless had to modify – and in some cases to radicalize – their views in order to respond to the new commercial realities.

As we have seen, the claim that a polity will only prosper if political power is exercised non-arbitrarily can be traced back to antiquity.[18] It rests on the simple observation that people will not be willing to invest time and energy in the pursuit of wealth unless they are reasonably confident that they will be able to enjoy whatever gains they might realize. This observation acquired new salience, however, when it was combined with the view that the modern age is one in which commerce provides the only reliable route to prosperity: If the economic well-being and even the survival of the state depends on the success that its citizens enjoy in the commercial realm, then it follows that even the would-be tyrant has an interest in moderating his rule. Thus Montesquieu writes that since the rise of commerce, "princes have had to govern themselves more wisely than they themselves would have thought, for it turned out that great acts [*grands coups*] of authority were so clumsy that experience itself has made known that only goodness of government brings prosperity." The same idea is expressed more sharply by the Scottish mercantilist James Steuart, who argues that "a modern œconomy...is the most effectual bridle ever was invented against the folly of despotism," because "the sovereign...finds himself so bound up by the laws of his political œconomy, that every transgression of them runs him into new difficulties." Hamilton

---

[18] The *locus classicus* is chapter 7 of Sallust's *Bellum Catilinae*; in the Greek context see also Herodotus, *Histories*, book 5, chapter 78.

puts the point in more positive terms, pointing out that "commerce is now perceived and acknowledged by all enlightened statesmen to be the most useful as well as the most productive source of national wealth, and has accordingly become a primary object of their political cares."[19]

As Benjamin Constant later observed, there are two features of a commercial economy that give it this politically beneficial effect. First, the substitution of mobile for immobile forms of property "makes the action of arbitrary power easier to elude," because property "becomes, in virtue of this change, almost impossible to seize." Second, the reliance on credit in commercial relationships "places authority itself in a position of dependence," because "to obtain the favours of wealth one must serve it." "Credit did not have the same influence among the ancients," he concludes, because "their governments were stronger than individuals, while in our time individuals are stronger than political power."[20] In other words, under modern conditions, what we now call the flight of capital provides the mechanism through which states are punished for failing to respect and promote the commercial activities of their citizens, as well as the publicly visible signal that allows such failures to be perceived – just as a decline in military prowess was thought both to herald and to bring about the more general decline of free societies in the pre-modern world. To paraphrase Machiavelli, there cannot be good laws where there is not good credit, and where there is good credit there must be good laws.[21]

Some early modern thinkers went so far as to predict that the pursuit of commerce would make the practice of warfare obsolete. Thus Montesquieu suggests, in what was perhaps the most far-reaching claim

---

[19] Montesquieu, *Spirit of the Laws*, p. 389 (book 21, chapter 20); James Steuart, *An Inquiry in the Principles of Political Economy* (1767), book 2, chapters 22, 13; Hamilton, *Federalist* 12. The influence of this line of argument in the 18th century is explored in some detail in Albert O. Hirschman's *The Passions and the Interests: Political Arguments for Capitalism Before Its Triumph* (Princeton, NJ: Princeton University Press, 1977), where the Montesquieu and Steuart passages are cited at pp. 72 and 83–5, respectively.

[20] Benjamin Constant, "The Liberty of the Ancients Compared with That of the Moderns" (1819), in idem, *Political Writings*, ed. Biancamaria Fontana (New York: Cambridge University Press, 1988), pp. 324–5; cf. idem, *The Spirit of Conquest and Usurpation and Their Relation to European Civilization* (1814), ibid., pp. 140–2 (part 2, chapter 18). Rousseau draws the opposite conclusion: "If all riches were public and visible," he argues, "if transfers of gold left a discernible mark and could not hide, there would be no instrument better suited for buying services, courage, loyalty, virtues; but in view of its secret circulation, it is even better suited for making plunderers and traitors, and putting the public good and freedom on the auction block": *Considerations on the Government of Poland* (1772) §11, *Later Political Writings*, p. 226.

[21] Machiavelli refers, of course, to "good arms": *The Prince*, chapter 12.

to be made about the political implications of the rise of commerce, that "[t]he natural effect of commerce is to lead to peace." This claim was historicized by Kant, who argues that "the spirit of commerce sooner or later takes hold of every people, and cannot exist side by side with war," and it was treated as a *fait accompli* by Constant, who concludes not only that "an age must come in which commerce replaces war," but that "[w]e have reached this age."[22] Three lines of argument were advanced in favor of this view. First, the rise of commerce was said to have removed the material incentives that states have traditionally had for going to war. Thus, after suggesting that war and commerce "are only two different means of achieving the same end, that of getting what one wants," Constant argues that technological advances in the realms of transportation and navigation – and in the destructive power of armies – ensure that in the modern era "even a successful war costs infallibly more than it is worth."[23] Second, the rise of commerce was said to have undermined the habits and dispositions that sustained a martial way of life in the first place. Montesquieu argues that by bringing people into regular contact with one another across national borders, commerce "cures destructive prejudices" and cultivates "gentle [*douces*] mores," and Constant points out that with the invention of firearms "[w]ar has lost its charm as well as its utility," so that "[m]an is no longer driven to it either by interest or by passion."[24] Third and finally, commerce and the related arts of manufacturing and finance demand the uninterrupted attention of those who are engaged in them. As Constant observes, in a commercial society "each individual, occupied with his speculations, his enterprises, the pleasures he obtains or hopes for, does not wish to be distracted from them other than momentarily, and as little as possible."[25] In short, the modern citizen has neither the time nor the inclination to meet the demands of active citizenship, still less of warfare – a problem that is compounded by the fact that modern societies, unlike their ancient counterparts, cannot rely on slave labor to provide the necessities of daily life.

---

[22] Montesquieu, *Spirit of the Laws*, p. 338 (book 20, chapter 2); Immanuel Kant, *Perpetual Peace: A Philosophical Sketch* (1795), in idem, *Political Writings*, ed. Hans Reiss, trans. H. B. Nisbet (New York: Cambridge University Press, 1970), p. 114 (emphasis removed); Constant, "Ancient and Modern Liberty," p. 313.

[23] Constant, "Ancient and Modern Liberty," p. 313–4; cf. *Spirit of Conquest and Usurpation*, pp. 52–5 (part 1, chapter 2).

[24] Montesquieu, *Spirit of the Laws*, pp. 338 (book 20, chapter 1); Constant, *Spirit of Conquest and Usurpation*, p. 55 (part 1, chapter 3).

[25] Constant, "Ancient and Modern Liberty," p. 315.

However, if the citizens of a commercial society do not have an inter-est (in either sense of the word) in cultivating the arts of war, it does not follow that they can afford to neglect them altogether. Indeed, the view that a commercial world would be a peaceful one was not universally shared even by those who agreed that the rise of commerce was the defin-ing feature of modern life. Thus Hamilton, writing for an audience that was deeply skeptical toward the idea of placing military power in the hands of the state, bluntly denies that "the spirit of commerce has a ten-dency to soften the manners of men, and to extinguish those inflammable humors which have so often kindled into wars": "Have there not been as many wars founded upon commercial motives since that has become the prevailing system of nations," he asks, "as were before occasioned by the cupidity of territory or dominion? Has not the spirit of commerce, in many instances, administered new incentives to the appetite, both for the one and for the other?"[26] On this point he echoes Hume, who had observed some thirty years earlier that "[n]othing is more usual, among states which have made some advances in commerce, than to look on the progress of their neighbours with a suspicious eye, to consider all trading states as their rivals, and to suppose that it is impossible for any of them to flourish, but at their expence."[27] Even Smith, whose *Wealth of Nations* remains the canonical defense of free trade, and who shared Montesquieu's view that commerce has rendered warfare obsolete as a means of acquisition, warns that "[a]n industrious, and upon that account a wealthy nation, is of all nations the most likely to be attacked" – adding that "unless the state takes some new measures for the public defence, the natural habits of the people [will] render them altogether incapable of defending themselves."[28]

---

[26] Hamilton, *Federalist 6*.

[27] Hume, "Of the Jealousy of Trade" (1758), *Political Essays*, p. 150. Despite its prevalence, Hume criticizes this kind of "jealousy" as misguided and self-defeating and concludes his essay by saying that "not only as a man, but as a BRITISH subject, I pray for the flourishing commerce of GERMANY, SPAIN, ITALY, and even FRANCE itself. I am at least certain, that GREAT BRITAIN, and all those nations, would flourish more, did their sovereigns and ministers adopt such enlarged and benevolent sentiments towards each other": ibid., p. 153. On the development of this line of thinking in the early modern period, see Istvan Hont, "Jealousy of Trade: An Introduction," in idem, *Jealousy of Trade*, esp. pp. 6–37, and cf. his "Free Trade and the Economic Limits to National Politics: Neo-Machiavellian Political Economy Reconsidered," ibid., pp. 185–266.

[28] Smith, *Wealth of Nations* V.i.15. Elsewhere, however, Smith laments the modern prac-tice of maintaining "great fleets and armies, who in time of peace produce nothing, and in time of war acquire nothing which can compensate the expence of maintaining them": ibid. III.iii.p.30.

Smith's suggestion that the "natural habits" of a commercial people need to be reformed if their security and independence are to be preserved could be taken to point in one of two directions: either toward the need to redouble the effort to promote the classical ideal of civic and martial virtue, despite the distractions and temptations that exist in a commercial world, or toward the need to identify a distinctively "modern" solution to the problem of maintaining collective security. The most influential proponent of the former position was of course Machiavelli himself, who held that "not gold, as the common opinion cries out, but good soldiers are the sinews of war," and who insists throughout his political writings on the superiority of citizen militias over mercenary and professional armies.[29] The political debates during and after the time of the Glorious Revolution in England – and during and after the American Revolution – are rife with neo-classical (or neo-Machiavellian) warnings that a free polity can only be defended by a politically vigilant citizenry organized into an effective militia.[30] Rousseau, writing for a Polish audience in the 1770s, echoes Machiavelli in challenging the claim that collective prosperity is a sufficient or even a necessary condition for collective security: "Is it certain that money is the sinews of war? Rich peoples have always been beaten and conquered by poor peoples....Money is at best the supplement of men, and the supplement will never be worth the thing itself."[31] Smith's friend Adam Ferguson worried that "the separation of professions...serves, in some measure, to break the bands of society" and

---

[29] Machiavelli, *Discourses on Livy*, book 2, chapter 10, quoting Harvey C. Mansfield and Nathan Tarcov's translation (Chicago: University of Chicago Press, 1996), p. 148. Cf. book 1, chapter 43; book 2, chapter 20; and *The Prince*, chapters 12–13.

[30] The seminal episode in Britain was the so-called Standing Army Controversy at the end of the 17th century; see especially John Trenchard and Walter Moyle, "An Argument, Shewing, that a Standing Army Is Inconsistent with a Free Government..."(1697), and Andrew Fletcher's "A Discourse of Government with Relation to Militias" (1698). For two useful discussions see Lois G. Schwoerer, *"No Standing Armies!": The Antiarmy Ideology in Seventeenth-Century England* (Baltimore, MD: Johns Hopkins University Press, 1974), and John Robertson, *The Scottish Enlightenment and the Militia Issue* (Edinburgh: J. Donald, 1985). The terms of the British debate were widely echoed in revolutionary America; see, for example, Josiah Quincy's "Observations on...the Boston Port Bill, with Thoughts on Civil Society and Standing Armies" (1774), and cf. Hamilton's defense of standing armies in *Federalist* 8 and 23–9. For a useful discussion, see Bernard Bailyn, *The Ideological Origins of the American Revolution* (Cambridge, MA: Harvard University Press, 1967), pp. 61–3, 112–16, 338–40, 354–8, and, for a more detailed account, Lawrence Delbert Cress, *Citizens in Arms: Army and Militia in American Society to the War of 1812* (Chapel Hill: University of North Carolina Press, 1982).

[31] Rousseau, *Considerations on the Government of Poland*, p. 225 (§11); on the superiority of militias to standing armies, see ibid., §12 passim.

held that "to separate the arts which form the citizen and the statesman, the arts of policy and war, is...to dismember the human character, and to destroy those very arts we mean to improve." An early critic of the *Wealth of Nations* argued that "it is surely better to be a little less rich and commercial, than by ceasing to be men, to endanger our existence as a nation," and warned his fellow Scots to "guard with jealous vigilance the constitution of our country, lest, like the greatest empire that ever was, that of the Romans in their decadency, we become so luxurious or effeminate, as to leave the use of arms to strangers and mercenaries."[32]

This line of argument did not go uncontested even in Machiavelli's day. Thus whereas Hume argues that "trade was never esteemed an affair of state till the last [17th] century" – adding, with Machiavelli in mind, that "even the ITALIANS have kept a profound silence with regard to it" – the historian James Hankins points out that for the Italian humanists of the 15th century, "[i]t was money which gave strength and vitality to the commonwealth and enabled it to defend itself against enemies," so that "[i]n an age of mercenary armies, cities without rich citizens would soon lose their liberty." This was the "common opinion" to which Machiavelli objected so vigorously.[33] The English republican Slingsby Bethel argued along similar lines in 1679 that "[f]rom trade there doth not only arise riches to the subjects, rendering a nation considerable, but also increase of revenue, and therein power and strength to the sovereign," concluding that "every nation is more or less considerable, according to the proportion it hath of trade." His contemporary John Locke agreed that "that Prince who shall be so wise and godlike as by established laws of liberty to secure protection and incouragement to the honest industry of Mankind against the oppression of power and narrownesse of Party will quickly be too hard for his neighbours." Montesquieu suggested somewhat hopefully that the citizens of a commercial society would "see that

---

[32] Adam Ferguson, *An Essay on the History of Civil Society* (1767), ed. Fania Oz-Salzberger (New York: Cambridge University Press, 1995), pp. 206–7, 218 (part 5, sections 3 and 4); Alexander Carlyle, "A Letter to His Grace the Duke of Buccleugh, on National Defence..." (1778). Both passages are cited in Richard Sher, "Adam Ferguson, Adam Smith, and the Problem of National Defense," *Journal of Modern History* 61 (1989) at pp. 244–5 and 247, respectively.

[33] Hume, "Of Civil Liberty" (1741; originally titled "Of Liberty and Despotism"), *Political Essays*, p. 52; James Hankins, "Humanism and the Origins of Modern Political Thought," in Jill Kraye, ed., *The Cambridge Companion to Renaissance Humanism* (New York: Cambridge University Press, 1996), p. 126. Jurdjevic argues that among the Florentine civic humanists Machiavelli was "a lone voice arguing for the suppression of private interests": "Virtue, Commerce, and the Enduring Florentine Republican Moment," p. 728.

their credit would be lost if it were conquered," and so "have a further motive to make efforts to defend its liberty." Hume himself held that "as private men receive greater security, in the possession of their trade and riches, from the power of the public, so the public becomes powerful in proportion to the opulence and extensive commerce of private men." In 1784 the editors of the *Pennsylvania Gazette* of Philadelphia went so far as to argue that "[t]o despise wealth, or to suppose it to be connected with principles unfavorable to the happiness of the state in its present commercial situation, is to depreciate the first of republican virtues, and to overturn the basis of freedom and empire in our country."[34]

Smith goes beyond the appeal to wealth as a foundation for security to argue that the extension of the division of labor – which is of course both a cause and an effect of the extension of commercial relations – has made the classical ideal of the citizen-soldier practically unattainable, and that modern societies should therefore apply the principle of the division of labor to the practice of warfare itself: to "render the trade of a soldier a particular trade, separate and distinct from all others." He offers a defense, in other words, of that old bane of republican polities: "a well-disciplined and well-exercised standing army." Indeed, he argues that standing armies are not only compatible with but "favourable to" liberty, provided that they are "placed under the command of those who have the greatest interest in the support of the civil authority, because they have themselves the greatest share of that authority."[35] Needless to say, a standing army is expensive to maintain even in peacetime, and so a world in which the national defense is entrusted to professional soldiers is a world in which

[34] Slingsby Bethel, *An Account of the French Usurpation upon the Trade of England* (1679), cited in Pincus, "Neither Machiavellian Moment nor Possessive Individualism," p. 717; Locke, *Second Treatise of Government* §42; Montesquieu, *Spirit of the Laws*, p. 327 (book 19, chapter 27); Hume, "Of Commerce" (1752), *Political Essays*, p. 94; *Pennsylvania Gazette*, "Hear the Other Side of the Question" (September 8, 1784), cited in Cathy Matson and Peter Onuf, "Toward a Republican Empire: Interest and Ideology in Revolutionary America," *American Quarterly* 37 (1985), p. 496.

[35] Smith, *Wealth of Nations* V.i.a.14, 34, 41. Smith concedes that the state may have other motives for fostering a "martial spirit" among the citizenry, namely, "to prevent that sort of mental mutilation, deformity, and wretchedness, which cowardice necessarily involves in it": ibid. V.i.f.60; cf. Smith, *Lectures on Jurisprudence* (Oxford: Clarendon Press, 1978) (B) 331–3 (1766). In the earlier course of lectures Smith places greater emphasis on the dangers of standing armies, naming them, along with the "Civill List" (i.e., the practice of royal patronage) as "the only things which can in any way endanger the liberty of the [British] subject." Here too he emphasizes the importance of ensuring that the army is loyal to the Parliament, and in particular to the Commons, rather than to the king himself: ibid. (A) v.1.179 (1763). Montesquieu advances a similar line of argument at *Spirit of the Laws*, book 5, chapter 19.

the military advantage belongs, all things being equal, to the wealthier, more economically advanced nations.[36] Thus Smith rejects Rousseau's claims for the military superiority of poor peoples, pointing out that "[i]n modern war the great expence of fire-arms gives an evident advantage to the nation which can best afford that expence." He concludes that whereas "[i]n antient times the opulent and civilized found it difficult to defend themselves against the poor and barbarous nations...[i]n modern times the poor and barbarous find it difficult to defend themselves against the opulent and civilized."[37] Here the argument for the pacific effects of the rise of commerce is brought full circle: If commerce has made warfare obsolete as a means of acquisition, the material demands of modern warfare make the pursuit of commerce obligatory as a matter of national security. Thus where Montesquieu and Constant had argued that commerce depends on freedom, Hume and Smith insist that freedom depends on, and may even arise from, the pursuit of commerce.[38]

3.4. WEALTH AND VIRTUE

The most far-reaching moral implications of the rise of commerce arise from the fact that the citizens of a commercial society depend not only on the goods but also on the good opinion of other people in order to realize their ends, and that they must therefore always act with an eye to their "market value." As traditional restrictions on the possession, use, and alienation of property – including property in one's own labor – were relaxed, it became difficult to avoid the conclusion that, as Thomas

---

[36] Franco Venturi points out that the "old republics" of the 18th century – Holland, Genoa, and Venice, for example – came to the same conclusion in practice that Smith had reached in principle: that they "could survive only if they withdrew from the conflicts of the great powers," that "the commercial state had to be neutral," and that "[t]he example of the classical republics was...the worst the modern ones could follow." "The argument was lively and manifold," he writes, "but the conclusion was unanimous": *Utopia and Reform in the Enlightenment* (New York: Cambridge University Press, 1971), p. 41. Cf. Rousseau, who argues that "[a]ny people which, because of its location, has no alternative than commerce or war is inherently weak; it is dependent on its neighbors; it is dependent on circumstances; it can never have any but a precarious and weak existence. Either it subjugates and changes its situation, or it is subjugated and is nothing. It can preserve its freedom only by being very small or very large": *Social Contract*, p. 76 (book 2, chapter 10).

[37] Smith, *Wealth of Nations* V.i.a.44.

[38] Hont draws a similar conclusion, arguing that in Hume "the causal nexus between liberty and commerce was reversed. Liberty, originally a prerequisite of commerce, became its most important political consequence": "Introduction" to *Jealousy of Trade*, p. 23.

Hobbes put it, "[t]he *Value*, or WORTH of a man, is as of all other things, his Price...and therefore is not absolute; but a thing dependant on the need and judgement of another."[39] Moreover, it soon became clear, as it may not have been to Hobbes, that the value judgments – the prices – with which we are confronted in a commercial society are not made in most cases by identifiable people but rather by the market itself, that is, by a decentralized and largely anonymous mechanism for aggregating information about the economic decisions of an indefinite number of people. It is difficult to overstate the challenge that this insight posed for traditional ways of thinking. As J. G. A. Pocock puts it, "[o]nce property was seen to have a symbolic value, expressed in coin or in credit, the foundations of personality themselves appeared imaginary or at best consensual: the individual could exist, even in his own sight, only at the fluctuating value imposed on him by his fellows, and these evaluations, though constant and public, were too irrationally performed to be seen as acts of political decision or virtue."[40]

In other words, the rise of commerce brought with it a clearer understanding of the depth and intricacy of the relationships of dependence that exist within and between commercial societies, and of the effect that this kind of dependence could be expected to have on the character – the virtue – of those who live in them. In this sense, early modern thinkers had even greater reason to be suspicious of commerce than their classical forebears. We have seen, however, that there is some ambiguity in republican thought about the nature both of arbitrary power and of virtue, and this created the conceptual space for a "republican" defense of even the most novel and apparently threatening features of commercial society. The most influential line of argument to be advanced along these lines was the claim that the well-being of the polity depends not on the fact that its citizens subordinate the claims of self-interest to those of virtue, but rather on the fact that they each pursue their private interests as diligently as they can. Quentin Skinner traces this way of thinking as far back as the 15th century, finding in Leonardo Bruni's "Oration for the Funeral of Nanni Strozzi" (1428) the view that "as long as each

---

[39] Thomas Hobbes, *Leviathan* (1651), ed. Richard Tuck (New York: Cambridge University Press, 1991), p. 63 (chapter 10; original emphasis). Hobbes goes on to make the related and equally commerce-friendly claims that "[t]he value of all things contracted for, is measured by the Appetite of the Contractors: and therefore the just value, is that which they be contented to give," and that "a mans Labour...is a commodity exchangeable for benefit, as well as any other thing": ibid., pp. 105, 171 (chapters 15 and 24).

[40] Pocock, *Machiavellian Moment*, p. 464.

individual pursues his own affairs 'with industry' and 'quickness in matters of business,' we may safely assume that the ultimate effect of such enlightened self-interest will be beneficial to the Republic as a whole."[41] If Renaissance humanists such as Bruni saw the pursuit of glory through material wealth as a matter of promoting a classical alternative to Christian asceticism,[42] by the 18th century this line of argument had been turned against the classical ideal of civic virtue itself. Indeed, if the pursuit of self-interest provides the most reliable path to collective prosperity, then it would seem to follow that *any* effort to promote virtue, whether classical or Christian, would be likely to do more harm than good. As Bernard Mandeville notoriously put it, "Fools only strive / To make a Great an Honest Hive."[43]

Despite the scandal that his writings provoked, many 18th-century thinkers came to agree with Mandeville in thinking that the rise of commerce required a shift away from the selfless and abstemious forms of behavior that are associated with success on the battlefield and toward the acquisitive and self-regarding forms of behavior that are associated with success in commerce. Hume wrote, for example, that "[t]he encrease and consumption of all the commodities, which serve to the ornament and pleasure of life, are advantageous to society; because, at the same time that they multiply those innocent gratifications to individuals, they are a kind of *storehouse* of labour, which, in the exigencies of state, may be turned to the public service." Smith, in his critique of Mandeville's "system," nevertheless agreed that "it is certain that luxury, sensuality, and ostentation are public benefits: since without the[se] qualities...the arts of refinement could never find encouragement, and must languish for want of employment."[44] Taken in itself, this line of argument did not

[41] Quentin Skinner, *The Foundations of Modern Political Thought* (New York: Cambridge University Press, 1978), vol. 1, p. 74.
[42] On this, see, for example, Hankins, "Humanism and Modern Political Thought," pp. 124–8, as well as Baron's "Franciscan Poverty and Civic Wealth."
[43] Bernard Mandeville, "The Grumbling Hive: or, Knaves Turn'd Honest" (1705) in idem, *The Fable of the Bees or Private Vices, Publick Benefits*, ed. F. B. Kaye (Oxford: Clarendon Press, 1924), vol. 1, p. 36. Mandeville echoes a view that had been set out by a series of 17th-century French moralists, most notably François de la Rochefoucauld, Pierre Nicole, and Pierre Bayle; for a useful overview, see Pierre Force, *Self-Interest Before Adam Smith: A Genealogy of Economic Science* (New York: Cambridge University Press, 2003). On Mandeville's influence on 18th-century social and political thought more generally, see especially E. J. Hundert, *The Enlightenment's Fable: Bernard Mandeville and the Discovery of Society* (New York: Cambridge University Press, 1994).
[44] Hume, "Of Refinement in the Arts" (1752; originally titled "Of Luxury"), *Political Essays*, p. 108 (original emphasis); Smith, *The Theory of Moral Sentiments* (Oxford: Clarendon

involve a repudiation so much as a rethinking of traditional republican ideas. After all, republican thinkers since at least the time of Aristotle had seen material self-sufficiency as a necessary condition for the practice of virtue.[45] The enjoyment of republican freedom had therefore always been thought to require a certain level of prosperity – at least for those who were not willing to endure the rigors of Sparta. Classical republican worries about prosperity arose at the point where the enjoyment of material goods tilted over into avarice, luxury, and effeminacy – at the point, in other words, where it began to pose a threat to civic and martial virtue, and thus to the freedom of the polity. This concern began to seem archaic and even perverse in a world in which the pursuit of wealth and luxury was thought to be conducive both to individual and to collective well-being. Thus Voltaire wrote in his satirical poem "Le Mondain" (1736) of "*Le superflu, chose très nécessaire.*"

Some defenders of commercial society (though not Mandeville himself) tried to soften the radical implications of this view by pointing out that the pursuit of commerce depends on and even instills virtues of its own. Montesquieu argues, for example, that "the spirit of commerce brings with it the spirit of frugality, economy, moderation, work, wisdom, tranquility, order, and rule [*règle*]," and he compares this commercial ethos favorably to the classical republican's selfless love of country, which he sardonically likens to the love that monks feel "for the very rule that afflicts them." The association of virtue with the prudent pursuit of self-interest is perhaps best exemplified in the writings of Benjamin Franklin, whose famous list of the thirteen moral virtues – composed of temperance, silence, order, resolution, frugality, industry, sincerity, justice, moderation, cleanliness, tranquility, chastity, and humility – bears a striking resemblance to Montesquieu's description of the commercial virtues.[46] This way of thinking departs from the classical view not only

Press, 1976 [1759/1790]), VII.ii.4.12. For a useful discussion, see John Robertson, "The Scottish Enlightenment at the Limits of the Civic Tradition," in Hont and Ignatieff, eds., *Wealth and Virtue*, esp. pp. 154–77 and, more generally, Christopher J. Berry, *The Idea of Luxury* (New York: Cambridge University Press, 1994), esp. chapter 6.

[45] Aristotle argues that "the best way of life, for individuals separately as well as for cities collectively, is the life of virtue duly equipped with such a store of requisites as makes it possible to share in the activities of virtue": *Politics*, book 7, chapter 1, quoting R. F. Stalley's revision of the Barker translation (New York: Oxford University Press, 1995 [1946]), p. 253, amended to give "virtue" rather than "goodness" as the translation of *aretē*. Cf. the *Nicomachean Ethics*, book 4, chapters 1–2 and Cicero, *On Duties*, book 2 §§55–60.

[46] Montesquieu, *Spirit of the Laws*, pp. 48, 42–3 (book 5, chapters 6 and 2); Franklin, *Autobiography*, part 2.

with respect to its content (frugality and industry were, after all, anathema to the free man of antiquity), but also and more importantly with respect to its ends: The commercial virtues aim not at the subordination of individual interests to the common good, but rather at the efficient pursuit of those interests. Moreover, instead of being attainable only by a cultured elite – one that has to be shielded from the materialism and instrumentalism that are endemic to commerce – virtue so understood is something that anyone can be said to possess insofar as they succeed in advancing their interests through prudent behavior over time. It is, like reason, the servant and not the ruler of the passions. Montesquieu concludes that "the laws of commerce perfect mores for the same reason that these same laws ruin mores": They provide a dependable, if in some respects distasteful, substitute for the loftier but more volatile ideal of civic virtue that lies at the heart of classical republicanism.[47]

Many thinkers saw this lowering of moral sights as a point in favor of commercial society. Smith's analysis in the *Wealth of Nations*, for example, is built on the assumption that "self-love" is the most reliable motivation for human action, and that only a "servile" man depends on the "humanity" of others for the satisfaction of his material needs.[48] However, not everyone saw the exchange of classical for commercial virtue as a good thing. Rousseau, for example, continued to defend the traditional republican view that it is the citizen of a commercial society who is servile, precisely because "[h]e must...constantly try to interest [others] in his fate and to make them really or apparently find their own profit in working for his," an obligation "which makes him knavish and artful with some, imperious and harsh with the rest, and places him under the necessity of deceiving all those he needs if he cannot get them to fear him and does not find it in his interest to make himself useful to them."[49]

---

[47] Montesquieu, *Spirit of the Laws*, p. 338 (book 20, chapter 1). This is of course the central argument of Hirschman's *The Passions and the Interests*. For a more detailed historical discussion, see Shelley Burtt, *Virtue Transformed: Political Argument in England, 1688–1740* (New York: Cambridge University Press, 1992); for an acute analysis of the ethical implications of the modern substitution of interest for classical virtue, see Harvey C. Mansfield, "Self-Interest Rightly Understood," *Political Theory* 23 (1995), esp. pp. 56–63.

[48] Smith, *Wealth of Nations* I.ii.2.

[49] Rousseau, *Discourse on the Origins and Foundations of Inequality Among Men* (1755), *Early Political Writings*, pp. 170–1. Smith quotes this passage at length in his "Letter to the Authors of the *Edinburgh Review*" (1756), *Essays on Philosophical Subjects*, ed. W. P. D. Wightman and J. C. Bryce (Oxford: Clarendon Press, 1980), pp. 252–3; elsewhere he refers to Rousseau as "an Author, more capable of feeling strongly than of analising accurately": "Of...the Imitative Arts" (c. 1777), ibid., p. 198.

Rousseau agrees with Smith in thinking that "[m]en can be moved to act only by their interest" but insists that "pecuniary interest is the worst of all, the vilest, the most liable to corruption, and even...the least and weakest in the eyes of anyone who knows the human heart well. In all hearts," he concludes, "there is naturally a reserve of great passions; when the only one left is the passion for money, it is because all the others, which should have been stimulated and encouraged, have been enervated and stifled."[50] Rousseau, like Smith, saw a necessary connection between commerce and prosperity in the modern age, and he does not hesitate, from the first of his political writings to the last, to draw the inference that the pursuit of virtue, and thus of freedom, requires a rejection of the comforts of modern civilization.

Although Rousseau's position was more consistent and thus more radical than most, a number of Renaissance and early modern thinkers agreed with him in seeing a connection between the traditional portrayal of the "servile" man and the "rational" egoism of *homo œconomicus*. Machiavelli's contemporary Francesco Guicciardini held, for example, that in Florence "the craving for riches erodes the desire for true glory [and] prevents the cultivation of the virtues."[51] Algernon Sidney warned his countrymen of those whose "slavish, vicious and base natures inclining them to seek only private and present advantages...easily slide into a blind dependence upon one who has wealth and power; and desiring only to know his will, care not what injustice they do, if they may be rewarded."[52] Locke's pupil the Third Earl of Shaftesbury complained that his contemporaries "have made virtue so mercenary a thing and have talked so much of its rewards that one can hardly tell what there is in it, after all, which can be worth rewarding. For to be bribed only or terrified into an honest practice bespeaks little of real honesty or worth."[53]

---

[50] Rousseau, *Considerations on the Government of Poland*, p. 226 (§11); for evidence that Smith shared this view, see his *Theory of Moral Sentiments* I.iii.2–3. On the influence of Rousseau on Smith's views more generally, see Dennis C. Rasmussen, *The Problems and Promise of Commercial Society: Adam Smith's Response to Rousseau* (University Park: Pennsylvania State University Press, 2008).

[51] Francesco Guicciardini, "How the Popular Government Should Be Reformed" (1512), in Jill Kraye, ed., *Cambridge Translations of Renaissance Philosophical Texts* (New York: Cambridge University Press, 1997), vol. 2, p. 230. Guicciardini likens his criticism of Florentine avarice to that of "the ancient writers who denounced the vices rampant in their own times": ibid.

[52] Algernon Sidney, *Discourses Concerning Government* (1683/1698), chapter 3 §19.

[53] Anthony Ashley-Cooper, Third Earl of Shaftesbury, "Sensus Communis, an Essay on the Freedom of Wit and Humour in a Letter to a Friend" (1709), in idem, *Characteristics of Men, Manners, Opinions, Times*, ed. Lawrence E. Klein (New York: Cambridge University Press, 1999 [1711]), p. 46.

Ferguson echoed Rousseau in arguing that when "[t]he individual considers his community so far only as it can be rendered subservient to his personal advancement or profit," then "men become either rapacious, deceitful, and violent, ready to trespass on the rights of others; or servile, mercenary, and base, prepared to relinquish their own." He concludes that "nations under a high state of the commercial arts, are exposed to corruption, by their admitting wealth, unsupported by personal elevation and virtue, as the great foundation of distinction, and by having their attention turned on the side of interest, as the road to consideration and honour."[54]

Even in the United States, which was to become the very model of a modern commercial republic, there were substantial doubts about the compatibility of commerce and republican virtue. Thomas Jefferson held, for example, that "[c]orruption of morals…is the mark set on those, who not looking up to heaven, to their own soil and industry…for their subsistence, depend for it on the casualties and caprice of customers." He later remarked, in a letter to John Jay, that "[c]ultivators of the earth are the most valuable citizens…the most vigorous, the most independant, the most virtuous…tied to their country and wedded to it's liberty and interests by the most lasting bonds," whereas "the class of artificers [are] the panders of vice, and the instruments by which the liberties of a country are generally overturned." Nor were such views confined to the party of Jefferson: John Adams, his political archenemy, wrote in the year of American independence (and of the publication of Smith's *Wealth of Nations*) that "the Spirit of Commerce," because it leads to "Servility and Flattery," is "incompatible with that purity of Heart and Greatness of soul which is necessary for an happy Republic." Madison, the architect of the Federal Constitution, argued in an anonymous essay published in 1792 that "[t]he class of citizens who provide at once their own food and their own raiment…are the best basis of public liberty, and the strongest bulwark of public safety," and that "the greater the proportion of this class to the whole society, the more free, the more independent, and the more happy must be the society itself."[55]

---

[54] Ferguson, *Essay on the History of Civil Society*, pp. 226–7, 241 (part 6, sections 1 and 3). Ferguson goes on to argue, like Rousseau, that "we must either, together with the commercial arts, suffer their fruits to be enjoyed, and even, in some measure, admired; or, like the Spartans, prohibit the art itself, while we are afraid of its consequences, or while we think that the conveniencies it brings exceed what nature requires." However, like Smith and unlike Rousseau, he is inclined to embrace the former alternative rather than the latter: ibid., p. 232 (part 6, section 2).

[55] Thomas Jefferson, *Notes on the State of Virginia* (1784), query 19; Jefferson, letter to John Jay, August 23, 1785; John Adams, letters to Mercy Otis Warren, April 16 and

It was Smith himself who gave the most far-reaching and influential response to this way of thinking, offering what Donald Winch has called "the best attempt, for its time, to provide some hypotheses concerning the problems of reconciling commercial realities with republican hopes."[56] Smith observes that the rise of commerce and manufacturing in British cities has "gradually introduced order and good government, and with them, the liberty and security of individuals among the inhabitants of the country, who had before lived in a continual state of war with their neighbours, and of servile dependency upon their superiors." Indeed, he suggests that this, "though it has been the least observed," was "by far the most important of all [its] effects," naming his friend "Mr. Hume" as "the only writer who...has hitherto taken notice of it." He argues, moreover, that it is precisely the impersonal nature of commercial relationships that gives them this freedom-promoting quality. A feudal tenant, he points out, "is as dependent upon the proprietor as any servant or retainer whatever and must obey him with as little reserve," because "[t]he subsistence of both is derived from his bounty, and its continuance depends upon his good pleasure." In a commercial economy, by contrast, "[e]ach tradesman or artificer derives his subsistence from the employment, not of one, but of a hundred or a thousand different customers," so that while he is "in some measure obliged to them all...he is not absolutely dependent upon any one of them." The same is true of the "customers" themselves: Although "the produce of [a wealthy man's] estate may be sufficient to maintain, and may perhaps actually maintain, more than a thousand people, yet as

January 8, 1776; James Madison, "Republican Distribution of Citizens" (1792). I should emphasize that the attitudes of the Founders toward commerce were decidedly more mixed, and in some respects more favorable, than these statements might suggest; for three rather different analyses, see Matson and Onuf, "Toward a Republican Empire;" Drew R. McCoy, *The Elusive Republic: Political Economy in Jeffersonian America* (Chapel Hill: University of North Carolina Press, 1980); and Appleby, *Capitalism and a New Social Order: The Republican Vision of the 1790s* (New York: NYU Press, 1984).

56 Donald Winch, "Commercial Realities, Republican Principles," in Martin van Gelderen and Quentin Skinner, eds., *Republicanism: A Shared European Heritage* (New York: Cambridge University Press, 2002), vol. 2, p. 310, and see more generally his *Adam Smith's Politics: An Essay in Historiographic Revision* (New York: Cambridge University Press, 1978). For a vigorous rejection of Winch's republican reading of Smith, see Edward J. Harpham, "Liberalism, Civic Humanism, and the Case of Adam Smith," *American Political Science Review* 78 (1984), pp. 764–74; for a more balanced view, see John Robertson, "Scottish Political Economy Beyond the Civic Tradition: Government and Economic Development in the *Wealth of Nations*," *History of Political Thought* 4 (1983), pp. 451–82, and cf. also Andreas Kalyvas and Ira Katznelson, *Liberal Beginnings: Making a Republic for the Moderns* (New York: Cambridge University Press, 2008), chapter 2.

those people pay for everything they get…there is scarce any body who considers himself as entirely dependent upon him."[57]

Smith appeals to a similar mix of economic and political considerations in defending the market as a means of arriving at value judgments. He argues that under conditions of "perfect liberty" – that is, when individuals are allowed to buy and sell commodities at whatever prices they are willing to accept – we should expect that on average just enough of each commodity will be produced to meet the effective demand, that resources will be moved into and out of various industries in response to changes in the relative supply of and demand for various commodities – including, of course, the various forms of skilled and unskilled labor – and that these changes will be revealed to producers and consumers by changes in relative prices.[58] Under such conditions, he famously concludes, "every individual…by directing [his] industry in such a manner as its produce may be of the greatest value," will be "led by an invisible hand to promote an end which was no part of his intention" and will thus promote the public good – understood in terms of material prosperity – "more effectually than when he really intends to promote it." The alternative – allowing economic policy to be dictated by the state – not only produces economically inferior outcomes, but grants "the statesman…an authority which could safely be trusted, not only to no single person, but to no council or senate whatever, and which would no-where be so dangerous as in the hands of a man who had folly and presumption enough to fancy himself fit to exercise it."[59] Thus Smith uses the republican fear of arbitrary power not only to attack the personalized forms of domination that existed in feudal society, but also to defend the depersonalized commercial relationships that were emerging to take their place. However, even he was moved at the end of his life to lament that the "disposition to admire, and almost to worship, the rich and the powerful, and to despise, or, at least, to neglect persons of poor and mean condition, though necessary both to establish and to maintain the distinction of ranks and the

---

[57] Smith, *Wealth of Nations* III.iv.4, 6, 12; V.i.b.7. Smith is presumably alluding to Hume's essays "Of Commerce" and "Of Refinement in the Arts." The moralistic roots of this line of argument are brought out more clearly in the *Lectures on Jurisprudence*, in which Smith argues that "[n]othing tends so much to corrupt mankind as dependency," and thus that "[t]he establishment of commerce and manufactures, which brings about…independencey, is the best police for preventing crimes": Smith, *Lectures on Jurisprudence* (B) 204–5.

[58] See especially *Wealth of Nations* I.vii passim.

[59] Ibid., IV.ii.10.

order of society, is, at the same time, the great and most universal cause of the corruption of our moral sentiments."[60]

3.5. A HOUSE DIVIDED

By shifting their focus from the realm of war to that of trade, and from the realm of self-government to that of voluntary exchange, the defenders of commercial society changed the terms of the debate about the meaning and implications of republican freedom in two different and overlapping ways. First, by making the security of the polity depend on its wealth, and by tying the acquisition of wealth to the pursuit of commerce, they severed the traditional connection between civic virtue and the common good. As we have seen, the classical republicans did not distinguish clearly between the demands of self-interest and virtue, or between individual and collective purposes, because they saw the control of arbitrary power as one of the most fundamental human interests, and because they could not conceive of a reliable way of achieving this end except through the vigilance of a virtuous citizenry. It was therefore possible for them to argue, as Aristotle did, that "[t]o aim at utility everywhere is utterly unbecoming...to those who have the character of freemen," and to deny, as Cicero did, that what is dishonorable can properly be called beneficial.[61] The insight that self-interested behavior can be socially useful – that private vice leads to public benefits – called this harmonization of the demands of virtue, enlightened self-interest, and the common good into question. The defenders of commercial society concluded that the long-standing ambiguity in republican thought between instrumental and intrinsic conceptions of the value of virtue should be resolved in favor of the instrumental view, and that the question of what constitutes virtuous behavior should be rethought along commercial lines.

Second, the defenders of commercial society – Smith foremost among them – sought to replace the traditional republican demand for transparency and accountability in the exercise of political power with a demand that power be exercised anonymously, impersonally, and above all nonpolitically, insofar as this was possible. In doing so they took advantage of a second long-standing ambiguity in republican thought, between procedural and substantive understandings of the nature of arbitrary power.

---

[60] Smith, *Theory of Moral Sentiments* I.iii.3.1. The chapter containing this passage was added to the sixth and final edition, dated 1790.

[61] Aristotle, *Politics*, p. 303 (book 8, chapter 3); Cicero, *On Duties*, book 3 passim.

Here again, the classical republicans did not distinguish clearly between the two possibilities, because they could not conceive of a way to ensure that power was exercised beneficially except through the proper design and supervision of political institutions, and here again, the insight that socially beneficial outcomes can arise from the self-interested actions of individuals called the traditional view into question. The defenders of commercial society argued that the traditional association of freedom with self-government was simply too cumbersome to be realized or even coherently pursued under modern conditions, especially in light of the fact that each of us, whenever we make an economic decision of any kind, has a marginal and largely unintended effect on the overall pattern of social outcomes. By shifting decision-making power from the political to the economic realm, they concluded, we are trading a process that is highly fallible and subject to abuse for one that is reliably beneficial – just as by substituting interest for virtue as the basis of social order, we are trading a lofty but volatile ideal for one that is less elevated but more dependable.

Another group of early modern thinkers, Rousseau most notably but by no means alone among them, objected on republican grounds not only to the rise of commercial society, but to the very idea that the pursuit of self-interest can properly be associated with individual or collective freedom. These thinkers remained loyal to the classical view that virtuous citizenship requires that individuals subordinate their personal interests to those of the political community, and they opposed the transfer of decision-making power from the political to the economic realm on the grounds that we cannot be considered free if we are subject to a power that we cannot control. Smith's appeal to an "invisible hand" that promotes ends that are no part of our intention seemed to them the very model of such a power. To the argument that arbitrary power should be judged by its effects rather than by the way in which it is exercised, they responded, in effect, that liberty consists not in having a generous master but in having none.[62]

Thus in a world where security and prosperity depend on the pursuit of commerce rather than war, it seems that we must either follow Smith and abandon or sharply circumscribe the demands of virtuous citizenship, perhaps redescribing as virtuous the egoistic forms of behavior that are associated with the commercial realm, or follow Rousseau and remain faithful to the classical ideal even at the expense

---

[62] Paraphrasing Cicero, *De re publica*, book 2 §43; Cicero refers to a "just" master.

of the material benefits that commerce brings. As we might expect, this disagreement about the compatibility of freedom and commerce is reflected in the efforts of early modern thinkers to make sense of the republican tradition itself. The leading figures in the classical republican tradition – Aristotle, Cicero, and even Machiavelli – had been willing to treat cultured Athens and ascetic Sparta, imperial Rome and insular Geneva, and turbulent Florence and serene Venice as equally legitimate (if not equally admirable) models of republican rule. The early modern thinkers, by contrast, often disagree, sometimes profoundly, about basic questions of classification. Whereas Montesquieu describes England as "a nation where the republic hides under the form of monarchy" and as the "one nation in the world whose constitution has political liberty for its direct purpose," Rousseau argues by contrast that if "[t]he English people thinks it is free; it is greatly mistaken, it is free only during the election of Members of Parliament; as soon as they are elected, it is enslaved, it is nothing" – adding sardonically that "[t]he use it makes of its freedom during the brief moments it has it fully warrants its losing it."[63] Similarly, whereas James Madison claimed to have found in the Federal Constitution "a republican remedy for the diseases most incident to republican government," his opponents accused him of fomenting "as deep and wicked a conspiracy as ever was invented in the darkest ages against the liberties of a free people."[64] Benjamin Constant goes so far as to place Sparta and Athens, the two leading republics of Greek antiquity, on opposite sides of a line dividing ancient from modern conceptions of liberty.[65]

The significance of these developments for our purposes does not lie in the fact that some thinkers were successful in working out a "republican" defense of commercial society – that part of the story is relatively familiar – and still less in the fact that their efforts were met with resistance from more traditionally minded thinkers. Rather, it lies in the fact that the rise of commerce forced thinkers of all stripes to

---

[63] Montesquieu, *Spirit of the Laws*, pp. 70, 156 (book 5, chapter 19; book 11, chapter 6); Rousseau, *Social Contract*, p. 114 (book 3, chapter 15). Rousseau grants, however, that the English "are closer to freedom than all the other" peoples of Europe: ibid., p. 51n (book 1, chapter 6).

[64] Madison makes the former claim at the end of *Federalist* 10; the latter was made by John Lansing, Jr., during the New York ratification debate that Madison was writing, in order to influence. Madison goes on to criticize the use of the term republican to describe the Dutch, Venetian, Polish, and English constitutions in *Federalist* 39.

[65] Constant, "Ancient and Modern Liberty," esp. pp. 312, 315–16.

confront squarely the ambiguities that had always been contained in the republican conception of freedom. Now, for the first time, there was a debate on republican grounds between those who argued that power should be considered non-arbitrary if and to the extent that it promotes (often through abstinence) the material well-being of those over whom it is exercised and those who held instead that the citizens of a republic should be protected from the arbitrary exercise of power – including economic power – even if this requires a substantial sacrifice of prosperity. There was also a debate between those who defined virtuous behavior as socially beneficial behavior, regardless of its motivations, and those who held that the demands of virtue and material gain are fundamentally opposed, and that to pursue the one is necessarily to abandon the other. As a result, the traditional picture of the free man as someone who displays his virtue by placing the public good ahead of his private interests was brought into competition with one that portrayed the free man as someone who advances the public good by attending to his private interests as diligently as possible. In short, the early modern debates about the rise of commerce raised a series of questions about the relationship between freedom and the market that remain central to our political culture even today.

We have seen that the immediate impact of the rise of commerce was not to make republican freedom obsolete, but rather to throw the longstanding disagreements about its practical implications into sharper relief: If the republican tradition was able to hang together, ideologically speaking, as long as its various ambiguities were not pressed too hard, the rise of commerce caused this fragile unity to come apart. Thus although the defense of commercial society that we have examined both reflected and helped to bring about a significant shift in modern thinking about freedom, it did not entail a repudiation of the republican view. These thinkers were still concerned with the control of arbitrary power and the cultivation of virtue, and they saw commerce – insofar as it could be relied on to generate wealth, tame social conflicts, and dissolve traditional relationships of dependence – as a tool for pursuing those ends. To this extent, they treated participation in the market as being instrumental to, and not constitutive of, the enjoyment of freedom properly speaking. The debate about the political implications of the rise of commerce was therefore not a debate in which competing conceptions of freedom were pitted against one another, but rather a debate about the extent to which a commonly accepted, if somewhat vaguely defined, conception of freedom was compatible with an increasingly influential set of norms and practices. We will now see how 18th-century thinkers such as Montesquieu, Hume, and Smith were able to weave this "commercial" brand of republican thought together with the juristic idea of "natural" liberty to defend an altogether new way of thinking, one that centered around the distinctive kind of freedom that is enjoyed in the market itself.

4

The Market Synthesis

> Their aim was the aim of kings: that needing nothing, and obeying no one, they might enjoy liberty, the mark of which is to live just as one pleases.
>
> Cicero, *On Duties*, book 1 §68 (Atkins trans.)

4.1. THE LOCKEAN LEGACY

We have seen that the debates about the political implications of the rise of commerce in the early modern period brought to the surface the long-standing tensions in republican thought between procedural and substantive conceptions of arbitrary power, and between instrumental and intrinsic conceptions of the value of virtue. As a result, early modern thinkers had to make a series of difficult choices about the meaning and implications of republican freedom that their forebears had been able to avoid, between options that their forebears may not have clearly recognized as such. The "republican" defense of commercial society that emerged in these debates represented a substantial departure in many ways from the classical republican view. The classical republican expects the free man to be independent; to depend on the market for the satisfaction of one's own wants and needs is to depend in a radical sense on the wants and needs of other people. The classical republican sees the pursuit and enjoyment of luxury as a threat to individual virtue, and thus to freedom itself; the flourishing of a commercial economy depends on the assumption that people will always want more material goods than they actually have. The classical republican expects the free man to be neither calculating nor self-interested; these are the defining features of *homo œconomicus*. Freedom in the classical republican tradition consists in being socially and legally set apart from one's fellows; markets are often praised for their blindness to status distinctions – or at least to those that cannot be expressed in economic terms.

Thus even those who were favorably disposed toward the rise of commerce had to admit that the norms and practices that prevail in commercial societies are very different from those that had been associated with free societies in the past. It is nevertheless the case, or so I have argued, that to the extent that a political defense of the rise of commerce was mounted, it was mounted in recognizably republican terms. This line of argument hinged on two related claims: first, that commerce has replaced war as the primary mode of interaction between societies in the modern world, and second, that governments, because they benefit from the prosperity of their citizens, have to exercise their power non-arbitrarily if they want to attract the desired level of commercial activity. The defenders of commercial society concluded that the self-regarding commercial virtues are superior to the traditional civic ones because they provide the most efficient route to collective prosperity, and because prosperity is a necessary condition for preserving the security and independence – and thus the freedom – of the modern state. Virtue stands in this way of thinking for the diligent and prudent pursuit of self-interest, especially in the economic realm, and power is said to be non-arbitrary if and to the extent that it refrains from interfering with virtuous behavior so defined. The promise of peace and prosperity that was associated with the rise of commerce was therefore said to provide grounds for extending commercial norms and practices even into the traditionally political areas of social life.

The critics of commercial society were generally willing to admit that under modern conditions the states that cultivate the arts of production and trade most assiduously are likely to be the most prosperous. However, they pointed out that in a commercial society both rulers and ordinary citizens depend on the good opinion of others – especially the wealthy – to achieve their ends, and that this kind of dependence is incompatible with the cultivation of civic virtue in the classical sense. As Rousseau put it, the citizen of a commercial society is "scheming, intense, greedy, servile and knavish ... forever at one of the two extremes of misery or opulence, of license or slavery, without any middle ground."[1] The defenders

---

[1] Jean-Jacques Rousseau, *Considerations on the Government of Poland* (1772) §11, quoting idem, *The Social Contract and Other Later Political Writings*, trans. and ed. Victor Gourevitch (New York: Cambridge University Press, 1997), p. 224. Gourevitch's translation is uncharacteristically loose: the French reads "*intrigant, ardent, avide, ambitieux, servile et fripon.*" Rousseau continues: "[I]f by chance you preferred to form a free,

of commercial society responded that although it is true that in the modern world the fate of individuals and even of entire states increasingly lies in the hands of the wealthy – and, in the limit, of unpredictable and ungovernable "market forces" – the overall effect of the rise of commerce has been to dissolve particular relationships of dependence and to provide historically unprecedented levels of prosperity. Moreover, the kind of dependence that we experience in the commercial realm is qualitatively different from the kind that we experience as political subjects. Thus to the extent that the aversion that we feel to being subject to arbitrary power arises from the fact, real or imagined, that an identifiable person or group is taking pleasure in our subjection, the relative anonymity of market relationships represents a distinct improvement.

I have suggested that the emergence of this commercial brand of republican thought in the early modern period was a necessary but not sufficient condition for the invention of market freedom, and that this further development was made possible by a synthesis of commercial republican and natural juristic ideas over the course of the 18th century. The present chapter will be devoted to fleshing out and defending this claim. I have so far ignored the important role that the juristic emphasis on the rule of law and the protection of individual rights played in the thought of 18th-century defenders of commercial society such as Montesquieu, Hume, and Smith – and the equally important role that these ideas played in the thought of critics of commercial society such as Rousseau and Adam Ferguson. We saw in Chapter 2, however, that the relationship between juristic and republican ideas *prior* to the 18th century was rather strained. On the one hand, the juristic idea of subjective natural rights provides a conceptually precise and ideologically powerful tool for defining the sphere of personal independence on which the enjoyment of republican freedom depends. On the other hand, the juristic preoccupation with ensuring that political power is exercised in accordance with the demands of natural law is not only compatible with, but was even said to require, the rule of a benevolent monarch. As a result, many natural jurists viewed the republican ideal of popular self-rule with a great deal of suspicion. This juristic brand of anti-republicanism is nicely, if somewhat quixotically, captured in the speech that Charles I

peaceful and wise nation which neither fears nor needs anyone, is self-sufficient and is happy; then you must adopt an altogether different method...make money contemptible and, if possible, useless, seek, find more powerful and more reliable springs to achieve great things": ibid., pp. 224–5.

made from the scaffold in 1649: "For the people...their Liberty and their freedom, consists in having of Government; those Laws, by which their life and their goods, may be most their own. It is not for having share in Government (sir) that is nothing pertaining to them. A Subject and a Sovereign are clean different things."

The fact that juristic and republican ideas can be found side by side in the work of a number of leading 18th-century thinkers suggests that the tensions between these two schools of thought were not irresolvable, and it is part of our task here to see how these thinkers were able to negotiate and finally to overcome them, at least to their own satisfaction. We left off our account of the development of juristic ideas about freedom with John Locke, who, as we have seen, was one of the first thinkers to associate natural liberty in the juristic sense with the republican concern to prevent the arbitrary exercise of power. As we now know, Locke's *Two Treatises* had only a limited impact on the thoughts and actions of his contemporaries.[2] It is nevertheless clear that by the middle of the 18th century the view that legitimate political rule rests on popular consent had become influential enough that Hume could treat it (without directly naming Locke as its author) as one of the two "systems of speculative principles" on which "the factions, into which this nation [*viz.*, Britain] is divided" rested – the other being the one against which Locke had directed his polemical energies, that "the DEITY is the ultimate author of all government."[3] The question of the nature and scope of the influence of Locke's political writings in the 18th century remains one of the most contentious topics of debate among historians of early modern political thought. Indeed, the contemporary revival of interest in the republican tradition was undertaken in large part with an eye toward overturning the once-conventional view that the political thought of that period was predominantly "Lockean-liberal" in character.[4] I will argue that the most

[2] On this, see, for example, Martyn P. Thompson, "The Reception of Locke's *Two Treatises of Government* 1690–1705," *Political Studies* 24 (1976), pp. 184–91 and, more recently, the introduction to Mark Goldie, ed., *The Reception of Locke's Politics* (London: Pickering & Chatto, 1999), vol. 1, esp. pp. xxii–xxiii, xxx–xxxiv. Goldie allows that the *Two Treatises* "had an esoteric éclat among advanced Whigs" in the 1690s: ibid., p. xxxi.

[3] David Hume, "Of the Original Contract" (1748), in idem, *Political Essays*, ed. Knud Haakonssen (New York: Cambridge University Press, 1994), pp. 186–7 (emphasis removed). Hume paraphrases the argument of the *Second Treatise* near the end of the essay, referring to its author only as "the most noted of [the] partizans" of the view that government was founded on an "original contract": ibid., p. 200.

[4] The canonical statement of the "Lockean-liberal" reading of American political thought is found in Louis Hartz, *The Liberal Tradition in America: An Interpretation of American Political Thought Since the Revolution* (New York: Harcourt, Brace, 1955). The most

striking fact about the political thought of this period is not that these two schools of thought were in competition with each other, but rather that key elements of both traditions were brought together for the first time into a single political vision.[5] The result, as we will see, was not a triumph of "liberal" over "republican" ideas, but rather a synthesis of the two into a qualitatively different conception of freedom that took economic rather than political life as its model.

4.2. LIBERTY AND THE LAW

We have seen that the juristic and republican traditions associate freedom with the rule of law in two different and, to some extent, conflicting ways. According to the natural jurists, the purpose of civil law is to ensure that human behavior conforms to the demands of natural law. Freedom is associated in this way of thinking with free (or autonomous) choice, which can be conceived either in positive terms, as choice in accordance with natural law, or in negative terms, as the ability to choose as one wishes within a legally defined sphere. In either case, freedom is *not* treated as a political value taken in itself, but rather, in the positive view, it is treated as an underlying property of human nature that makes moral behavior possible, or, in the negative view, as a morally neutral category of action that has to be regulated for the sake of justice and social order. Republicans hold, by contrast, that the purpose of law is to prevent the arbitrary exercise of power. They are therefore concerned not only with the content of law, but also with the way in which it is made and the means by which rulers are constrained to obey it in practice. The

influential republican criticisms of Hartz's view are found in Bernard Bailyn, *The Ideological Origins of the American Revolution* (Cambridge, MA: Harvard University Press, 1967) and Gordon S. Wood, *The Creation of the American Republic, 1776–1787* (New York: W. W. Norton, 1969). Part 3 of J. G. A. Pocock's *The Machiavellian Moment: Florentine Political Thought and the Atlantic Republican Tradition* (Princeton, NJ: Princeton University Press, 1975) provides a seminal statement of the republican or (as Pocock prefers to say) "civic humanist" reading of early modern Anglo-American political thought more generally. For two notable and generally sympathetic critiques of Pocock's position, see Isaac Kramnick, *Republicanism and Bourgeois Radicalism: Political Ideology in Late Eighteenth-Century England and America* (Ithaca, NY: Cornell University Press, 1990) and the essays collected in Joyce Appleby, *Liberalism and Republicanism in the Historical Imagination* (Cambridge, MA: Harvard University Press, 1992), especially chapters 4, 6, 11, and 13.

[5] For another recent effort to demonstrate the historical interdependence of liberal and republican ideas, see Andreas Kalyvas and Ira Katznelson, *Liberal Beginnings: Making a Republic for the Moderns* (New York: Cambridge University Press, 2008). Kalyvas and Katznelson define the term republican more loosely than I have here.

distinction is subtle but significant: Republicans seek to ensure that the
authors and executors of the law are accountable to those on whom it is
binding, and they associate freedom with the ability of citizens to ensure
that this is the case. Here freedom, rather than justice or peace, is the first
end to be pursued in public life, and the rule of law is treated as a means
for achieving that end.

However, because the republican defense of the rule of law contains
the same ambiguity about the meaning of arbitrary power that we have
identified in republican thought more generally, it is not always clear
what criteria republicans should use to determine whether the laws have
been made and applied non-arbitrarily in a given case. According to what
I have called the "substantive" understanding of arbitrary power, the test
will be whether a given system of laws serves the interests of those who
are bound by it. This raises the obvious question of what those interests
are and how we should determine whether they have been served in a
given case. In its pure form, this line of argument is consistent with,
though it does not strictly entail, the juristic (and Lockean) view that
political rule is legitimate only if it conforms to the demands of natural
law. However, the more traditional republican position, which we can
find in Locke as well, is that the only reliable way to ensure that political
power is exercised non-arbitrarily is by giving those who are subject to
it a say in determining how it is exercised. This line of argument rests on
what I have called the "procedural" understanding of arbitrary power
and points toward the equally traditional republican project of designing
accountable political institutions.

As we have seen, the classical republicans sought to take each of these
positions into account: Power cannot be considered non-arbitrary simply
because it is subject to procedural checks, nor can it be considered non-
arbitrary simply because it is exercised benevolently. Rather, the classical
republicans saw the control of arbitrary power and the display of virtue
as complementary aims: The test of whether political power is *substantively* non-arbitrary is whether its exercise (or non-exercise) promotes the
cultivation and practice of virtue among the citizenry, and the absence of
procedurally arbitrary power is seen as a necessary condition for realizing this end. It follows that for republicans the relationship between
liberty and the law has both negative and positive dimensions, just as it
does for the natural jurists: The function of law is not only to shield us
from the arbitrary exercise of power – thereby making the cultivation of
virtue possible – but also to mold us into virtuous citizens and to create
the social conditions under which we can display whatever virtue we may

have. Just as the rise of commerce exposed the tension between the substantive and procedural understandings of arbitrary power, so too did it expose the tension between the positive and negative understandings of the relationship between liberty and the law. The ensuing efforts to disentangle these positions gave rise to a synthesis of juristic and republican ideas about freedom in which the classical republican commitment to virtuous citizenship came to play a distinctly subordinate role.

An early example of this kind of syncretism is found in the writings of John Trenchard and Thomas Gordon, whose pseudonymous *Cato's Letters* (1720–3) stand as one of the most eloquent and influential expressions of Lockean political thought in the first half of the 18th century.[6] Taken together, *Cato's Letters* provide a discourse on the meaning of English liberty and the necessary conditions for its preservation. However, two different conceptions of liberty can be found in the text: one rooted in the republican concern with checking arbitrary power, the other in the juristic concern with defining the limits of rightful action and of legitimate political authority. Thus Gordon begins the sixty-second letter, titled "An Enquiry Into the Nature and Extent of Liberty," by defining liberty in juristic and even proto-Millian terms as "the power which every man has over his own actions, and his right to enjoy the fruit of his labour, art, and industry, as far as by it he hurts not the society, or any members of it."[7] However, he goes on to characterize this sphere

---

[6] Pocock, in keeping with his tendency to minimize the influence of Locke's political writings in the 18th century, has argued that Cato's thought is predominantly "neo-Harringtonian" in character: See especially *Machiavellian Moment*, pp. 467–77. However, although the Harringtonian language of virtue, corruption, and the balance of property can indeed be found in *Cato's Letters* (see especially ##35, 84, 85, and 91), so too do many crucial passages (most notably in #59, but cf. ##11, 33, 38, 45, 55, 60, and 62) echo and even closely paraphrase Locke's *Second Treatise*. For two readings of Cato that emphasize his debt to Locke, see Ronald Hamowy, "*Cato's Letters*, John Locke, and the Republican Paradigm," *History of Political Thought* 11 (1990), pp. 273–94 and Michael P. Zuckert, *Natural Rights and the New Republicanism* (Princeton, NJ: Princeton University Press, 1994), pp. 297–319; for a recent defense of the "neo-Harringtonian" reading, see Eric Nelson, *The Greek Tradition in Republican Thought* (New York: Cambridge University Press, 2004), pp. 139–44. It is worth pointing out in this connection that Cato, although he often espouses Lockean views, never credits these views to Locke and indeed mentions Locke by name only twice (##105 and 116), both times in passing and in his capacity as a philosopher rather than a political thinker. By contrast, two of the letters (##26 and 37) consist almost entirely of extended (and attributed) quotations from the writings of Locke's contemporary and fellow radical Whig Algernon Sidney. Harrington's name does not appear in the text at all.

[7] John Trenchard and Thomas Gordon, *Cato's Letters, or, Essays on Liberty, Civil and Religious, and Other Important Subjects*, ed. Ronald Hamowy (Indianapolis: Liberty Fund, 1995), vol. 1, p. 427. In #59, also by Gordon, the Lockean roots of this line of

of individual liberty as something that is not only due to us as a matter of right, but that is necessary for the cultivation and practice of virtue. "Liberty is," he argues, "to live upon one's own terms; slavery is, to live at the mere mercy of another; and a life of slavery is, to those who can bear it, a continual state of uncertainty and wretchedness." Indeed, where the natural jurists hold that self-preservation is the first duty imposed by natural law, Gordon notes approvingly that "to many men, and to many other creatures, as well as men, the love of liberty is *beyond* the love of life." He concludes with the unmistakably republican observation that "[the] passion for liberty in men, and their possession of it, is of that efficacy and importance, that it seems the parent of all the virtues," so that "in free countries there seems to be another species of mankind, than is to be found under tyrants."[8]

"Cato" sounds even more like a republican when he discusses questions of governance. "Power," Gordon writes in the twenty-fifth letter, "is like fire; it warms, scorches, or destroys, according as it is watched, provoked, or increased." It follows, as Trenchard puts it in the sixtieth letter, that a "free country" is one in which "the power and sovereignty of magistrates...[is] so qualified, and so divided into different channels, and committed to the direction of so many different men, with different interests and views, that the majority of them could seldom or never find their account in betraying [the people's] trust," that is, one in which "the concerns of all [are] directed by all, as far as possibly can be."[9] (Gordon is careful to emphasize in the thirty-seventh letter that the British system, having been purged of its Stuart excesses, meets this standard: "[O]ur government is a thousand degrees nearer a-kin to a commonwealth," he argues, "than it is to absolute monarchy." Trenchard adds in the eighty-fifth letter that "liberty may be better preserved by a well poised monarchy, than by any popular government."[10]) However, institutional checks alone do not suffice. Gordon points out in the seventieth letter that "[t]he emperors of Rome were as absolute with the shew of a Senate,

---

argument are even clearer: "All men are born free; liberty is a gift which they receive from God himself; nor can they alienate the same by consent, though possibly they may forfeit it by crimes. No man has power over his own life, or to dispose of his own religion; and cannot consequently transfer the power of either to any body else: Much less can he give away the lives and liberties, religion or acquired property of his posterity, who will be born as free as he himself was born, and can never be bound by his wicked and ridiculous bargain": ibid., vol. 1, pp. 406–7; cf. Locke, *Second Treatise* §§22–3, 172, 182.

[8] *Cato's Letters*, vol. 1, p. 430 (emphasis added).
[9] Ibid., vol. 1, pp. 186, 417–8.
[10] Ibid., vol. 1, p. 262; vol. 2, p. 613.

and the appearance of the people's choosing their praetors, tribunes, and other officers of the commonwealth, as the eastern monarchs are now without these seeming checks, and this shew of liberty." He therefore urges his fellow Britons to remember that their freedom can only be preserved through vigilance: "As you love your liberties exercise your virtue: they depend upon it." The other half of the republican view – that virtue depends on free government – is stated in the ninety-fourth letter, in which Trenchard and Gordon, writing jointly, argue in characteristically vivid terms that "[t]here is scarce such a thing under the sun as a corrupt people, where the government is uncorrupt: it is that, and that alone, which makes them so, and to calumniate them for what they do not seek, but suffer by, is as great impudence as it would be to knock a man down and then rail at him for hurting himself."[11]

Thus we find in *Cato's Letters* – and, as we will see, in the writings of a number of other 18th-century thinkers – the synthesis of republican and juristic ideas that is so conspicuously absent in the medieval period and that is only tentatively explored even in Locke. The *Letters* appeal to liberty, understood in terms of the absence of arbitrary power, as the first good to be pursued in public life; to mixed and limited government as its institutional corollary; to virtue as the precondition for and product of liberty so understood; and to natural and inalienable rights as a way of defining the sphere of action within which neither the state nor our fellow citizens can interfere, except arbitrarily. However, this synthesis required – or perhaps it would be more accurate to say that it reflected – a fundamental rethinking of the premises of classical republican thought. Most notably, Cato treats virtue as a means to the preservation of juristic liberty rather than as an end in itself; to refer again to the terminology that I introduced in Chapter 1, he favors an instrumental over an intrinsic understanding of the value of virtue. Indeed, Gordon argues in the sixty-second letter that "entering into political society, is so far from a departure from... natural right, that to preserve it was the *sole reason* why men did so." There is no trace in *Cato's Letters*, any more than there is in Locke, of the classical view that the life of virtuous citizenship should be valued for its own sake, and still less that it should be taken as the proper aim of political society. As Trenchard dryly remarks in the opening words of the sixty-first letter, "[t]he most reasonable meaning that can be put upon this apothegm, that *virtue is its own reward*, is, that it seldom meets with any other."[12]

---

[11] Ibid., vol. 2, pp. 505, 510, 673.
[12] Ibid., vol. 1, pp. 427 (emphasis added), 420 (original emphasis).

Cato's treatment of the *content* of virtue departs no less sharply from
the classical view. As Gordon puts it in the fortieth letter, "[w]hen the
passions of men do good to others, it is called virtue and publick spirit;
and when they do hurt to others, it is called selfishness, dishonesty, lust,
and other names of infamy." In other words, Cato measures virtue – or,
more precisely, suggests that most people measure virtue – not by the
character or motivations of those who display it, but rather by the social
benefits to which it leads. Indeed, as the appeal to the "passions" may
suggest, Cato's conception of virtue, and of human behavior more generally, is rooted in a Hobbesian psychology that holds that human beings
are fundamentally egoistic. Gordon writes in the same letter that "[f]or
men to act independently of their passions, is a contradiction! since their
passions enter into all that they do, and are the source of it." He adds in
the thirty-first letter that "[o]f all the passions which belong to human
nature, self-love is the strongest, and the root of all the rest; or, rather,
all the different passions are only several names for the several opera-
tions of self-love."[13] Thus despite his eloquent words about the priority
of liberty over life, Gordon views the blessings of liberty in strictly instrumental terms, arguing in the sixty-second letter – this time in a Lockean
tone of voice – that "[t]rue and impartial liberty is...the right of every
man to pursue the natural, reasonable, and religious dictates of his own
mind; to think what he will, and act as he thinks, provided he acts not
to the prejudice of another; to spend his own money himself, and lay out
the produce of his labour his own way; and to labour for his own pleasure and profit." The same point is stated in more frankly egoistic terms
in the sixty-eighth letter, also by Gordon, which begins with the observation that "it is the ambition of all men to live agreeably to their own
humours and discretion."[14]

Thus although *Cato's Letters* contain both republican and juristic
ideas about the relationship between liberty and the law, the former are
nevertheless strictly subordinated to the latter. As Gordon puts it in the
sixty-eighth letter:

To live securely, happily, and independently, is the *end* and *effect* of liberty...and
only to be found in free countries, where power is fixed on one side, and property secured on the other; where the one cannot break bounds without check,
penalties or forfeiture, nor the other suffer diminution without redress; where the

[13] Ibid., vol. 1, pp. 279–80, 222.
[14] Ibid., vol. 1, pp. 429, 483.

people have no masters but the laws, and such as the laws appoint; [and] where both laws and magistracy are formed by the people or their deputies.[15]

This synthesis of republican and juristic ideas was undeniably a major ideological achievement – and I do not mean to suggest that it was Cato's achievement alone – but it was vulnerable to two significant objections. First of all, if it is true, as Cato maintains and as later 18th-century thinkers tend to agree, that human beings are fundamentally motivated by self-interest,[16] then it is not clear that we can depend on them to display the virtue that is, by Cato's own account, a necessary condition for the preservation of free government. Second of all, by conceiving of rights as the legal corollaries of "the ambition of all men to live agreeably to their own humours and discretion," rather than as the moral corollaries of duties that we owe to God as our creator, these thinkers raise the question of whether we can depend on citizens to respect the rights of their fellows, and further, whether it is prudent or even coherent to rest the legitimacy of political rule on the claim that they have consented to do so. The political thought of the later 18th century was largely devoted to addressing one or the other of these concerns.

4.3. "THE DEFECT OF BETTER MOTIVES"

As I have suggested, the juxtaposition of republican and juristic ideas about freedom is not unique to Cato in the 18th century. Indeed, it can be found not only in thinkers who were favorably disposed toward the rise of commerce, such as Montesquieu, Hume, Smith, and Cato himself, but even in as vigorous a critic of commercial society as Rousseau. In each case, the problem of reconciling the aim of maintaining a free government with the aim of allowing citizens to pursue their own ends – or, put otherwise, of ensuring that citizens display the qualities of character that are necessary to preserve their freedom – looms large. For Rousseau, the challenge is to reconcile a juristic, and thus essentially voluntaristic, conception of political obligation with a classical conception of virtue as the fulfillment of human personality: To use his terminology,

---

[15] Ibid., vol. 1, pp. 483–4 (emphasis added).
[16] For an examination of the role that the appeal to self-interest played in 18th-century moral and political thought, see Pierre Force, *Self-Interest Before Adam Smith: A Genealogy of Economic Science* (New York: Cambridge University Press, 2003) and for a classic statement, see Albert O. Hirschman, *The Passions and the Interests: Political Arguments for Capitalism Before Its Triumph* (Princeton, NJ: Princeton University Press, 1977).

the enjoyment of civil and moral freedom requires that each citizen be persuaded to place the general will ahead of his own particular will.[17] Citizenship – and, indeed, the act of founding a polity in the first place – is thus in his view a pedagogical project: it requires that the will of each citizen be molded in such a way that he comes to prefer, and thus to choose, the freedom that republican citizenship offers over the material and psychic enticements of modern civilization. Rousseau insists that this project can be sustained only if and insofar as the polity in question is sheltered from the corrupting effects of commerce.[18]

If republican critics of commercial society such as Rousseau follow their classical forebears in emphasizing the positive association of the rule of law with the cultivation of virtue, the commercial republicans associate the rule of law instead with the negative aim of defining a sphere of action that is immune from arbitrary interference. They therefore detach the socially beneficial effects of virtuous behavior from the larger ideal of self-realization: Virtue, insofar as it is seen as a matter of public concern, is in this way of thinking something of instrumental rather than intrinsic value. This raises the question, as Rousseau never tired of pointing out, of whether a political system that treats self-regarding behavior as both the foundation and the end of social life can be relied on to generate the other-regarding norms of behavior on which the preservation of free government – and thus of juristic liberty itself – depends. As we have seen, Cato responds to this concern simply by exhorting his fellow citizens to be more virtuous, and this was – and indeed remains – a prominent strand of republican discourse.[19] However, a more innovative group of thinkers

---

[17] See especially Rousseau, *Social Contract*, book 1, chapters 6–8, as well as book 1, chapter 2 of the so-called *Geneva Manuscript*. My use of gendered language is considered, because Rousseau's is an exclusively male conception of citizenship.

[18] On the corrupting effects of commerce, see, for example, Rousseau, *Social Contract*, book 3, chapter 15 and *Considerations on the Government of Poland* §11. On the pedagogical dimensions of Rousseau's conception of citizenship, see, for example, Patrick Riley, *The General Will Before Rousseau: The Transformation of the Divine into the Civic* (Princeton, NJ: Princeton University Press, 1986), chapter 5, esp. pp. 243–8; on the problem of founding in Rousseau, see, for example, Bonnie Honig, "Between Decision and Deliberation," *American Political Science Review* 101 (2007), pp. 1–18.

[19] Among 18th-century thinkers, the bare appeal to classical virtue as a necessary supplement to commercial self-interest is perhaps most notably made by Adam Ferguson in his *Essay on the History of Civil Society* (1767). For two contemporary examples of such an appeal, made from different perspectives and for different purposes, see Michael J. Sandel, *Democracy's Discontent: America in Search of a Public Philosophy* (Cambridge, MA: Harvard University Press, 1996) and Richard Dagger, *Civic Virtues: Rights, Citizenship, and Republican Liberalism* (New York: Oxford University Press, 1997).

followed Rousseau in seeing a fundamental conflict between the self-regarding nature of life in a commercial society and the other-regarding demands of republican citizenship. They sought to show that juristic and republican freedom – the legitimate pursuit of self-interest and the effective checking of arbitrary power – can nevertheless be enjoyed within the same political order. We have already seen that these thinkers were able to forge a republican response to the rise of commerce by emphasizing the connection between the pursuit of commerce, the control of arbitrary power, and the preservation of national security and independence, and that in doing so they exposed the conceptual ambiguities in the republican conception of freedom. As we will now see, their efforts to resolve the tension between juristic and republican freedom led to a loosening of the connection not only between republican freedom and civic virtue, but also between juristic freedom and republican government itself.

Two of the more sophisticated efforts along these lines are found in the writings of Montesquieu and Hume, who, although they hold conflicting views on the question of how freedom is best preserved under modern conditions, nevertheless agree on the more fundamental question of what freedom itself consists in. Montesquieu argues that "[p]olitical liberty in a citizen is that tranquility of spirit which comes from the opinion each one has of his security," adding that "in order for him to have this liberty the government must be such that one citizen cannot fear another citizen." Liberty so understood, he concludes, "in no way consists in doing what one wants," but rather in "the right to do everything the laws permit." Hume argues along similar lines that a free government is one that "in the usual course of administration, must act by general and equal laws, that are previously known to all the members and to all their subjects," because "a legal authority, though great, has always some bounds, which terminate both the hopes and pretensions of the person possessed of it."[20] Thus Montesquieu and Hume agree with the classical republicans

---

[20] Montesquieu, *The Spirit of the Laws*, trans. Anne Cohler, Basia Miller, and Harold Stone (New York: Cambridge University Press, 1989 [1748]), pp. 157, 155 (book 11, chapters 6 and 3); Hume, "Of the Origin of Government" (1777), *Political Essays*, p. 23; "Whether the British Monarchy Inclines More to Absolute Monarchy, or to a Republic" (1741), ibid., p. 30. Ferguson agrees that "[w]here the citizen is supposed to have rights of property and of station, and is protected in the exercise of them, he is said to be free" and adds that "[n]o person is free, where any person is suffered to do wrong with impunity": *Essay on the History of Civil Society* (1767), ed. Fania Oz-Salzberger (New York: Cambridge University Press, 1995), p. 150 (part 3, section 6). Adam Smith, too, defines "the liberty of every individual" as "the sense which he has of his own security": *An Inquiry into the Nature and Causes of the Wealth of Nations* (Oxford: Clarendon Press, 1979 [1776]), V.i.b.25.

in associating freedom with the absence of arbitrary (extralegal) power held either by rulers or by private citizens. Like Locke, however, they raise doubts as to whether freedom so understood requires the existence of republican institutions. Part 1 of Montesquieu's *Spirit of the Laws* centers around the claim that, whereas monarchical and republican governments rest on different "principles" of behavior – the former on honor, the latter on virtue – both are nevertheless free in the sense that they are each subject to the rule of law and can be contrasted with despotism on those grounds. Hume puts the point more succinctly, arguing that "[i]t may now be affirmed of civilized monarchies, what was formerly said in praise of republics alone, *that they are a government of Laws, not of Men*."[21]

As I have suggested, however, Montesquieu and Hume do not agree on the question of how freedom is best preserved under modern conditions; indeed, they took opposite sides in the dispute between the "Country" and "Court" parties that divided British politics for much of the 18th century. Montesquieu, who from 1729 to 1731 stayed in England as a guest of Lord Bolingbroke, the leading figure in the Country opposition, includes a lengthy paean to English liberty in the eleventh book of his *Spirit of the Laws* that toes the Country line by attributing the genius of the English Constitution to its success in keeping the legislative, executive, and judicial powers distinct and independent of one another. Political liberty is found, he argues, "only in moderate governments," that is, in governments where "power...check[s] power by the arrangement of things." This claim provides the basis for his famous defense of the separation of powers: When legislative and executive power are united in the same hands, he argues, then "one can fear that the same monarch or senate that makes tyrannical laws will execute them tyrannically."[22]

---

[21] Montesquieu, *Spirit of the Laws*, books 2–3 passim; Hume, "Of Civil Liberty" (1741; originally "Of Liberty and Despotism"), *Political Essays*, p. 56 (original emphasis). Elsewhere Hume argues that the English government is "neither wholly monarchical, nor wholly republican" and adds that "the republican part of the government...is obliged, for its own preservation, to maintain a watchful *jealousy* over the magistrates, to remove all discretionary powers, and to secure every one's life and fortune by general and inflexible laws": "Of the Liberty of the Press" (1742), *Political Essays*, pp. 1–2 (original emphasis).

[22] Montesquieu, *Spirit of the Laws*, pp. 155, 157 (book 11, chapters 4 and 6). A more precise translation of the latter passage – and one that better captures the practical dynamics of arbitrary rule – would be to say that "one can fear that the same monarch or senate *would make* tyrannical laws *in order to execute them* tyrannically" (*ne fasse...pour les exécuter...*). For bibliographic evidence of Montesquieu's debt to Bolingbroke on this point, see Robert Shackleton, "Montesquieu, Bolingbroke, and the Separation of Powers," *French Studies* 3 (1949), pp. 25–38.

By contrast, a government in which these powers check one another will be resilient against what James Madison, a student of Montesquieu on this point, aptly termed "the defect of better motives."[23] As we have seen, Montesquieu, unlike Madison, holds that a monarchy can be free in this sense, but only if the power of the king is limited in such a way that he is constrained to obey and faithfully execute the laws of his kingdom. Whatever regime is in place, freedom depends on the countervailing presence of "intermediate powers": an independent legislature (such as the British Parliament), an independent judiciary (such as the French *parlements*, whose influence Montesquieu hoped to restore), and a hereditary nobility.[24]

Hume agrees with Montesquieu in thinking that republican government is not the only alternative to despotism under modern conditions: "Private property," he argues, "[is] almost as secure in a civilized EUROPEAN monarchy, as in a republic; nor is danger much apprehended in such a government, from the violence of the sovereign; more than we commonly dread harm from thunder, or earthquakes, or any accident the most unusual and extraordinary."[25] However, whereas Montesquieu follows the Country party in insisting on the need for a strict separation of legislative, executive, and judicial powers, Hume was perhaps the most influential defender of the Court view that the enhancement of executive power, and in particular the exercise of royal prerogative through the influence of the king's ministers in Parliament, was an appropriate and indeed necessary feature of public life in a commercial republic such as

---

[23] The quoted passage is from *Federalist* 51; for Madison's debt to Montesquieu on the question of the separation of powers, see especially *Federalist* 47. This is not to say that Madison, any more than Montesquieu, discounts the importance of virtue altogether: In *Federalist* 57 he argues that "[t]he aim of every political constitution is, or ought to be, first to obtain for rulers men who possess most wisdom to discern, and most virtue to pursue, the common good of the society; and in the next place, to take the most effectual precautions for keeping them virtuous whilst they continue to hold their public trust," and he warned the delegates to the Virginia ratifying convention on June 20, 1788, that "[t]o suppose that any form of government will secure liberty or happiness without any virtue in the people, is a chimerical idea."

[24] See, for example, Montesquieu, *Spirit of the Laws*, book 2, chapter 4; book 5, chapter 11; book 8, chapter 6.

[25] Hume, "Of Civil Liberty," p. 55. Hume goes on to argue that "[a]varice, the spur of industry, is so obstinate a passion, and works its way through so many real dangers and difficulties, that it is not likely to be scared by an imaginary danger, which is so small, that it scarcely admits of calculation": ibid. Montesquieu argues, by contrast, that "public business is for the most part as suspect to the merchants in monarchies as it appears safe to them in republican states," so that "great commercial enterprises are not for monarchies, but for the government by many": *Spirit of the Laws*, p. 340 (book 20, chapter 4).

England had become.[26] Thus although he endorses the traditional republican claim that mixed government is favorable to liberty,[27] he nevertheless downplays the differences between the liberties that are enjoyed in England and in France, the latter of which he describes as "the most perfect model of pure monarchy." He even goes so far as to suggest that the French should look not to constitutional checks, but rather to the interests of the monarch himself to curb the arbitrary power of the state: "If a prince or minister...should arise, endowed with sufficient discernment to know his own and the public interest, and with sufficient force of mind to break through ancient customs, we might expect to see these abuses remedied; in which case, the difference between that absolute government and our free one, would not appear so considerable as at present." Indeed, the close connection between the interests of the monarch and those of his subjects – and the tendency of republics to take on unsustainable levels of public debt – led Hume to conclude that "though all kinds of government be improved in modern times, yet monarchical government seems to have made the greatest advances towards perfection."[28]

Whatever their differences – and they are on the whole differences of judgment rather than principle – Montesquieu and Hume agree in

[26] See especially Hume, "Of the Independency of Parliament" (1741), *Political Essays*, pp. 24–7, and "Whether the British Government Inclines More to Absolute Monarchy, or to a Republic." Elsewhere Hume argues that the pervasive corruption in British political life "is chiefly to be ascribed to our established liberty, when our princes have found the impossibility of governing without parliaments, or of terrifying parliaments by the phantom of prerogative": "Of Refinement in the Arts" (1752; originally "Of Luxury"), *Political Essays*, p. 111.

[27] "When there offers, therefore, to our censure and examination, any plan of government, real or imaginary, where the power is distributed among several courts, and several orders of men, we should always consider the separate interest of each court, and each order; and, if we find, that, by the skilful division of power, this interest must necessarily, in its operation, concur with public, we may pronounce that government to be wise and happy. If, on the contrary, separate interest be not checked, and be not directed to the public, we ought to look for nothing but faction, disorder, and tyranny from such a government. In this opinion I am justified by experience, as well as by the authority of all philosophers and politicians, both ancient and modern": "Of the Independency of Parliament," p. 25.

[28] Hume, "Of Civil Liberty," pp. 56–7. Montesquieu expresses agreement on this point in an early *pensée*, writing that "[t]he sole advantage that a free people has over any other, is the security in which each person lives that the caprice of a single man cannot deprive him of his goods or his life," and adding that "[t]hat security is no greater in England than in France, and...was hardly greater in several ancient Greek republics which were divided into two factions": *Pensée* 1802 (1728), translated and cited in Nannerl O. Keohane, "Virtuous Republics and Glorious Monarchies: Two Models in Montesquieu's Political Thought," *Political Studies* 20 (1972), p. 392. Cf. also *Spirit of the Laws*, book 12, chapter 1.

thinking that civic virtue in the classical sense is not necessary for the preservation of political liberty, and they attribute the absence of this kind of virtue in the modern world to the rise of commerce. Montesquieu observes, for example, that where "[t]he political men of Greece who lived under popular government recognized no other force to sustain it than virtue…[t]hose of today speak to us only of manufacturing, commerce, finance, wealth, and even luxury."[29] Hume agrees that the classical ideal of civic virtue is "too disinterested and too difficult to support" under modern conditions, so that "it is requisite to govern men by other passions, and animate them with a spirit of avarice and industry, art and luxury."[30] To the extent that virtue has a role to play in modern political life, they argue, its content is defined not by the degree and quality of one's involvement in public life, but rather by the extent to which one respects the juristic liberties and, in particular, the property of one's fellow citizens. "The spirit of commerce," as Montesquieu puts it, "produces in men a certain feeling for exact justice, opposed on the one hand to banditry and on the other to those moral virtues that make it so that one does not always discuss one's own interests alone and that one can neglect them for those of others."[31] Hume goes so far as to argue that a "civilized" commercial society is likely to produce better citizens than the "barbarous" polities of antiquity, prosperous enough to resent and resist the intrusions of arbitrary power, but also prosperous enough to realize that they have something to lose from political instability and agitation: "[They] submit not to slavery, like the peasants, from poverty and meanness of spirit; and having no hopes of tyrannizing over others, like

---

[29] Montesquieu, *Spirit of the Laws*, p. 22 (book 3, chapter 3). This remark is closely paraphrased by Rousseau, who notes disapprovingly that "[t]he ancient politicians forever spoke of morals and of virtue; ours speak only of commerce and of money": *Discourse on the Arts and Sciences* (1750), part 2, in idem, *The Discourses and Other Early Political Writings*, trans. and ed. Victor Gourevitch (New York: Cambridge University Press, 1997), p. 18. Montesquieu later makes the striking observation that where "[o]ther nations have made commercial interests give way to political interests: England has always made its political interests give way to the interests of its commerce": *Spirit of the Laws*, p. 343 (book 20, chapter 7).

[30] Hume, "Of Commerce" (1752), *Political Writings*, p. 100. Cf. Locke, whose unpublished note on "Labour" (1693) betrays a lingering and decidedly un-Humean prejudice against luxury: "Would [governments] suppress the arts and instruments of luxury and vanity and bring those of honest and useful industry in fashion," he argues, then "[t]he populace…would not be so easy to be blown into tumults and popular commotions by the breath and artifice of designing or discontented grandees": "Labour," in *Political Essays*, ed. Mark Goldie (New York: Cambridge University Press, 1997), p. 328.

[31] Montesquieu, *Spirit of the Laws*, p. 339 (book 20, chapter 2); cf. Smith, *Lectures on Jurisprudence* (Oxford: Clarendon Press, 1978) (B) 327 (1766).

the barons, they are not tempted, for the sake of that gratification, to submit to the tyranny of their sovereign"; as a result, "[f]actions are...less inveterate, revolutions less tragical, authority less severe, and seditions less frequent." Hume concludes that commerce, far from being incompatible with the enjoyment of freedom, "is rather favourable to liberty, and has a natural tendency to preserve, if not produce a free government."[32]

Not all of the defenders of commercial society were so confident that it would "naturally" generate the habits of thought and action that are necessary for its preservation. Hume's friend Adam Smith points out, for example, that although "the interest of the labourer is strictly connected with that of the society, he is incapable either of comprehending that interest, or of understanding its connection with his own," because "[h]is condition leaves him no time to receive the necessary information, and his education and habits are commonly such as to render him unfit to judge even though he was fully informed." The mercantile and manufacturing classes, by contrast, "have generally an interest to deceive and even to oppress the public, and...accordingly have, upon many occasions, both deceived and oppressed it." Smith adds that the opinions of the laborer may be heard "upon some particular occasions," but only "when his clamour is animated, set on, and supported by his employers, not for his, but their own particular purposes."[33] Indeed, he warns that if left to run its course, "the progress of the division of labour" – which is, of course, inextricably bound up with economic progress – will render "the great body of the people...as stupid and ignorant as it is possible for a human creature to become...altogether incapable of judging...the great and extensive interests of [their] country."[34]

Smith concludes that it is the duty of the state to see that its citizens are educated in such a way that they are able to perform their duties as citizens. However, like Hume and unlike Rousseau, he holds that the aim of civic education is not to make it possible for the people to play an active

---

[32] Hume, "Of Refinement in the Arts," pp. 112, 109, 111. Hume is echoing and perhaps alluding here to Aristotle's claim that the "best constitution...for the majority of cities and the majority of mankind" is one in which "there is a large middle class": *Politics*, book 4, chapter 11, quoting R. F. Stalley's revision of the Barker translation (New York: Oxford University Press, 1995 [1946]), pp. 157, 159. Aristotle, unlike Hume, does not provide any suggestions as to how a large middle class might be created, counting it simply as "the greatest of blessings" if one is present: ibid., p. 159.

[33] Smith, *Wealth of Nations* I.xi.p.9–10.

[34] Ibid., V.i.f.49–50; I have changed the order in which these passages appear in the text. Cf. Smith, *Lectures on Jurisprudence* (B) 329–30.

role in government, but rather to prevent them from interfering unduly with its just administration:

> An instructed and intelligent people are always more decent and orderly than an ignorant and stupid one. They feel themselves, each individually, more respectable, and more likely to obtain the respect of their lawful superiors, and they are therefore more disposed to respect those superiors. They are more disposed to examine, and more capable of seeing through, the interested complaints of faction and sedition, and they are, upon that account, less apt to be misled into any wanton or unnecessary opposition to the measures of government.[35]

This line of argument is stated even more strongly by Adam Ferguson, who, writing anonymously against American independence, argues that "the essence of political Liberty is such an establishment as gives power to the wise, and safety to all," adding that "popular Assemblies" represent "a power, which is of all others the most unstable, capricious, and arbitrary: bound by no law, and subject to no appeal." Ferguson concludes, with Montesquieu, Hume, and Smith, that "Democracy and Aristocracy are...inferior in this respect to certain species of monarchy, where law is more fixed and the abuses of power are better restrained."[36]

The disagreement between Smith and Hume about the effects of commerce on individual virtue, like the corresponding disagreement between Montesquieu and Hume about the relative merits of monarchical and mixed government, should not obscure the fact that each of these thinkers agrees with Cato in treating virtue, insofar as it is a matter of public concern, as a means to the preservation of juristic liberty rather than as an end in itself (Ferguson's is a more complicated case[37]). By distancing themselves from the classical association of virtue with the fulfillment of human personality, these thinkers raise the question of what kind of virtue promotes the enjoyment of freedom as they understand it and of whether commercial society tends to cultivate, or at least not to corrupt, virtue so understood. They respond, as we have seen, by arguing that the

---

[35] Smith, *Wealth of Nations* V.i.f.61.

[36] Ferguson, *Remarks on a Pamphlet Lately Published by Dr. Price*...(London: T. Cadell, 1776), pp. 8–9. Ferguson is responding to Richard Price's enormously influential *Observations on the Nature of Civil Liberty, the Principles of Government, and the Justice and Policy of the War with America* (1776).

[37] For a useful discussion of Ferguson's treatment of virtue, see David Kettler, *The Social and Political Thought of Adam Ferguson* (Columbus: Ohio State University Press, 1965), chapters 6–7.

virtuous citizen is one who is, as Smith puts it, "decent and orderly," that is, who refrains from interfering not only in the private affairs of others, but in the affairs of the government itself as long as it is duly protecting the rights of its citizens.[38] This line of argument represents a substantial departure from the premises of classical republican thought; indeed, we are not far here from Locke's definition of liberty itself as a kind of property. However, as we will now see, these thinkers do not rest the defense of juristic liberty, as Locke does, on an appeal to divine purposes; rather they rest it on an appeal to the good of society as a whole. They thereby raise a series of questions about the relationship between individual and collective interests that are no less pregnant with implications for the relationship between republican and juristic freedom.

4.4. "NONSENSE UPON STILTS"

We have seen that the 18th-century defenders of commercial society developed a way of talking about freedom that was a genuine synthesis of republican and juristic ideas, combining the negative republican view that freedom depends on the enjoyment of personal security within a legally defined sphere and the negative juristic view that freedom consists in the exercise of discretionary choice within that sphere. What distinguishes these thinkers most clearly from their more traditional predecessors and contemporaries is their belief that the classical republican ideal of virtuous citizenship is no longer viable in the modern world. From this premise they drew the natural conclusion that the question of whether the practice of virtue is a necessary condition for the enjoyment of freedom – and the question of what virtue itself consists in – should be fundamentally rethought. In particular, they turned away from the classical association of virtue with active citizenship and devotion to the common good, focusing instead on the qualities of diligence and prudence that are necessary for success in a commercial society, and on the norms of deference to the laws and to the legally established authorities that

[38] The logic of this position is brought out nicely by Hirschman, who points out that "there is another side to the insight that the modern economy, its complex interdependence and growth constitute so delicate a mechanism that the *grands coups d'autorité* of despotic government become impossible. If it is true *that the economy must be deferred to*, then there is a case not only for constraining the imprudent actions of the prince but for repressing those of the people, for limiting participation, in short, for crushing anything that could be interpreted by some economist-king as a threat to the proper functioning of the 'delicate watch'": *The Passions and the Interests*, p. 124 (original emphasis).

are necessary for the orderly management of such a society. Although these thinkers agree on the importance of cultivating virtue in this rather limited sense, their views on the desirability of maintaining a republican form of government are rather mixed. Indeed, republican ideas play a distinctly subordinate role in this way of thinking, providing at most a statement of the necessary means for achieving the more fundamental end of protecting juristic liberty, and serving at times as little more than a set of rhetorical tropes for warning about the dangers of greed, envy, and factionalism.

This position has obvious ideological advantages: If commerce leads citizens away from the public sphere, it also complicates and deepens their private ties to one another, and to many 18th-century thinkers – and, no doubt, to many ordinary people – this seemed a trade-off well worth making.[39] However, this depoliticized conception of public life also has certain ideological vulnerabilities. In particular, the 18th-century defenders of commercial society had to confront more squarely than their predecessors the question of how the existence of individual rights, and especially of rights to property, can be defended. Here, the juristic and republican traditions begin to pull once again in opposite directions. From a juristic standpoint the obligation to respect individual rights is ultimately derived from the obligation that we each have under natural law to preserve the human species and to be good stewards of the creation that we have been given in common. The challenge in this way of thinking is to ensure that human beings, corrupt and fallible as they are, are nevertheless compelled to respect the rights of their fellows. The solution is to empower a central authority – a sovereign or state – to enforce them. From a republican standpoint, by contrast, the secure enjoyment of individual rights is a necessary condition for the existence of a vibrant public sphere: Rights protect citizens from the arbitrary exercise of power, thereby making it possible for them to cultivate their virtue and to pursue the common good as they see it. It follows that rights must be politically actionable; that is, their enjoyment must depend not on the good will of a benevolent ruler, but rather on the vigilance of the citizens themselves.

---

[39] As Pocock puts it, "if [the individual] could no longer engage directly in the activity and equality of ruling and being ruled…he was more than compensated for his loss of antique virtue by an indefinite and perhaps infinite enrichment of his personality, the product of the multiplying relationships, with both things and persons, in which he became progressively involved": "Virtues, Rights, and Manners: A Model for Historians of Political Thought," in idem, *Virtue, Commerce, and History: Essays on Political Thought and History* (New York: Cambridge University Press, 1985), p. 49.

As we have seen, elements of each of these positions are brought together in Locke, who argues that the legitimacy of political rule depends on the consent of those who are subject to it, and that freedom consists in obedience to no other political authority than the one to which we have consented. We have also seen that, despite the republican overtones of his argument, Locke conceives of consent in de jure rather than de facto terms: It can be improperly given, as when an individual or group consents to their own enslavement, and improperly withheld, as when an individual or group disobeys, resists, or seeks to overthrow a government that is in fact ruling justly.[40] This raises the question of how the appeal to a natural standard of justice can be reconciled with the claim that the authority to decide whether that standard has been met should be placed in the hands of the people themselves, and indeed of each person taken singly.[41] After all, as Locke himself was well aware, we often disagree about what our natural rights to life, liberty, and property entail, and thus about when they have been violated in a given case. This line of argument led Hume to conclude that the appeal to an "original contract" has anarchic implications: "[N]othing is a clearer proof," he argues, "that a theory of this kind is erroneous, than to find, that it leads to paradoxes, repugnant to the common sentiments of mankind, and to the practice and opinion of all nations and all ages." Jeremy Bentham, writing in the wake of the French Revolution, put the point even more sharply, accusing the defenders of natural rights of promoting a view that was not only "dangerous nonsense," but "rhetorical nonsense – nonsense upon stilts."[42]

Needless to say, these thinkers did not reject the idea of individual rights altogether; rather, they sought to justify their existence and define their scope by appealing to the good of society rather than to the purposes of God or the consent, counterfactual or otherwise, of the individuals concerned. Hume argues, for example, that we are obliged to observe "the natural duties of justice and fidelity" not because "we have given a tacit promise to that purpose," but rather because "the commerce and intercourse of mankind, which are of such mighty advantage, can have no security where men pay no regard to their engagements." Bentham

---

[40] On the illegitimacy of "voluntary" slavery, see especially Locke, *Second Treatise* §§23–4; on the illegitimacy of resisting a just government, see ibid., §§226, 230.

[41] As Locke puts it, "where the Body of the People, *or any single Man*, is deprived of their Right, or is under the Exercise of a power without right, and have no Appeal on Earth, there they have a liberty to appeal to Heaven, whenever they judge the Cause of sufficient moment": ibid., §168 (emphasis added).

[42] Hume, "Of the Original Contract," p. 200; Jeremy Bentham, "Anarchical Fallacies" (c. 1796), article 2, sentence 1.

argues along similar lines that just as "there is no right, which ought not to be maintained so long as it is upon the whole advantageous to the society that it should be maintained, so there is no right which, when the abolition of it is advantageous to society, should not be abolished." "[T]he exercise of the rights allowed to and conferred upon each individual," he concludes, "ought to have no other bounds set to it by the law, than those which are necessary to enable it to maintain every other individual in the possession and exercise of such rights as...is consistent with the greatest good of the community." Even Edmund Burke, who was hardly a Benthamite in his political views, holds that "[i]f civil society be made for the advantage of man, all advantages for which it is made become his right," and, conversely, that "[t]he rights of men in governments are their advantages."[43]

By resting the defense of individual rights on considerations of social utility rather than on the consent of the governed, Hume, Bentham, Burke, and like-minded thinkers[44] sought to avoid the seemingly anarchic implications of a position that combines, as Locke's does, a juristic appeal to natural liberty with a quasi-republican appeal to popular sovereignty. However, if these thinkers sought to limit the grounds on which something can be regarded as a right, the rise of commerce dramatically expanded the grounds on which something can be regarded as property – the most conspicuous, and most conspicuously Lockean, example being the "property" that individuals were now said to have in their own labor. Indeed, as real property was increasingly displaced by or convertible into mobile property, it became possible and even customary to take the very fact that something can be exchanged for something else of value as grounds for treating it as property. Moreover, as J. G. A. Pocock observes, "defining something as property was becoming hard to distinguish from defining it as commodity," and thus as something that its owner had the right to alienate – to sell – at will.[45] Rights to possession therefore became

---

[43] Hume, "Of the Original Contract," p. 196; Bentham, "Anarchical Fallacies," article 2, sentence 1; article 4, proposition 3 (emphasis removed); Edmund Burke, *Reflections on the Revolution in France* (1790), ed. J. G. A. Pocock (Indianapolis: Hackett, 1987), pp. 51, 54.

[44] See, for example, William Paley's *Principles of Moral and Political Philosophy* (1785), book 6, chapter 3, which repeats Hume's critique of contractarianism (adding a distinctly non-Humean theological twist), and which served as a leading textbook on the subject through the middle of the 19th century.

[45] J. G. A. Pocock, "The Political Limits to Premodern Economics," in John Dunn, ed., *The Economic Limits to Modern Politics* (New York: Cambridge University Press, 1990), pp. 124–5.

hard to distinguish from rights to exchange: If to sell one's property (or one's labor) is to lose one's freedom in the classical republican sense, to be prevented from doing so is to be prevented from exercising one's freedom in this new, commercial sense.

Instead of being seen as the stable foundation of human personality, property was now seen in dynamic terms as something to be used or traded according to the interests of the individuals concerned. This commercialized conception of the relationship between property and consent turns Locke's position on its head: Rather than serving as a counterfactual condition for the legitimacy of political rule, consent is now treated as a constitutive feature of social life, an activity in which individuals are continuously engaged as they pursue their interests by making voluntary exchanges in the marketplace. In other words, if the juristic appeal to natural rights was (and is) intended to limit the discretionary power of individuals in the public sphere, with the rise of commerce it also came to stand for the idea that an entire social order could – and should – be built out of the consensual actions of individuals in the private sphere. Thus Keith Michael Baker points out, for example, that in the writings of Abbé Sieyès (1748–1836), "the notion of the social contract is generalised into the principle of constant exchange underlying the logic of the division of labour and the progress of society towards greater complexity. In this idiom, freedom is not secured against domination by a single contractual act; instead it is indefinitely extended by a constantly proliferating system of contracts/exchanges generating an ever-increasing satisfaction of human needs." Joyce Appleby finds a similar development in 18th-century Anglo-American thought more generally: "A hundred years earlier [*viz.*, in the 17th century] ... people spoke of the state of nature, a predicament, and civil society, a solution. A century and a quarter of economic development had dramatically enhanced public opinion about voluntary human actions, and society was the word that emerged to represent the uncoerced relations of people living under the same authority."[46]

---

[46] Keith Michael Baker, "Political Languages of the French Revolution," in Mark Goldie and Robert Wokler, eds., *The Cambridge History of Eighteenth-Century Political Thought* (New York: Cambridge University Press, 2006), pp 639–40; Joyce Appleby, *Capitalism and a New Social Order: The Republican Vision of the 1790s* (New York: NYU Press, 1984), p. 23. Baker points out that "Sieyès's early ideas were shaped by an extended confrontation with Quesnay and the physiocrats, on the one hand, and with Adam Smith and the Scottish school on the other": *Inventing the French Revolution: Essays on French Political Culture in the Eighteenth Century* (New York: Cambridge University Press, 1990), p. 245.

The canonical statement of this line of argument is found not in Locke, but rather in Smith's "obvious and simple system of natural liberty," in which "[e]very man, as long as he does not violate the laws of justice, is left perfectly free to pursue his own interest his own way, and to bring both his industry and capital into competition with those of any other man, or order of men," and in which the duties of the state are limited to protecting its citizens against external enemies, securing the necessary conditions for just and orderly exchange, and providing those public goods "which it can never be for the interest of any individual, or small number of individuals, to erect and maintain." The aim of this "obvious and simple system" is to approximate as closely as possible what Smith refers to elsewhere as a condition of "perfect" liberty, one in which each person is free to offer their goods – including their labor – for sale at a price of their own choosing, to buy or not buy goods at a given price, and to choose and change occupations as they please. When perfect liberty obtains, Smith argues, the market price of commodities will tend to converge to their "natural price" – that is, the cost of bringing them to market plus what he refers to as the "ordinary rate of profit" – and an efficient allocation of resources will be achieved as productive resources are brought into and out of play in response to changes in effective demand. This is, he concludes, the only way to ensure "the progress of the society towards real wealth and greatness" by "increasing the real value of the annual produce of its land and labour."[47]

Smith, like the other defenders of commercial society, rests his defense of perfect liberty squarely on the empirical claim that the best way to advance the well-being of society is to allow individuals to dispose of their property as they please. However, his defense of individual rights, unlike Hume's and Bentham's, does not rest solely on considerations of social utility. "[W]hen a single man is injured," he argues, "we demand the punishment of the wrong that has been done to him, not so much from a concern for the general interest of society, as from a concern for that very individual." Smith defines "injury" as harm, first, to "that which we are possessed of," and second, to that of which "we have only the

---

[47] Smith, *Wealth of Nations* IV.ix.50–1; on "perfect" liberty, see in particular I.vii.6, 30; I.x.a.1. Smith is careful to emphasize that this is an ideal: "If a nation could not prosper without the enjoyment of perfect liberty and perfect justice, there is not in the world a nation which could ever have prospered. In the political body, however, the wisdom of nature has fortunately made ample provision for remedying many of the bad effects of the folly and injustice of man; in the same manner as it has done in the natural body, for remedying those of his sloth and intemperance": ibid., IV.ix.28.

expectation" because of agreements that we have entered into. "The most sacred laws of justice," he concludes, "are the laws which guard the life and person of our neighbour; the next are those which guard his property and possessions; and last of all come those which guard what are called his personal rights, or what is due to him from the promises of others."[48] For Smith, as for later market theorists, the distribution of property in a given society is not just because it is socially optimal, but rather because it is the product of voluntary exchanges on the part of the individuals concerned. He therefore takes the Lockean claim that "[t]he property which every man has in his own labour, as it is the original foundation of all other property, so it is the most sacred and inviolable" to mean that government interference in the labor *market* is "a manifest encroachment upon the just liberty both of the workman, and of those who might be disposed to employ him." Indeed, this principle of non-interference applies in Smith's view to the operation of any market whatsoever: "[t]o prohibit a great people...from making all that they can of every part of their own produce, or from employing their stock and industry in the way that they judge most advantageous to themselves," he argues, "is a manifest violation of the most sacred rights of mankind."[49]

Here again we have a synthesis of the commercial republican claim that rights to property and exchange should be respected as a matter of social utility and the juristic claim that they should be respected as a

---

[48] Smith, *The Theory of Moral Sentiments* (Oxford: Clarendon Press, 1976 [1759/1790]) II.ii.3.10, II.ii.2.2; cf. Hume, *An Enquiry Concerning the Principles of Morals*, chapter 3 and Bentham, *An Introduction to the Principles of Morals and Legislation*, chapter 1. On the derivation of "personal rights" from "contract," see also Smith, *Lectures on Jurisprudence* (A) ii.42 (1762–3). Smith's unfinished book on jurisprudence was notoriously destroyed after his death, and there is some question as to whether he succeeds in deriving a coherent theory of justice from his sentimentalist theory of moral judgment – and if so, what that theory is. My argument here does not rest on any particular answer to that question. For a useful discussion, see Knud Haakonssen, *The Science of a Legislator: The Natural Jurisprudence of David Hume and Adam Smith* (New York: Cambridge University Press, 1981), chapter 4, and more recently Michael L. Frazer, *The Enlightenment of Sympathy: Justice and the Moral Sentiments in the Eighteenth Century and Today* (New York: Oxford University Press, 2010), chapter 4.

[49] Ibid., I.x.c.12; IV.vii.b.44. Smith is referring in the former passage to the laws regulating apprenticeships, and in the latter to the British treatment of the American colonists. On the fallacy of attributing to Locke a full-blown defense of a free market in labor, see, for example, E. J. Hundert, "Market Society and Meaning in Locke's Political Philosophy," *Journal of the History of Philosophy* 15 (1977), pp. 33–44, which seeks to rebut C. B. Macpherson's influential claim that Locke provides "a moral foundation for bourgeois appropriation": *The Political Theory of Possessive Individualism: Hobbes to Locke* (New York: Oxford University Press, 1962), quoted at p. 221.

matter of justice. The tension between these positions is finessed in Smith, as it is in market ideology more generally, by the empirical claim that it is precisely the policy of justice that leads to the greatest welfare of society as a whole. The definition of liberty that he appeals to in making this line of argument resembles Hobbes's conceptually pioneering but politically stillborn effort to define the "liberty of subjects" in purely negative terms. However, where Hobbes sought to neutralize the appeal to the language of liberty on the part of political subjects, Smith makes the absence of restrictions on voluntary exchange a leading measure of the legitimacy of political rule. In his hands the synthesis of commercial republican and juristic ideas takes an explicitly market-centered form: The proper aim of a system of law is not simply to ensure that human behavior is kept within the bounds of justice, but to facilitate the efficient exchange of goods and services by maximizing the amount of natural liberty that is enjoyed by each individual. Freedom so understood consists in, rather than simply being realized through, the pursuit of individual interests in the marketplace. It is associated on the one hand with the impersonal operation of a decentralized and largely anonymous mechanism for determining social outcomes – the "invisible hand" of the market – and on the other hand with the right of individuals to exercise their natural liberty within the legal and material constraints that are defined by that mechanism. This is, of course, the market conception of freedom with which we are now familiar.

4.5. MARKET FREEDOM

I hope to have shown that the empirical and conceptual objections to which the Lockean doctrine of government by consent was subject brought it into contact with commercial republicanism, another newly emerging ideological position with seemingly anarchic implications. Each of these schools of thought sought to resolve a long-standing tension in the republican conception of freedom: the commercial republicans by favoring an instrumental over an intrinsic conception of the value of virtue, and the Lockean liberals by favoring a substantive over a procedural conception of the nature of arbitrary power. And each has certain ideological advantages taken on its own: The Lockean appeal to natural rights offers a clearer set of criteria for identifying the presence of arbitrary power than the classical republicans had been able to provide, and the commercial republican appeal to the incentives that states have to promote the commercial activities of their citizens offers a means of checking arbitrary power that was more robust and less demanding than the classical republican appeal to civic virtue. However, each of these positions also suffers from a corresponding ideological vulnerability. The Lockean view that the legitimacy of political rule rests on the consent of the governed, and that consent can only legitimately be given to governments that respect the natural rights of their subjects, raises the question of how individuals and governments can be constrained to respect those rights in practice. After all, government is necessary in Locke's view precisely because we often disagree about what our natural rights entail, and the threat that consent might be withdrawn and revolution undertaken can only be invoked, as he admits, in exceptional cases. Similarly, the commercial republican view that self-interested behavior can have collectively beneficial consequences raises the question of whether the habits of thought and action that are generated by a commercial society are compatible with the traditional republican aim of creating the conditions under which individuals can cultivate and display their virtue.

The Lockean claim that the "Industrious and Rational" have a natural right, and indeed a God-given duty, to "improve" the earth through their labor[50] made it possible for the 18th-century defenders of commercial society to tie their position to something loftier than the pursuit of wealth and luxury, and to portray the abuse of political power as something more than a matter of inefficient administration. They were therefore better able than their 16th- and 17th-century predecessors had been to respond to the accusation that the rise of commerce has made citizenship into a purely mercenary proposition and the citizen into little more than an anonymous cog in a larger economic machine. Indeed, the claim that we each have a sacred right to life, liberty, and property and a corresponding duty to provide for our own well-being proved to be more than a match rhetorically speaking for the traditional republican appeal to civic virtue and the common good. For their part, the commercial republicans provided the Lockeans with a conception of resistance to arbitrary power that extended beyond mere consent, tacit or otherwise, to political rule into the day-to-day world of commercial transactions. The project of securing justice was therefore not restricted to those exceptional, revolutionary moments of crisis in which the very legitimacy of political rule is called into question. As the idea of a social order built out of individual acts of consent came to occupy a central place in the theoretical imagination of the 18th century, the idea of a political order based on the

50 Locke, *Second Treatise* §34.

same principles began to seem less mysterious and radical than it had in the original Lockean formulation. After all, not only do we consent to commercial transactions all the time, but we each have an interest in seeing that the commercial realm continues to function in an orderly way. Indeed, the supposed efficacy of the market in generating wealth for all people made it possible for the defenders of market freedom to sweep aside the moral restrictions that natural jurists, including Locke, had placed on market activity since at least the time of Thomas Aquinas.[51]

Thus, as I suggested at the beginning of this chapter, the most striking feature of the 18th-century debates about the meaning and value of freedom is not the existence of a conflict between liberals and republicans, but rather the weaving together of two distinct theories of freedom – each of which emerged, as we have seen, out of a much older tradition of thought – into a new and predominantly market-centered view. According to this way of thinking, the proper aim of government is not, as in classical republicanism, simply to enact the will of a virtuous citizenry as filtered through a properly designed set of political institutions, or, as in Lockean liberalism, simply to protect the natural rights of its citizens. Rather, the aim is to ensure the smooth functioning of commerce by allowing individuals to dispose of their property – including the property that they have in their labor – as they see fit, thereby advancing the security and prosperity of the polity as a whole. Whereas the classical republicans saw the subordination of economic to political concerns as a necessary condition for the enjoyment of freedom, the cause of freedom and that of commerce were now said to be closely linked. Whereas the classical republicans sought to subordinate individual interests to the common good, the defenders of market freedom, despite (or because of?) their professed belief in the ultimate harmony between individual and collective interests, placed the ever-present possibility of conflict between the individual and the state at the center of attention and described it as a conflict in which freedom itself was at stake.

The defenders of market freedom did not abandon the commercial republican claim that markets, as the most efficient means of generating and distributing wealth, are socially beneficial; they simply added the claim that markets are to be valued because they provide the greatest

---

[51] See, for example, Istvan Hont and Michael Ignatieff, "Needs and Justice in the *Wealth of Nations*: An Introductory Essay," in idem, eds., *Wealth and Virtue: The Shaping of Political Economy in the Scottish Enlightenment* (New York: Cambridge University Press, 1983), pp. 1–44.

scope for the exercise of individual liberty. The defense of market freedom, and of market society more generally, has always consisted in a somewhat unstable amalgam of these two lines of argument:[52] Markets are favored on the one hand because they promote what Smith calls the "real wealth and greatness" of society, and when counter-arguments are advanced against this claim they are rejected, usually through an appeal to anti-paternalism, on the grounds that even socially beneficial interference with markets infringes on what Smith calls the "just liberty" of the individual.[53] The resilience of the market conception of freedom, like the resilience of the republican conception that it displaced, is due in large part to its ability to hold these two ways of thinking – one individual and personal, the other collective and impersonal – in fruitful tension with each other. Indeed, there is a sense in which these two lines of argument reinforce each other: Whether we believe that the exercise of individual liberty in the marketplace provides the best means of advancing the interests of society as a whole, or that the expansion of individual liberty is itself the end that we should pursue in public life, we are assured in either case that by attending to our own interests without conscious regard for the common good, we are meeting our social obligations in the most efficient possible way. This is an enormously liberating point of view: a vision of a world that, once the right rules are in place, runs by itself. The effort to bring such a world into being has always been one of the central aims of market ideology, from the *ordre naturel* of the Physiocrats (to whose founder, François Quesnay, Smith intended to dedicate his *Wealth of Nations*) to the "self-regulating market" of

---

[52] A similar observation is made by John Dunn, who points out that "the conception of the bourgeois liberal republic is a precarious fusion of the two very different modern idioms of ethical thought – deontological theories ascribing rights to all human beings in virtue of their humanity (or perhaps more narrowly to all human agents in virtue of their agency), and consequentialist theories assessing the distribution of utilities or preferences, or more broadly, welfare outcomes, and deeply preoccupied, accordingly, with questions of social, political and economic causation": "The Identity of the Bourgeois Liberal Republic," in Biancamaria Fontana, ed., *The Invention of the Modern Republic* (New York: Cambridge University Press, 1994), quoted at p. 219.

[53] The delicate balance between the claims of justice and utility in Smith's economic thought is brought out especially clearly in his defense of free trade in grain, where he argues that "[t]o hinder...the farmer from sending his goods at all times to the best market, is evidently to sacrifice the ordinary laws of justice to an idea of publick utility, to a sort of reasons [sic] of state; an act of legislative authority which ought to be exercised only, which can be pardoned only in cases of the most urgent necessity": ibid., IV.v.b.39. On Smith's involvement in the 18th-century Corn Law debates, see Emma Rothschild, *Economic Sentiments: Adam Smith, Condorcet, and the Enlightenment* (Cambridge, MA: Harvard University Press, 2001), chapter 3.

19th-century laissez-faire to the "spontaneous order" of Friedrich Hayek and the Austrian school.[54]

I began this book by suggesting that much of the appeal of market freedom can be traced to the fact that it aims at the removal of constraint as such, thus allowing the partisan of freedom to bracket disagreements about the proper ends of public life from discussions about freedom itself. We can now see how this way of thinking, seemingly incoherent though it is, fits hand-in-glove with the norms and practices of market societies: In such societies individuals are not only absolved of responsibility for consciously pursuing the common good (which is said to be realized, if at all, through the unhindered operation of the market), they are encouraged to think of their own sphere of free action in purely individualistic terms, as one that the state is obliged to respect as a matter of right. Constraints on individual choice therefore appear as a loss of freedom *tout court*, to be defended by appealing not to a broader conception of freedom as participation in a free man's ethos or obedience to natural law, but rather to the competing presence of a qualitatively different – and, often enough, presumptively inferior – value. Instead of serving as a shorthand for an entire way of life, which combines under one heading a pattern of social relationships and a standard of individual behavior, freedom becomes a particular value that has to be traded off against other values in public life.[55] It is this way of thinking that makes it possible for Isaiah Berlin to

[54] For a useful compendium of Quesnay's writings and an analysis of Physiocratic thought more generally, see Ronald L. Meek, *The Economics of Physiocracy: Essays and Translations* (Cambridge, MA: Harvard University Press, 1963). Smith's intention to dedicate the *Wealth of Nations* to Quesnay prior to the latter's death is reported in Dugald Stewart's "Account of the Life and Writings of Adam Smith, LL.D." (1794); see Smith, *Essays on Philosophical Subjects*, ed. W. P. D. Wightman and J. C. Bryce (Oxford: Clarendon Press, 1980), p. 304. For a seminal analysis of the emergence and influence of the idea of the "self-regulating market" in the 19th century, see Karl Polanyi, *The Great Transformation: The Political and Economic Origins of Our Time* (Boston: Beacon Press, 1944). On the idea of spontaneous order or "catallaxy," see especially Hayek's *Law, Legislation and Liberty* (Chicago: University of Chicago Press, 1973–9). Hayek himself credits the idea that social order can be "the result of human action but not of human design" to Adam Ferguson, although Ferguson puts the idea to somewhat different use: see ibid., vol. 1, p. 20, and cf. Ferguson's *Essay on the History of Civil Society*, p. 119 (part 3, section 2).

[55] As James T. Kloppenberg observes, "[w]hen independence lost its identification with benevolence, when self-interest was no longer conceived in relation to [an] egalitarian standard...then freedom itself, especially the freedom to compete in the race for riches without the restraint of natural law, became an obstacle in the way of justice." Kloppenberg traces this development to "the early alliance between the virtues of republicanism and the virtues of liberalism," although he defines these terms rather differently than I have here: "The Virtues of Liberalism: Christianity, Republicanism, and

argue, as if it were a matter of plain common sense, that "[e]verything is what it is: liberty is liberty, not equality or fairness or justice or culture, or human happiness or a quiet conscience."[56] In other words, the market conception of freedom makes it possible to detach the problem of removing constraints from the larger political context in which it necessarily appears – ironically, the very detachment against which Berlin protests in the quoted passage. Any effort to revive the republican conception of freedom must therefore begin, *pace* Berlin, by showing that there *is* a sense in which a commitment to freedom entails a commitment to values such as equality, fairness, justice, culture, and happiness. Yet the contemporary theorist of freedom is in the paradoxical position of being unable to do this without seeming to pose a threat to the value of freedom itself.

Ethics in Early American Political Discourse," in idem, *The Virtues of Liberalism* (New York: Oxford University Press, 1998), pp. 35, 37.
[56] Isaiah Berlin, "Two Concepts of Liberty" (1958/1969), in idem, *Liberty*, ed. Henry Hardy (New York: Oxford University Press, 2002), p. 172.

5

Republicanism in Eclipse

It can happen that the constitution is free and that the citizen is not. The citizen can be free and the constitution not. In these instances, the constitution will be free by right and not in fact; the citizens will be free in fact and not by right.

Montesquieu, *The Spirit of the Laws*, book 12, chapter 1 (Cohler, Miller, & Stone trans.)

5.1. DEMOCRATIZATION AND INDUSTRIALIZATION

We have traced the close association between freedom and the market in Western political thought to the contingent fact that the rise of modern commercial societies in early modern Europe appeared as a threat to the freedom of the people concerned, and that the conception of freedom that was inherited from classical antiquity was ambiguous and flexible enough that it could be used to defend as well as to criticize this development. The resulting ideological crisis created the conceptual space for the invention of market freedom, a view that was built out of a synthesis of republican and juristic ideas. In particular, the commercial republican claim that the pursuit of self-interest provides the most reliable path to collective prosperity was woven together with the Lockean appeal to consent as the foundation of legitimate political rule – the difference being that consent was now seen as something that *is* given day to day and moment to moment in the market, rather than as something that *was* given at a hypothetical founding moment. The defenders of market freedom, by tying individual liberty to justice (the right to make, and the duty to observe, contracts) as well as to social utility (the realization of prosperity, and thus of national greatness) were therefore able to show, at least to their own satisfaction, that the emerging commercial order would promote the enjoyment of peace and security as well as freedom. As a result, it became possible to treat individual liberty, understood as the absence of constraint, as a good in itself, and even as a maximand in political life.

If this line of argument sheds light on the historical development of debates about the meaning and value of freedom, it also raises a new set of questions about the state of those debates today. Why, we might ask, has it been necessary for contemporary scholars to *revive* the republican conception of freedom if central elements of the republican position were carried forward into the modern, market-centered view? If the republican association of freedom with the control of arbitrary power and the practice of virtue played a central role in the invention of market freedom, then how was this way of thinking so thoroughly lost from view that it now takes some effort to recapture its original meaning? How in particular did the debates about the meaning and value of freedom come to center not around the relationship between republicanism and the market, as they had in the early modern period, but rather around the relationship between negative and positive liberty? What can account, in other words, for the gradual eclipse of the republican conception of freedom over the course of the 19th and 20th centuries, and does the fact that this eclipse took place cast doubt on the relevance of republican ideas today?

Here again we should start by taking into account the practical challenges to which the thinkers in question were responding. If the 18th century was the century of the rise of commerce and the demise of absolute monarchy, the 19th century was the century of democratization and industrialization, in which popular sovereignty became a practical reality as well as a theoretical premise, and large-scale industrial production replaced trade as the salient feature of a modern economy. Each of these developments was influentially framed in republican terms. In particular, the emergence of mass democracy gave rise to fears of "majority tyranny": The expansion of the suffrage and the decline of the countervailing power of monarchic and aristocratic institutions created the specter of an unchecked popular will with access not only to the traditional mechanisms of state coercion, but also to the more insidious power of public opinion, with its capacity both to socialize and to ostracize. Those who associated democracy with the threat of majority tyranny were motivated, in other words, by the traditional republican concern to prevent the arbitrary exercise of power by a particular social class.

Similarly, the emergence of mass production gave rise to fears of "wage slavery": The material well-being and even the survival of an increasing number of people was now tied to the vagaries of the labor market, and an increasing proportion of remunerative work was monotonous at best, and often debilitating and dangerous as well. Here again the new industrial economy raised traditional republican concerns, this time having to do with the corruption of character that follows from material insecurity and personal dependence.

Despite the republican nature of the concerns that they raised, the ultimate impact of these developments was to call into question the uneasy synthesis of republican and liberal ideas about freedom that had been worked out over the course of the 18th century. As long as it was taken for granted that all people share an interest in promoting the smooth functioning of commerce, these two ways of thinking reinforced one another: The exercise of power by the state was considered non-arbitrary insofar as it did not interfere with the property rights – including, crucially, rights of exchange – of its citizens, and the virtuous man was one who prudently managed his own property while respecting the property rights of others. However, the insight that majority rule brings with it the threat of class legislation served as a reminder that a polity can be free in the sense of being self-governing without being free in the sense of providing for the secure enjoyment of property. Similarly, the insight that democracy brings with it the twin dangers of political apathy and social conformity served as a reminder that individuals can be free in the sense of being allowed to order their lives as they please while nevertheless lacking the virtue that is needed to sustain a free society. Above all, the insight that the newly enfranchised working class was the plaything of economic forces beyond its control made it clear that the classical republican image of the free man as independent proprietor–cum–virtuous citizen, and even the more modest commercial republican image of the free man as prudent manager of his property, did not provide a plausible description of modern social and political life.

Taken in themselves, each of these observations is of course impeccably republican; indeed, when set against the ideological innovations of the 18th century, they represent something of a return to a more traditional republican view. The commercial republicans responded to the rise of commerce by highlighting the social and political benefits of manufacturing and trade, by pointing out that commerce tends to dissolve traditional relations of dependence, and by emphasizing that a certain kind of virtue is necessary for success in the commercial realm. To be a proponent of republican freedom in the 19th century, by contrast, was to be committed on the one hand to fighting against the rising tide of economic modernization, and on the other hand to shoring up the "intermediate powers" that had once checked the popular will – or, failing that, to finding less overtly inegalitarian means of achieving the same end. As it became difficult to avoid the conclusion that there are no viable alternatives to mass democracy and mass production under modern conditions, the debate about the meaning and value of freedom became a debate in which both sides associated freedom with unconstrained choice rather than individual independence. As a result, disagreement centered no longer on the practical question of how citizens might best be shielded from the arbitrary exercise of power, but rather on the more abstract question of what counts as a choice. Thus where it had been possible for thinkers such as Montesquieu, Hume, and Smith to offer a constructive and even progressive republican response to the rise of modern commercial societies, the rise of democratization and industrialization made it tempting to conclude that the republican tradition has little to offer to the modern world except for an atavistic appeal to an idealized past.

5.2. MAJORITY RULE AND MAJORITY TYRANNY

The dangers of majority tyranny were most influentially described in the work of Alexis de Tocqueville, who is arguably the last thinker to have made a genuinely original contribution to the development of republican thought. Tocqueville's writings center around an analysis of the "equality of conditions" that exists in modern democracies, a phenomenon that not only "gives a certain direction to public spirit, a certain turn to the laws, new maxims to those who govern, and particular habits to the governed," but also "creates opinions, gives birth to sentiments, suggests usages, and modifies everything it does not produce." He argues that equality so understood is the defining feature of modern social life, and that the question is therefore not whether polities should be organized along egalitarian or inegalitarian lines, but rather whether they can be organized in such a way that equality is enjoyed along with, rather than to the exclusion of, freedom.[1] Tocqueville uses the word "freedom," moreover,

---

[1] Alexis de Tocqueville, *Democracy in America* (1835/1840), quoting Harvey C. Mansfield and Delba Winthrop's translation (Chicago: University of Chicago Press, 2000) at p. 3 (introduction). This concern with the relationship between equality and freedom is the common thread that runs through Tocqueville's thought; he begins the discussion of freedom in his study of the French Revolution, for example, by remarking that "[i]t was

in a straightforwardly republican sense: although he concedes that there must always be "one social power superior to all the others," he nevertheless insists that "freedom [is] in peril when that power finds no obstacle before it that can restrain its advance and give it time to moderate itself." The power of the majority is especially dangerous in his view because it operates directly on the beliefs and desires of those who are subject to it. "Under the absolute government of one alone," he observes, "despotism struck the body crudely, so as to reach the soul; and the soul, escaping from those blows, rose gloriously above it; but in democratic republics, tyranny does not proceed in this way; it leaves the body and goes straight for the soul."[2]

Thus Tocqueville inverts the classical criticism of democracy – a view that can be traced back at least as far as Plato – to argue that "anarchy is not the principal evil that democratic centuries will have to face, but the least." "[W]hat is most repugnant to me in America," he writes, "is not the extreme freedom that reigns there, it is the lack of a guarantee against tyranny."[3] However, he agrees with the classical republicans in thinking that the problem with majority tyranny is not that it keeps us from doing what we want – again, the power of the majority is dangerous precisely because it shapes our desires in such a way that we *want* to conform[4] – but rather because it corrupts the character of those who are subject to it. Indeed, Tocqueville goes so far as to argue that there is no country with "less independence of mind and genuine freedom of discussion…than in America," and that "[a]mong the immense crowd that flocks to a political career in the United States," there are "few men indeed who show that virile candor, that manly independence of thought, that…forms the salient feature of great characters."[5] In the concluding chapters of *Democracy in America*, he argues more broadly that because democratic citizens are equal in power and therefore have only a limited ability to influence one another, they will be tempted to withdraw from the public realm even as they look to the state for help in pursuing

---

almost twenty years ago that, speaking of another society, I wrote almost exactly what I am now about to say": *The Old Regime and the Revolution* (1856), quoting Alan S. Kahan's translation (Chicago: University of Chicago Press, 1998), vol. 1, p. 87 (preface).

[2] Tocqueville, *Democracy in America*, pp. 241, 244 (vol. 1, part 2, chapter 7).

[3] Ibid., pp. 640, 241 (vol. 2, part 4, chapter 1; vol. 1, part 2, chapter 7); cf. Plato, *Republic* 557a–564a.

[4] "The majority is vested with a force, at once material and moral, that acts on the will as much as on actions, and which at the same time prevents the deed and the desire to do it": *Democracy in America*, p. 243 (vol. 1, part 2, chapter 7).

[5] Ibid., pp. 244, 247.

their private ends. Over time this pattern of behavior will give rise, he warns, to "an innumerable crowd of like and equal [*semblables et égaux*] men who revolve on themselves without repose, procuring the small and vulgar pleasures with which they fill their souls," while "an immense tutelary power...takes charge of assuring their enjoyments and watching over their fate." The result, he concludes, will be a "softer" but more profound kind of despotism that "finally reduces each nation to being nothing more than a herd of timid and industrious animals," "losing little by little the faculty of thinking, feeling, and acting by themselves, and thus...gradually falling below the level of humanity."[6]

Here again Tocqueville is not concerned about majority tyranny because it keeps democratic citizens from doing as they please. Rather, he fears that if they *are* left to as they please, then they will voluntarily submit to the authority of a benevolent but arbitrary power and become incapable of cultivating the strength of character and independence of mind – the virtue – that is befitting of, and that is ultimately only available to, free men.[7] However, if his diagnosis of the problem is traditional, the solutions that he proposes are less so. Like the American Founders, Tocqueville takes it for granted that there is no place for fixed status hierarchies in the modern world, and that the classical republican strategy of preventing the arbitrary exercise of power by allowing distinct social classes – nobles and plebs, aristocrats and commoners – to check one another is therefore obsolete. The challenge, then, is to find democratic analogs for the freedom-enhancing function that these class conflicts once served. Tocqueville's best-known response to this dilemma centers around the claim that voluntary associations of individually weak but collectively powerful citizens can "take the place of the powerful particular persons whom equality of conditions has made disappear": "when plain citizens associate," he argues, "they can constitute very opulent, very influential, very strong beings – in a word, aristocratic persons."[8] He also praises the decentralization of political power under a federal system

---

[6] Ibid., pp. 663, 665 (vol. 2, part 4, chapter 6). On the tendency toward "individualism" in democracies, see more generally ibid., vol. 2, part 2, chapters 2–4.

[7] "The natural inclination of their minds and hearts leads them to it, and it is enough that they not be held back for them to arrive at it": ibid., p. 645 (vol. 2, part 4, chapter 3). Or, as Tocqueville later put it, "despotism favors the development of all the vices to which [democratic] societies are especially prone, and thus pushes them in the direction in which they are already inclined to go": *The Old Regime and the Revolution*, p. 87 (preface).

[8] Tocqueville, *Democracy in America*, pp. 492, 668 (vol. 2, part 2, chapter 5 and part 4, chapter 7). On the importance of voluntary associations in American public life, see more generally vol. 1, part 2, chapter 4 and vol. 2, part 2, chapters 5–7.

and highlights the important role that an independent judiciary and an educated legal class, a free press, a culture of religious observance, and even the study (within limits) of Greek and Latin literature have to play in sustaining American liberty.[9] As different as these various norms and practices are from one another, the underlying claim that he makes on their behalf is always the same: that they help to counter the "natural" democratic tendency toward individualism, isolation, and apathy, and thus toward centralization, paternalism, and despotism. In short, they force democratic citizens to be free.[10]

A similar line of argument can be found in the political writings of John Stuart Mill, who was by his own account profoundly influenced by Tocqueville's analysis of modern democracy and who provides, after Tocqueville, the most far-reaching and influential discussion of the dangers of majority tyranny in the 19th century.[11] Like Tocqueville, Mill

[9] On federalism see ibid., vol. 1, part 1, chapter 5; on lawyers and the judiciary, vol. 1, part 2, chapter 8; on the press, vol. 1, part 2, chapter 3 and vol. 2, part 2, chapter 6; on religion, vol. 1, part 2, chapter 9 and vol. 2, part 1, chapters 5–7; on classical literature, vol. 2, part 1, chapter 15. For an overview of the leading mechanisms for preventing democratic despotism, see ibid., vol. 2, part 4, chapter 7.

[10] "Only freedom can bring citizens out of the isolation in which the very independence of their circumstances has led them to live, can daily force them to mingle, to join together through the need to communicate with one another, persuade each other, and satisfy each other in the conduct of their common affairs": *The Old Regime and the Revolution*, p. 87 (preface). Cf. ibid., p. 163 (part 2, chapter 10), where Tocqueville remarks that in England "freedom always forced [the aristocracy] to stay in touch with one another, in order to be able to reach an understanding when necessary," and *Democracy in America*, p. 487 (vol. 2, part 2, chapter 4), where he argues that in the United States "[l]ocal freedoms...constantly bring men closer to one another, despite the instincts that separate them, and force them to aid each other."

[11] Mill hailed the first volume of *Democracy in America* as "a book with which...all who would understand, or who are called upon to exercise influence over their age, are bound to be familiar" – adding, rather amusingly, that "[t]he book is such as Montesquieu might have written, if to his genius he had superadded good sense": "De Tocqueville on Democracy in America" (I) (1835), in idem, *Collected Works*, ed. J. M. Robson (Toronto: University of Toronto Press, 1963–91), vol. 18, quoted at pp. 57–8. In his review of the second volume, Mill described Tocqueville's work as "the first philosophical book ever written on Democracy, as it manifests itself in modern society," adding that its author "has earned the double honor of being the first to make the attempt, and of having done more toward the success of it than probably will ever again be done by any one individual": "De Tocqueville on Democracy in America" (II) (1840), ibid., pp. 156–7. He later remarked that "[the] shifting of my political ideal from pure democracy, as commonly understood by its partisans, to the modified form of it, which is set forth in my *Considerations on Representative Government*...dates its commencement from my reading, or rather study, of M. de Tocqueville's *Democracy in America*": *Autobiography*, chapter 6, in *Collected Works*, vol. 1, quoted at p. 199. For some doubts about the extent of Tocqueville's influence on Mill, see H. O. Pappé, "Mill and Tocqueville," *Journal of the History of Ideas* 25 (1964), pp. 217–34.

associates majority tyranny more closely with the threat of social conformity than of state coercion.[12] However, rather than point to the "equality
of conditions" as the source of the problem, he looks instead to the ascendance of what he calls "bourgeois opinion," an ascendance whose effects
are felt, he argues, no less strongly in aristocratic England than in democratic America, and which he sees as a distinguishing feature of modern
commercial society rather than of democracy itself. Thus in his review
of the second half of *Democracy in America*, Mill chides Tocqueville for
"ascrib[ing] to equality of conditions several of the effects naturally arising from the mere progress of national prosperity, in the form in which
that progress manifests itself in modern times." Equality is, he insists,
"one of the incidental effects of the progress of industry and wealth…
not therefore to be confounded with the cause," and "[t]he defects which
M. de Tocqueville points out in the American, and which we see in the
modern English mind, are the ordinary ones of a commercial class." "The
evil," he concludes, in a strikingly republican formulation, "is not in
the preponderance of a democratic class, but of *any* class," and the proper
response is not to cultivate aristocratic habits of behavior in an otherwise
homogeneous citizenry, but rather to check the power of the newly ascen-
dant bourgeoisie.[13]

It is therefore not surprising that when Mill turned, some twenty years
later, in his *Considerations on Representative Government*, to the problem of finding institutional remedies for the shortcomings of democratic
rule, he gave special attention to the problem of ensuring that "no class,
and no combination of classes likely to combine, shall be able to exercise
a preponderant influence in the government."[14] It is notable, however,
that in the later work he associates majority tyranny with the dominance
of the "labouring" rather than of the "commercial" class. In particular,
although Mill saw progress toward universal suffrage – including

---

[12] Mill introduces the concept of majority tyranny at the beginning of *On Liberty* with a
reference to *Democracy in America* and goes on to argue, echoing Tocqueville, that it is
"more formidable than many kinds of political oppression, since, though not usually
upheld by such extreme penalties, it leaves fewer means of escape, penetrating much
more deeply into the details of life, and enslaving the soul itself": *On Liberty* (1859),
Collected Works, vol. 18, quoted at p. 220 (chapter 1).

[13] Mill, "De Tocqueville on Democracy in America" (II), pp. 191–2, 196 (emphasis
added). For a discussion of Mill's political thought that emphasizes his debt to classical republicanism, see Nadia Urbinati, *Mill on Democracy: From the Athenian Polis to
Representative Government* (Chicago: University of Chicago Press, 2002).

[14] Mill, *Considerations on Representative Government* (1861), *Collected Works*, vol. 19,
p. 446 (chapter 6).

women's suffrage – as "absolutely necessary to an enlarged and elevated conception of good government," he nevertheless worried that over time "the great majority of voters in most countries, and emphatically in this [i.e., in England], would be manual laborers," and thus that "the twofold danger, that of too low a standard of political intelligence, and that of class legislation, would...exist in a very perilous degree." Mill's response to the threat of majority tyranny seeks to avoid each of these dangers: A well-designed system of representative government would ensure, he argues, not only that "laborers and their affinities on one side, employers of labor and their affinities on the other, [are] in the arrangement of the representative system, equally balanced," but also that "education as such" is given "the degree of superior influence due to it, and sufficient as a counterpoise to the numerical weight of the least educated class."[15] If the first project appeals to the traditional republican aim of achieving a durable balance of power between competing interests, the second appeals to the more distinctively Millian aim of empowering an intelligentsia whose regard for the common good somehow transcends those interests.[16]

Thus although Mill was in many ways an egalitarian of a fairly radical stripe, he was not an egalitarian when it came to matters of governance. He does insist that every citizen should be given a political voice, and does so

---

[15] Ibid., pp. 472–3, 447, 477 (chapters 8 and 6). This concern to balance the interests of different economic classes represents a marked departure from Mill's earlier view that "the theory of *class-representation*" is the "master fallacy" in discussions of representative government, that "[t]he only interest which we wish to be consulted is the general interest, and that, therefore, is the only one which we desire to see represented": "Rationale of Representation" (1835), *Collected Works*, vol. 18, pp. 43, 45 (original emphasis). As late as 1848 Mill held that "views of things taken from the peculiar position of the working classes are not likely to predominate or have at all more than their just influence, even in a legislature chosen by universal suffrage": "On Reform," *Collected Works*, vol. 25, p. 1105.

[16] Each of these arguments in favor of weighted representation would seem to be at odds with Mill's claim that "in a really equal democracy, every or any section [of the people] would be represented, not disproportionately, but proportionately," and that to arrange things otherwise is "contrary to all just government, [and] above all, contrary to the principle of democracy, which professes equality as its very root and foundation." It is this line of argument that leads Mill to endorse Thomas Hare's system of proportional representation through transferable votes. His enthusiasm for Hare's voting scheme does not seem to rest, however, on its egalitarian credentials, but rather on the view that "[o]f all modes in which a national representation can possibly be constituted, this one affords the best security for the intellectual qualifications desirable in the representatives," that "[i]n no other way...would Parliament be so certain of containing the very *élite* of the country": *Considerations on Representative Government*, chapter 7, quoted at pp. 449, 455–6.

on traditional republican grounds: "the rights and interests of every or any person are only secure from being disregarded when the person interested is himself able, and habitually disposed to stand up for them," he argues, and "the general prosperity attains a greater height, and is more widely diffused, in proportion to the amount and variety of the personal energies enlisted in promoting it."[17] However, the idea that everyone should be given an *equal* political voice is, Mill insists, "in principle wrong, because [it] recognize[s] a wrong standard, and exercise[s] a bad influence on the voter's mind.... [O]ne person is *not* as good as another; and it is reversing all the rules of rational conduct, to attempt to raise a political fabric on a supposition which is at variance with [this] fact."[18] Mill argues instead for a system of "universal, but graduated suffrage" in which "every one is entitled to some influence, but the better and wiser to more than others." In other words, he suggests that the "better and wiser" should be given more votes than their fellow citizens.[19] Moreover, because he is willing, in the absence of "a really national education or a trustworthy system of general examination," to treat economic status as a proxy for intelligence, Mill's plural voting scheme gives disproportional representation not only to the educationally but also to the economically advantaged classes.[20] It

[17] Ibid., p. 404 (chapter 3); Mill calls these the "self-protection" and "self-dependence" principles and says that they are "of as universal truth and applicability as any general propositions which can be laid down respecting human affairs": ibid.

[18] Ibid., p. 478 (chapter 8); "Thoughts on Parliamentary Reform" (1859), *Collected Works*, vol. 19, p. 323 (original emphasis). It is important to emphasize that Mill did not apply this line of argument to democracies alone: "In a numerous aristocracy, as well as in a democracy, the sole chance for considerate and wise government lies not in the wisdom of the democracy or of the aristocracy themselves, but in their willingness to place themselves under the guidance of the wisest among them. And it would be difficult for democracy to exhibit less of this willingness than has been shown by the English aristocracy in all periods of their history, or less than is shown by them at this moment": "Tocqueville on Democracy in America" (I), p. 79.

[19] Mill, *Considerations on Representative Government*, chapter 8 passim, quoted at pp. 478–9. In the *Considerations* Mill suggests only that the better-educated classes should be given "two or more" votes; in the "Thoughts on Parliamentary Reform" (pp. 324–5), where he first defends the idea of plural voting, he proposes that "at least" five or six votes be given to the most highly educated classes.

[20] "An employer of labor is on the average more intelligent than a laborer; for he must labor with his head, and not solely with his hands. A foreman is generally more intelligent than an ordinary laborer, and a laborer in the skilled trades than in the unskilled. A banker, merchant, or manufacturer is likely to be more intelligent than a tradesman, because he has larger and more complicated interests to manage." Mill is careful to add, however, that "[i]n all these cases it is not the having merely undertaken the superior function, but the successful performance of it, that tests the qualifications," that "it [is] entirely inadmissible, unless as a temporary makeshift, that the superiority of influence

therefore responds to each of the "twofold dangers" that he associates with majority rule: "The distinction in favour of education, right in itself, is further and strongly recommended by its preserving the educated from the class legislation of the uneducated" – although he is careful to add, in good republican fashion, that "it must stop short of enabling them to practise class legislation on their own account."[21]

History has not been kind, as Tocqueville might have predicted, to this brand of intellectual elitism, and Mill is better remembered today as the author of *On Liberty* than of the *Considerations on Representative Government*.[22] This fact has had profound implications for the reception of his political thought. When read in light of his other political writings, the central argument of *On Liberty* – that people should learn to think and act for themselves or, failing that, that they should allow others to do so – can be recognized as a variation on the traditional republican claim that tyranny can only be prevented if citizens display an independence of thought and action that does not come to them naturally. However, when Mill's defense of individual liberty is detached from his broader defense of plural voting and mixed government, then its republican character becomes harder to see. That is, if the power of the state is *necessarily* the power of the majority, as the argument of *On Liberty* seems to assume, then it follows that the only way to prevent majority tyranny is by placing strict limits on the sphere within which the state can legitimately act. This is, of course, the aim of the so-called harm principle.[23] Similarly, if

---

should be conferred in consideration of property" as such, and most importantly that it must "be open to the poorest individual in the community to claim [the] privileges" of plural voting "if he can prove that, in spite of all difficulties and obstacles, he is, in point of intelligence, entitled to them": *Considerations on Representative Government*, pp. 475, 474, 476 (chapter 8).

[21] Ibid., p. 476 (chapter 8).

[22] Mill himself was under no illusions about the popularity of his proposal: He admits in the *Considerations* that "[p]lural voting…is not likely to be soon or willingly adopted," but he adds that "as the time will certainly arrive when the only choice will be between this and equal universal suffrage, whoever does not desire the last can not too soon begin to reconcile himself to the former": ibid. He later remarked that "[a]s far as I have been able to observe, it [*viz.*, his defense of plural voting] has found favour with nobody: all who desire any sort of inequality in the electoral vote, desiring it in favour of property and not of intelligence or knowledge": *Autobiography*, p. 261 (chapter 7).

[23] "The only purpose for which power can be rightfully exercised over any member of a civilized community, against his will, is to prevent harm to others," a principle which Mill argues is "entitled to govern absolutely the dealings of society with the individual in the way of compulsion and control, whether the means used be physical force in the form of legal penalties, or the moral coercion of public opinion": *On Liberty*, p. 223 (chapter 1).

the power of the majority is largely extra-political in nature – if it is exercised as much through informal practices of praise and blame as through the traditional mechanisms of state coercion – then it follows that the only way to cultivate virtue in a democratic society is by promoting a spirit of non-conformity and toleration among the citizenry itself.[24] In other words, the republican critique of majority rule, when combined with the democratic view that the majority is the final arbiter of all political disputes, is indistinguishable from the liberal view that the pursuit of liberty is a matter of defining "the nature and limits of the power which can be legitimately exercised by society over the individual," and that "[t]he only freedom which deserves the name is that of pursuing our own good in our own way."[25]

Thus to the extent that Tocqueville and Mill frame the problem of majority tyranny in republican terms – as a matter of creating a durable balance of power among the various factions in society – their solutions are out of joint with the democratic character of modern political life. To the extent that they frame the problem in voluntaristic terms – as a matter of promoting habits of independence and self-reliance through extra-political means – their position can be defended more straightforwardly by appealing to the liberal language of limited government and toleration than to the republican language of mixed government and virtue. In Tocqueville's case, this shift from a republican to a liberal frame does some violence to the content of his thought: Although he does not provide a formal definition of freedom, he consistently associates it with the absence of arbitrary power rather than the absence of constraint.[26] Mill, by contrast, though he was no less committed to the control of arbitrary power, never wavered from the Benthamite – and emphatically non-republican – view that "[l]iberty, in its original sense, means freedom

---

[24] "The disposition of mankind, whether as rulers or as fellow-citizens, to impose their own opinions and inclinations as a rule of conduct on others, is so energetically supported by some of the best and by some of the worst feelings incident to human nature, that it is hardly ever kept under restraint by anything but want of power; and as the power is not declining, but growing, unless a strong barrier of moral conviction can be raised against the mischief, we must expect, in the present circumstances of the world, to see it increase": ibid., p. 227 (chapter 1).

[25] Ibid., pp. 217, 226.

[26] See, for example, the preface to *The Old Regime and the Revolution* (p. 88), where Tocqueville asks "[w]hat person could be naturally base enough to prefer dependence on the caprice of one man, rather than follow laws which he himself has helped to make, if he thought his country had the virtues necessary to make good use of freedom."

from restraint," and that "[i]n this sense, every law, and every rule of morals, is contrary to liberty."[27] The central question for Mill is therefore not, as it is for Tocqueville, how the love of freedom and the love of equality can be reconciled, but rather what the limits of state power, and thus of individual liberty, should be. This is, of course, exactly the form in which the debate about the relationship between freedom and democracy has come down to us today, and so it is not surprising that it is Mill rather than Tocqueville who is now seen as the 19th-century theorist of freedom *par excellence*.

5.3. WAGE LABOR AND WAGE SLAVERY

Slavery has of course always been the paradigmatic example of unfreedom in republican thought, as indeed it is in nearly all branches of political thought. However, from classical times up through the 19th century, it was widely believed that anyone who was obliged to sell their labor in exchange for a wage was not far removed from that precarious and degraded social condition. This fear of wage slavery was based not only on the fact that wage labor is, like slave labor, typically menial, but also and more profoundly on the fact that the wage laborer, like the slave and unlike the skilled craftsman or independent proprietor, depends on the good will of another person – an employer – for his subsistence. In other words, wage labor was said to lead to a loss of freedom because it has a degrading effect on the bodies and minds of those who are engaged in it and because it imposes a relationship of dependence, with all of the servility and corruption that such a relationship entails. Thus Aristotle lumps slaves, "mechanics" [*banausoi*], and laborers together under the category of those who perform "necessary tasks" in the city, distinguishing between them only on the grounds that "slaves do them for individuals," whereas "mechanics and laborers…do them for the community" as a whole. He concludes that mechanics and laborers, like slaves, would not

---

[27] Mill, "Periodical Literature: Edinburgh Review" (1824), *Collected Works*, vol. 1, p. 296. Mill continues in a Hobbesian vein: "A despot, who is entirely emancipated from both [laws and moral rules], is the only person whose freedom of action is complete. A measure of government, therefore, is not necessarily bad, because it is contrary to liberty; and to blame it for that reason, leads to confusion of ideas." This idea is expressed more succinctly in the first chapter of *On Liberty* (p. 220), where Mill argues that "[a]ll that makes existence valuable to any one, depends on the enforcement of restraints upon the actions of other people." I am grateful to Piers Norris Turner for bringing the earlier passage to my attention.

be admitted to citizenship in the ideal city.[28] Cicero shares Aristotle's view, arguing that "all those workers who are paid for their labour and not for their skill have servile and demeaning employment," and adding the more distinctively republican claim that "the very wage is a contract to servitude."[29]

Cicero's remark notwithstanding, the specter of wage slavery does not play a prominent role in classical and early modern republican thought, presumably because it was widely assumed that only a small proportion of the population would ever be permanently obliged to sell their labor for a wage, and that those people were unlikely to be fit for republican citizenship in any case. The rise of industrial capitalism, along with the gradual elimination of property qualifications for voting, called each of these assumptions into question. The 19th century therefore saw the emergence of a vigorous debate over the question of whether the emergence of a growing class of people who had no realistic prospect of earning their living in any other way posed a threat not only to their freedom, but to the freedom of the larger society to which they belonged. Like the 18th-century debate about the political implications of the rise of commerce, this debate centered around the question of whether the enjoyment of republican freedom is possible under modern economic conditions. However, where the commercial republicans were able to respond to this question in the affirmative, and thus to redefine the terms of republican citizenship for the modern age, the 19th-century critics of wage slavery failed to identify an alternative to large-scale industrial production that was both practically viable and recognizably republican. This failure led, as we will see, to a decline in the role that republican ideas had to play in debates about political economy, thereby contributing to the eclipse

[28] Aristotle, *Politics*, book 3, chapter 5, quoting R. F. Stalley's revision of the Barker translation (New York: Oxford University Press, 1995 [1946]) at p. 95. Aristotle is careful to emphasize that mechanics "often become rich," and that it is the absence of virtue rather than of wealth that makes them unfit for citizenship: ibid., p. 96. Cf. Hobbes: "[T]he difference...between a *free citizen* and a *slave* [is] that the FREE MAN is one who serves only the commonwealth, while the SLAVE serves also his fellow citizen": *On the Citizen* (1642), trans. Richard Tuck and Michael Silverthorne (New York: Cambridge University Press, 1998), pp. 111–12 (chapter 9; original emphasis).

[29] Marcus Tullius Cicero, *On Duties*, book 1 §150, quoting Margaret Atkins's translation (New York: Cambridge University Press, 1991), at p. 58. The Latin *servitutis* is derived from *servus*, or slave. Locke, by contrast, draws a strict distinction between servitude and slavery: "a Free-man makes himself a Servant to another, by selling him, for a certain time, the Service he undertakes to do, in exchange for Wages he is to receive," whereas slaves, "being Captives taken in a just War, are by the Right of Nature subjected to the Absolute Dominion and Arbitrary Power of their Masters": *Second Treatise of Government* §85.

of republican freedom as a tool for addressing the challenges of modern social and political life.

The dangers of wage slavery were most vigorously debated in the United States, which was at the time the most democratic and arguably the most economically advanced country in the world.[30] The American Founders hoped that these two facts would complement one another; that the absence of a fixed social hierarchy, along with the presence of a frontier that offered the possibility of free-holding citizenship to all men (excluding, of course, the Native Americans and African slaves), provided a unique opportunity to establish a genuine and lasting republic in the modern world. With the War of 1812, this vision of a republic that was both agrarian and commercial ran aground on the geopolitical realities of international trade,[31] but the belief that economic conditions in America were uniquely favorable to free government proved to be more resilient. Tocqueville finds, for example, that in Jacksonian America even the "servant" – a term that he, like Aristotle and Cicero, uses to describe wage laborers as well as domestic servants in the narrower sense – "carries into servitude some of the virile habits to which independence and equality had given birth." He attributes this fact to the ubiquitous, temporary, and voluntary nature of the wage labor relationship: "American servants do not believe themselves degraded because they work," he argues, "for everyone around them works," and "[t]hey do not feel themselves debased by the idea that they receive a wage, for the President of the United States works for a wage as well." More importantly, the "servitude" of the wage laborer is qualitatively different from that of the slave because it rests on "the temporary and free accord of two wills"; "[o]ne is not naturally inferior to the other; he only becomes so temporarily by the fact of a contract."[32]

This idealized portrait of an egalitarian, consensual, and "virile" wage-labor economy is of course hard to square with the realities of industrial production, and to his credit Tocqueville does not entirely blink this

[30] For a useful overview of these debates, see part 2 of Michael J. Sandel's *Democracy's Discontent: America in Search of a Public Philosophy* (Cambridge, MA: Harvard University Press, 1996), esp. chapter 6.
[31] For an influential discussion of the political economy of the American Founders, see Drew R. McCoy, *The Elusive Republic: Political Economy in Jeffersonian America* (Chapel Hill: University of North Carolina Press, 1980); for a contrasting view, see Joyce Appleby, *Capitalism and a New Social Order: The Republican Vision of the 1790s* (New York: NYU Press, 1984).
[32] Tocqueville, *Democracy in America*, pp. 551, 526, 549–50 (vol. 2, part 3, chapter 5; vol. 2, part 2, chapter 18).

fact. Industrial workers, he argues, "generally have little enlightenment, industry, and resources; [and] are therefore almost at the mercy of their master... for they have scarcely any property other than [the labor of] their arms." These workers, he argues, are trapped "in a vicious circle they can in no way escape": The nature of the work that they do "render[s] them unsuited for every other labor," and the asymmetrical bargaining position in which they find themselves with respect to their employers ensures that they will become "easier to oppress as they become poorer." Tocqueville insists that this "state of dependence and misery" is "an exceptional fact and contrary to everything that surrounds it," but he nevertheless warns his readers that "there is none graver or that deserves more to attract the particular attention of the legislator."[33] Nor was he alone in holding this view; indeed, by mid-century it had become something of a commonplace to argue that the increasing prevalence of wage labor posed a grave threat to individual liberty and thus to the preservation of a free society. The preacher, journalist, and sometime Transcendentalist Orestes Brownson wrote in 1840, for example, that wage labor is "a cunning device of the devil for the benefit of tender consciences who would retain all the advantages of the slave system without the expense, trouble and odium of being slaveholders." His contemporary Mike Walsh – an Irish-born journalist and labor organizer who was later elected to the U.S. Congress – bluntly warned his working-class readers in 1845 that "you are slaves, and none are better aware of the fact than the heathenish dogs who call you freemen."[34]

Needless to say, rhetorical flourishes like this drew much of their force from the fact that chattel slavery was actually being practiced on

[33] Ibid., p. 557 (vol. 2, part 3, chapter 7). I have changed the order in which these passages appear in the text, and the bracketed phrase is a clarificatory interpolation by the translators. Cf. ibid., pp. 656–7 (vol. 2, part 4, chapter 5), where Tocqueville argues that "the industrial class" – which "carries despotism within itself" – "has been enriched from the debris of all the others; it has grown in number, in importance, in wealth; it grows constantly; almost all those who are not part of it are linked to it, at least in some place; after having been the exceptional class, it threatens to become the principal class, and so to speak, the sole class." Cf. also vol. 2, part 2, chapter 20, where Tocqueville endorses Adam Smith's conclusions regarding the economic benefits and human costs of the division of labor and warns that the rise of industrial production could lead to the creation of a "manufacturing aristocracy."

[34] Cited in Eric Foner, *Free Soil, Free Labor, Free Men: The Ideology of the Republican Party before the Civil War* (2nd ed., New York: Oxford University Press, 1995 [1970]), p. xviii. For an overview of Walsh's colorful career, see Sean Wilentz, *Chants Democratic: New York City and the Rise of the American Working Class* (New York: Oxford University Press, 1984), pp. 326–35.

American soil. Indeed, the language of slavery was often used to describe the predicament of the factory worker precisely in order to draw a moral equivalence between the Southern planter and the Northern industrialist. George Fitzhugh, one of the leading Southern defenders of slavery, argued for example that "[c]apital commands labor, as the master does the slave" – adding, as Brownson had that capitalism is inferior to slavery in that it sets "a master, without the obligations of a master" over "slaves, without the rights of slaves."[35] The Republican party's "free labor" response to this line of argument is captured nicely in a message that President Lincoln delivered to Congress at the end of 1861.[36] The bulk of the message consists, as we might expect, of a report on the progress of the nascent Civil War, but Lincoln turns at the end to the more fundamental question of "whether it is best that capital shall *hire* laborers, and...induce them to work by their own consent, or *buy* them, and drive them to it without consent." In responding he does not argue, as we might expect, that consent is morally superior to coercion; rather he contends that "there is not, of necessity, any such thing as the free hired laborer being fixed to that condition for life." Alluding, as he so often did, to his own modest background, Lincoln argues instead that "[t]he prudent, penniless beginner in the world, labors for wages awhile, saves a surplus with which to buy tools or land for himself; then labors on his own account another while, and at length hires another beginner to help him." Thus in contrast to the permanent bondage imposed by chattel slavery, a wage-labor economy "opens the way to all – gives hope to all, and consequent energy, and progress, and improvement of condition to all."[37]

What is striking about this line of argument is the fact that it seems to grant the premise of the slaveholders' case. That is, Lincoln seems tacitly

---

[35] George Fitzhugh, *Cannibals All! Or, Slaves Without Masters* (1857), ed. C. Vann Woodward (Cambridge, MA: Harvard University Press, 1960), quoted at p. 17. In his previous book Fitzhugh had gone so far as to argue that "slavery is a form, and the very best form, of socialism": *Sociology for the South: Or the Failure of Free Society* (Richmond: A. Morris, 1854), pp. 27–8. Foner notes that "[i]t is one of the more tragic ironies of this complex debate that, in the process of attempting to liberate the slave, the abolitionists did so much to promote a new and severely truncated definition of freedom for both blacks and whites": "Abolitionism and the Labor Movement in Antebellum America," reprinted in idem, *Politics and Ideology in the Age of the Civil War* (New York: Oxford University Press, 1980), quoted at p. 64.
[36] For a broader discussion of the Republican party's position on this question, see Foner's *Free Soil, Free Labor, Free Men*, passim.
[37] Abraham Lincoln, "Annual Message to Congress," December 3, 1861 (original emphasis).

to admit that if it *were* the case that the wage laborer was "of necessity…
fixed to that condition for life," then the claim that he is free would be
substantially weakened. Despite the remarkable resilience in American
political culture of the rags-to-riches story and the image of the self-made
man, it became increasingly clear as the 19th century progressed that most
people were in fact "fixed to the condition" of wage labor. By 1870, for
example, when occupational data were first included in the U.S. Census,
roughly two-thirds of working Americans in the North reported that they
were dependent on someone else for employment,[38] and the closing of the
frontier at the end of the century dealt the final blow to the Jeffersonian
vision of free-holding citizenship for all.[39] These developments placed the
republican association of freedom with economic independence under
enormous pressure, and the later 19th century saw a series of efforts to
reconcile the ideal of independent proprietorship with the demands of
industrial production. The most notable of these was the effort to promote workers' cooperatives as an alternative to wage labor, and thus to
replace the hierarchical and authoritarian capitalist factory with a workplace based on principles of individual autonomy and collective self-
rule.[40] Despite a brief florescence in the 1880s and a long afterlife in the
form of the rather nebulous ideal of "industrial democracy," cooperative

[38] This figure is cited in Daniel T. Rodgers, *The Work Ethic in Industrial America,
1850–1920* (Chicago: University of Chicago Press, 1978), p. 37.
[39] The classic account is Frederick Jackson Turner's: "[T]hat restless, nervous energy;
that dominant individualism, working for good and for evil, and withal that buoyancy
and exuberance which comes with freedom – these are traits of the frontier, or traits
called out elsewhere because of the existence of the frontier. Since the days when the
fleet of Columbus sailed into the waters of the New World, America has been another
name for opportunity, and the people of the United States have taken their tone from
the incessant expansion which has not only been open but has even been forced upon
them.… And now, four centuries from the discovery of America, at the end of a hundred
years of life under the Constitution, the frontier has gone, and with its going has closed
the first period of American history": "The Significance of the Frontier in American
History" (1893).
[40] Mill was an early and enthusiastic proponent of cooperative production: "Eventually, and
in perhaps a less remote future than may be supposed, we may, through the co-operative
principle, see our way to a change in society, which would combine the freedom and
independence of the individual, with the moral, intellectual, and economical advantages
of aggregate production; and which, without violence or spoliation, or even any sudden
disturbance of existing habits and expectations, would realize, at least in the industrial
department, the best aspirations of the democratic spirit, by putting an end to the division of society into the industrious and the idle, and effacing all social distinctions but
those fairly earned by personal services and exertions": *Principles of Political Economy,
with Some of Their Applications to Social Philosophy* (1848), *Collected Works*, vol. 3,
p. 793 (book 4, chapter 7).

production failed to make significant inroads in the industrial economy. Much the same can be said of later efforts to secure the independence of the working class through profit-sharing schemes, the replacement of hourly with piecework compensation, and so on.[41]

As it became increasingly difficult to reconcile the traditional republican claim that freedom requires economic independence with the realities of modern economic life, the tension between the aim of securing everyone against the arbitrary exercise of power and the aim of guaranteeing to everyone the right to do as they please with their property was thrown into ever sharper relief. As long as the market actor could plausibly be associated with the classical image of the free-holding citizen, then these two conceptions of freedom could be used almost interchangeably: The right to free exchange on which a market economy depends could be treated as a corollary of the right to the secure ownership of property on which republican freedom had always rested. With the emergence of a class of otherwise free citizens who owned nothing of value except for their own capacity to work, it became clear that it is possible to be free in the sense of having the right to trade one's property for something else of value – to sell one's labor in exchange for a wage – while nevertheless remaining unfree in the sense of being dependent on an employer and, more broadly, on the availability of remunerative work for one's material well-being. From a republican standpoint, the freedom to sell one's labor to the highest bidder is not properly speaking freedom at all, as the various critics of wage slavery never tired of pointing out. From the standpoint of market freedom, by contrast, the effort to preserve or enhance the security of the working class by blocking or regulating voluntary transactions between consenting adults is a manifest and even paradigmatic encroachment on individual liberty.

As a result of these developments, the debate over what Michael Sandel has called the "political economy of citizenship" shifted over the course of the 19th century from the question of how the economic independence of workers might best be preserved to the question of when an agreement – a contract – between an employer and an employee can be considered truly voluntary.[42] According to the strict laissez-faire view,

[41] For a useful overview, see Rodgers, *Work Ethic in Industrial America*, chapter 2, and cf. Sandel, *Democracy's Discontent*, pp. 185–9, 197–200.
[42] Sandel, *Democracy's Discontent*, part 2 passim. Although I agree with Sandel in seeing a shift in American political thought from a republican to a "voluntarist" conception of freedom at around the turn of the 20th century, I follow Philip Pettit in thinking that it was a fear of dependence rather than a desire to play an active role in politics that

of course, the very fact that a contract has been entered into – assuming that its terms are mutually understood and that coercive force has not been applied – is enough to show that the parties acted freely. This association of freedom with the sanctity of contracts provided the ideological basis for a largely successful campaign, undertaken most notably in the courts, to resist or overturn the various efforts to insulate workers from the harsh realities of industrial capitalism through minimum-wage and maximum-hours laws, workplace safety regulations, and so on. For their part, the defenders of working-class interests began to focus less on identifying alternatives to wage labor and more on trying to reduce the asymmetry of bargaining power between employers and employees. As Samuel Gompers, the founder of the American Federation of Labor, put it in 1899, "we are living under the wage system, and so long as that lasts it is our purpose to secure a continually larger share for labor."[43] The language of freedom of contract – of what L. T. Hobhouse called "true consent"[44] – was therefore used to defend the very reforms that the proponents of laissez-faire opposed. This is, again, exactly the form in which the debate about the relationship between freedom and the market has come down to us today.

5.4. THE MARKET VERSUS THE STATE

In some ways, then, the terms of the late 19th- and early 20th-century debates about the meaning and value of freedom are immediately familiar. Herbert Spencer, for example, who was perhaps the most influential proponent of laissez-faire in the Victorian period, offers a straightforward defense of negative liberty, arguing that "the liberty which a citizen enjoys is to be measured, not by the nature of the governmental machinery he lives under...but by the relative paucity of the restraints it imposes on him." His contemporary T. H. Green, one of the founders of what became known as "social" liberalism, argues by contrast that "the mere removal of compulsion, the mere enabling a man to do as he likes, is in itself no contribution to true freedom," and that freedom consists instead in the "positive power or capacity of doing or enjoying

---

motivated the republican response to industrialization: see Pettit, "Reworking Sandel's Republicanism," *Journal of Philosophy* 95 (1998), pp. 93–4.

[43] Quoted in Sandel, *Democracy's Discontent*, p. 198.

[44] "True consent is free consent, and full freedom of consent implies equality on the part of both parties to the bargain": L. T. Hobhouse, *Liberalism* (New York: Cambridge University Press, 1994 [1911]), p. 43 (chapter 4).

something *worth* doing or enjoying."[45] However, the debate in which these thinkers were engaged, unlike the more purely conceptual debate about negative and positive liberty that was set into motion with the publication of Isaiah Berlin's "Two Concepts of Liberty" in 1958, was explicitly concerned with the question of the proper relationship between the state and the market. Spencer focuses on the contrast between what he calls the *"régime* of status" and the *"régime* of contract" and insists that a free society is one in which "each, having freedom to use his powers up to the bounds fixed by the like freedom of others, obtains from his fellow-men as much for his services as they find them worth in comparison with the services of others." Green holds, by contrast, that "freedom of contract, freedom in all the forms of doing what one will with one's own, is valuable only as a means to an end," namely, "freedom in the positive sense...the liberation of the powers of all men equally for contributions to a common good." He concludes that it is "the business of the state...to maintain the conditions without which a free exercise of the human faculties is impossible."[46] For Spencer and his like-minded contemporaries, the state poses the single greatest threat to individual liberty; for Green and the other "social" liberals, true freedom can only be realized by political means.

What is immediately striking about the laissez-faire position in this debate is the fact that it combines a call for the removal of restraints on individual choice with an appeal to larger social forces whose operation is said to be both inexorable and beneficial. Spencer argues, for example, that "[t]he poverty of the incapable, the distresses that come upon the imprudent, the starvation of the idle, and [the] shoulderings aside of the weak by the strong...are the decrees of a large, far-seeing benevolence" that "[n]o power on earth, no cunningly-devised laws of statesmen, no world-rectifying schemes of the humane, no communist panaceas, no reforms that men ever did broach or ever will broach, can diminish...one jot." Indeed, the effort to mitigate these harms, "[i]nstead of diminishing suffering...eventually increases it" by "favour[ing] the multiplication of those worst fitted for existence, and, by consequence, hinder[ing] the

---

[45] Herbert Spencer, *The Man Versus the State* (1884), in idem *Political Writings*, ed. John Offer (New York: Cambridge University Press, 1994), p. 77; T. H. Green, "Liberal Legislation and Freedom of Contract" (1881), in idem, *Lectures on the Principles of Political Obligation and Other Writings*, ed. Paul Harris and John Morrow (New York: Cambridge University Press, 1986), p. 199 (emphasis added).
[46] Spencer, *Man Versus State*, p. 167; cf. pp. 63, 79, 156; Green, "Liberal Legislation," p. 200.

multiplication of those best fitted for existence."⁴⁷ Spencer's American contemporary and admirer William Graham Sumner argues along similar lines that "[i]t is impossible to understand society except we think of it as held and governed by forces which maintain equilibrium in it...so that when we seem most free to adopt such plans as we please, we find ourselves actually controlled by facts in the nature of man and of the earth." Freedom does not consist for Sumner in doing as one likes, but rather in "intelligent acceptance of the conditions of earthly life": The free man "must conform to the conditions in which he finds himself. He must obey." Sumner therefore agrees with Spencer in thinking that those who criticize economic freedom on the grounds that it "bears harshly on the weak" overlook the fact that "'the strong' and 'the weak' are terms which admit of no definition unless they are made equivalent to the industrious and the idle, the frugal and the extravagant." He concludes that "if we do not like the survival of the fittest, we have only one possible alternative, and that is the survival of the unfittest."⁴⁸ The Austrian economist Ludwig von Mises puts the point most succinctly of all, arguing that capitalism "is the only possible social system."⁴⁹

This association of economic freedom with submission to larger social forces is echoed and even amplified in the writings of Mises's student Friedrich Hayek, who was perhaps the most sophisticated and influential defender of market freedom in the 20th century. Hayek differs from Spencer and Sumner in refusing to credit economic success to superior "fitness," emphasizing instead that "in competition chance and good luck are often as important as skill and foresight in determining the fate of different people." Indeed, he goes so far as to suggest that the assignment of individual responsibility for economic outcomes is something of a convenient fiction: "Though a man's conviction that all he achieves is due solely to

⁴⁷ Spencer, *Social Statics* (New York: D. Appleton, 1890 [1851]), pp. 354, 356, 416 (chapter 25 §6, chapter 28 §4); these passages are reprinted in *Man Versus State*, pp. 130–1. Elsewhere Spencer puts the point even more bluntly: "If they are sufficiently complete to live, they *do* live, and it is well that they should live. If they are not sufficiently complete to live, they die, and it is best that they should die": *Social Statics*, p. 415 (chapter 28 §4; original emphasis).
⁴⁸ William Graham Sumner, "Liberty and Discipline" (1890), in idem, *Earth-Hunger and Other Essays*, ed. Albert Galloway Keller (New Haven, CT: Yale University Press, 1913), pp. 167–8; Sumner, "The Influence of Commercial Crises on Opinions about Economic Doctrines" (1879), in idem, *The Forgotten Man and Other Essays*, ed. Albert Galloway Keller (New Haven, CT: Yale University Press, 1918), p. 225.
⁴⁹ Ludwig von Mises, *Liberalism: The Classic Tradition*, trans. Ralph Raico (Indianapolis: Liberty Fund, 2005 [1927]), p. 61.

his exertions, skill, and intelligence may be largely false," he writes, "it is apt to have the most beneficial effects on his energy and circumspection," and "if the smug pride of the successful is often intolerable and offensive, the belief that success depends wholly on him is probably the pragmatically most effective incentive to successful action."[50] Despite this important point of difference, however, Hayek agrees with Spencer and Sumner in thinking that a social order in which individuals are allowed to make their own economic decisions will be one in which those decisions are shaped and even determined by forces beyond their control. If anything, Hayek's appreciation of the role that chance plays in determining economic outcomes gives him a greater appreciation of the limits of individual agency in a market society. "A complex civilization like ours," he argues, "is necessarily based on the individual's adjusting himself to changes whose cause and nature he cannot understand: why he should have more or less, why he should have to move to another occupation, why some things he wants should become more difficult to get than others." Indeed, "not only the mass of men, but, strictly speaking, *every* human being is led by the growth of civilization into a path that is not of his own choosing."[51]

Instead of trying to insulate individuals from the hardships to which they are exposed in a market economy, the defenders of market freedom see hardship, and the self-discipline to which it gives rise, as a necessary condition for social progress. Thus Mises writes, in language that would no doubt have horrified Lincoln and the "free labor" Republicans, that "there is only *one* argument" against slavery "which can and did refute all others – namely, that free labor is incomparably more productive than slave labor." Because "[t]he slave has no interest in exerting himself fully," whereas "[t]he free worker...knows that the more his labor accomplishes, the more he will be paid," it follows that "[o]nly free labor can accomplish what must be demanded of the modern industrial worker." Here again we have an appeal to an inexorable process whose purposes individuals are made to serve: "It is true," Mises admits, "that all this straining and struggling to increase their standard of living does not make men any happier. Nevertheless, it is in the nature of man to strive for an improvement in his material condition." Hayek agrees with Mises in thinking that "[p]rogress is movement for movement's sake,"

---

[50] Friedrich A. Hayek, *The Road to Serfdom* (Chicago: University of Chicago Press, 1944), p. 112; Hayek, *The Constitution of Liberty* (Chicago: University of Chicago Press, 1960), pp. 82–3.
[51] Hayek, *Road to Serfdom*, p. 223; *Constitution of Liberty*, p. 50 (emphasis added).

and that "[t]he question whether, if we had to stop at our present stage of development, we would in any significant sense be better off or happier than if we had stopped a hundred or a thousand years ago is probably unanswerable." He nevertheless insists that "[i]t was men's submission to the impersonal forces of the market that in the past has made possible the growth of a civilization," and that "it is by thus submitting that we are every day helping to build something that is greater than any one of us can fully comprehend."[52]

We might ask, of course, why a social order in which we submit to forces that we do not understand and follow paths that we did not choose, and in which wealth and "progress" are pursued for their own sake and not for the sake of human happiness or flourishing, should be associated with the enjoyment of freedom. When confronted with this question the defenders of market freedom tend to abandon the language of negative liberty, appealing instead to the republican association of freedom with the absence of arbitrary power. This is clearest in the case of Hayek, who argues that "the range of physical possibilities from which a person can choose at a given moment has no direct relevance to freedom," which should be measured instead by "the possibility of a person's acting according to his own decisions and plans, in contrast to the position of one who [is] irrevocably subject to the will of another, who by arbitrary decision could coerce him to act or not to act in specific ways." "[T]he only alternative," he insists, "to submission to the impersonal and seemingly irrational forces of the market is submission to an equally uncontrollable and therefore arbitrary power of other men."[53] Mises argues along similar lines that unless we limit the state "solely and exclusively [to] guaranteeing the protection of life, health, liberty, and private property against violent attacks," then the individual will become "a slave of the community, bound to obey the dictates of the majority."[54] For Sumner, the test of freedom is not whether "a man may do as he has a mind to," but rather whether he is "guaranteed by law and civil

---

[52] Mises, *Liberalism*, pp. 4, 148 (original emphasis); Hayek, *Constitution of Liberty*, p. 41; *Road to Serfdom*, p. 224. Mises goes on to argue, somewhat perplexingly, that the aim of liberalism as he conceives it is "to diminish suffering, to increase happiness": *Liberalism*, p. 151.

[53] Hayek, *Constitution of Liberty*, p. 12; *Road to Serfdom*, p. 224. Hayek goes on to argue that "[w]hether or not I am my own master and can follow my own choice and whether the possibilities from which I must choose are many or few are two entirely different questions": *Constitution of Liberty*, p. 17.

[54] Mises, *Liberalism*, pp. 30, 32.

institutions the exclusive employment of all his own powers for his own welfare."[55] Even Spencer, who as we have seen measures freedom by the "paucity of the restraints" that are placed on individuals, echoes Mises and Hayek in associating socialism with slavery in the specific sense of "labour[ing] under coercion to satisfy another's desires."[56]

Hayek concludes that when the state is limited to enforcing rules governing the possession and exchange of property and individuals are allowed (or obliged) to order their lives within the material constraints that are generated by the application of those rules, then "the laws of the state have the same significance...as the laws of nature" in the sense that the constraints that they impose are "generally the result of circumstances in which the person to be coerced has placed himself."[57] What is odd about this line of argument is the fact that markets do not in fact make it possible for individuals to foresee the consequences of their economic choices – of training for a certain line of work, taking or refusing a certain job, making certain investment decisions, and so on. It is therefore hard to argue that the constraints that individuals face in the market are the result of circumstances in which they have placed themselves: Although we sometimes talk about the market as being governed by certain "laws" (most notably the "law" of supply and demand), no one can predict what outcomes the operation of those "laws" will yield over even relatively modest periods of time. If this *were* possible, then the guiding assumption of classical economic theory – that no agent or agency can aggregate information as efficiently as a competitive market – would collapse.[58] It is no accident, then, that the defenders of market freedom define coercion

---

[55] Sumner, "The Forgotten Man" (1883), in *The Forgotten Man and Other Essays*, p. 472.
[56] Spencer, *Man Versus State*, pp. 95–6. Spencer's argument on this point finds a notable echo in Robert Nozick, who argues that "[t]axation of earnings from labor is on a par with forced labor": "If people force you to do certain work, or unrewarded work, for a certain period of time, they decide what you are to do and what purposes your work is to serve apart from your decisions. This process whereby they take this decision from you makes them a *part-owner* of you; it gives them a property right in you": *Anarchy, State, and Utopia* (New York: Basic Books, 1974), p. 172 (original emphasis).
[57] Hayek, *Constitution of Liberty*, p. 142; see more generally ibid., chapter 10 and *Road to Serfdom*, chapter 6, where he argues that the rule of law "make[s] it possible to foresee with fair certainty how the authority will use its coercive powers in given circumstances and to plan one's individual affairs on the basis of this knowledge" (p. 80), and that "it is more important that there should be a rule applied always without exceptions than what this rule is" (p. 88).
[58] For a seminal statement of Hayek's position on this question, see his "The Use of Knowledge in Society," *American Economic Review* 35 (1945), pp. 519–30.

172The Invention of Market Freedom

in such a way that it means being made to serve the ends of an identifiable person or group, because by hypothesis when we act in the market we promote ends that are, to paraphrase Adam Smith, no part of our – *or of anyone else's* – intention. This piece of conceptual sleight-of-hand makes it possible for Hayek to argue that "[e]ven if the threat of starvation to me and perhaps to my family impels me to accept a distasteful job at a very low wage, even if I am 'at the mercy' of the only man willing to employ me, I am not coerced by him or anybody else. So long as the act that has placed me in my predicament is not aimed at making me do or not do specific things, so long as the intent of the act that harms me is not to make me serve another person's ends, its effect on my freedom is not different from that of any natural calamity – a fire or a flood that destroys my house or an accident that harms my health."[59]

From this point of view, the decision to hand a given range of social outcomes over to the market appears as an absolute gain from the standpoint of freedom, because the constraints to which individuals are thereby subject do not appear on the ledger books. We have, as Hayek puts it, the "[f]reedom to order our own conduct in the sphere where material circumstances force a choice upon us." It is nevertheless clear that such an arrangement does not bring about a *reduction* in the number of constraints that individuals face, but rather a *conversion* of those constraints from a relatively personal to a relatively impersonal form. Individuals may indeed "feel" freer in a market society because and to the extent that they do not have the unpleasant feeling – so central to the salience of republican freedom – of being subject to the will of a identifiable agent. No one in particular is responsible when we are harmed in the market: The power against which we hone our wits or before which we cringe cannot take pleasure in, or even be aware of, our discomfiture. Hayek is explicit on this point; after arguing that "the competitive system is the only system designed to minimize by decentralization the power exercised by man over man," he concedes (in a footnote) that "there will always be *something* that determines everything that happens, and in this sense the amount of power existing must always be the same. But this is not true of the power consciously wielded by human beings." We should nevertheless prefer the "impersonal and seemingly irrational forces of the market" to the "equally uncontrollable and therefore arbitrary power of other men" not only because of the superior efficiency of markets in

[59] Hayek, *Constitution of Liberty*, p. 137.

generating and distributing wealth, but also because there is a real sense in which we "feel" freer in a market society. As Hayek acutely remarks, "[i]nequality is undoubtedly more readily borne, and affects the dignity of a person much less, if it is determined by impersonal forces than when it is due to design."[60]

Thus the defenders of market freedom endorse the republican conception of freedom in a rather one-sided way: Instead of trying to ensure that political power is exercised in accordance with commonly approved ends, they call for the dispersion of power to market agents, and thus to market "forces" that generate outcomes that no one can predict and for which no one in particular can be held responsible. These thinkers agree with their successors in the negative liberty tradition that there is an inverse relationship between the extent of individual liberty and the extent of political authority – that it is, in Spencer's phrase, a matter of "the man versus the state." However, if the "free" market allows individuals to decide whether or not to buy or sell a given commodity at a given price, it is nevertheless the case that in a well-functioning market the prices themselves, and thus the opportunities that are available to a given individual, appear as exogenous constraints; features of the social order for which, again, no one (except in certain cases of "market failure") is directly responsible. The distinction between the collective and the individual dimensions of freedom – between public and private, state and market – is maintained in this way of thinking by appealing to a prior distinction between the personal and the impersonal exercise of power, and to the further claim that impersonally imposed constraints – for example, adverse market outcomes such as poverty and unemployment – do not count as freedom-reducing. As we will now see, many thinkers who were opposed to unfettered capitalism – and, in some cases, to capitalism itself – held the opposite view about the relationship between freedom and impersonality and therefore called the association of markets with freedom radically into question.

---

[60] Hayek, *Road to Serfdom*, pp. 231, 224, 117. Ironically a similar conclusion was reached some two centuries earlier by Rousseau, the archenemy of commercial society, who contrasts "dependence on things, which is from nature" with "dependence on men, which is from society" and argues that "[i]f the laws of nations could, like those of nature, have an inflexibility that no human force could ever conquer, dependence on men would then become dependence on things again…and freedom which keeps man exempt from vices would be joined to morality which raises him to virtue": *Emile: or On Education* (1762), book 2, quoting Allan Bloom's translation (New York: Basic Books, 1979), p. 85.

5.5. SELF-REALIZATION AND SELF-RULE

We might gloss the line of argument that we have just examined by saying that a market society maximizes our freedom in the sense that it confronts us least painfully with the limits of our agency, and indeed we have seen that this is the position that the more sophisticated defenders of market freedom adopt on reflection. According to a contrasting point of view, however, the realization of human freedom requires that we confront the limits of our agency, critically examine the conditions under which they arise, and seek either to transcend or to reconcile ourselves to them insofar as this is possible. For the proponents of this positive conception of freedom, whose roots lie in the practical philosophy of Kant and Hegel, and before that in the political thought of Rousseau, freedom consists in rational self-determination; that is, it requires that the social structures and relationships in which we find ourselves be the result of a process of critical reflection, or at least that they can consistently be regarded as having arisen from such a process. From this point of view, it is precisely the anonymity and "bruteness" of the constraints that we face in the market – and the egoistic attitude that we are encouraged to take toward those constraints – that makes it a freedom-reducing institution. Thus although Hegel agrees with Smith in thinking that in a market economy self-regarding individuals are led as if by an invisible hand to promote the good of all, he nevertheless insists that the market, embedded as it is in the broader realm of civil society, serves at best as a precondition for, or "moment" in, the realization of "concrete" freedom, which is achieved only when the individual *consciously* identifies his own purposes with those of the larger community.[61]

There is some question, of course, as to whether Hegel can consistently hold this positive conception of freedom while remaining committed to

---

[61] In Hegel's words, "*concrete freedom* requires that personal individuality and its particular interests should reach their full *development*," that is, "that they should, on the one hand, *pass over* of their own accord into the interest of the universal, and on the other, knowingly and willingly acknowledge this universal even as their own *substantial spirit*, and *actively pursue it* as their *ultimate end*": G. W. F. Hegel, *Elements of the Philosophy of Right* (1821), ed. Allen W. Wood, trans. H. B. Nisbet (New York: Cambridge University Press, 1991), p. 282 (§260; original emphasis). For Hegel's (rather oblique) endorsement of the logic of the "invisible hand," see, for example, ibid., §199. For a useful analysis of the various ways in which this conception of freedom might be understood – one that concludes that Hegel's political thought is best thought of as a brand of "civic humanism" – see Alan Patten, *Hegel's Idea of Freedom* (New York: Oxford University Press, 1999).

the claim that participation in a market economy plays a necessary, if limited, role in its realization.[62] This question is posed in an especially radical form by Karl Marx, who agrees with Hegel in thinking that markets offer only an illusory kind of freedom. "[I]n imagination," he writes, "individuals seem freer under the dominance of the bourgeoisie than before, because their conditions of life seem accidental; in reality, of course, they are less free, because they are more subjected to the violence of things." For Marx, however, freedom depends not on establishing the priority of state over civil society, but rather on overturning the capitalist mode of production and the entire political and legal apparatus on which it rests. Real freedom requires, in short, "the abolition of bourgeois individuality, bourgeois independence, and bourgeois freedom." Once this has been done, he argues, then the "community of revolutionary proletarians" will "put...the conditions of the free development and movement of individuals under their control," and the productive resources that capitalism has generated will be placed in the service of all people: "*All-round* dependence, this natural form of the *world-historical* co-operation of individuals, will be transformed by this communist revolution into the control and conscious mastery of these powers, which, born of the action of men on one another, have till now overawed and governed men as powers completely alien to them."[63]

If this line of argument is easier to reconcile with the claim that market relationships are freedom-reducing, it threatens to make positive liberty into an unattainable ideal. Indeed, many of Marx's successors held that although capitalism is indeed dehumanizing and exploitative, it is nevertheless an irreducible feature of modern life. Max Weber, for example, agrees with Marx in thinking that "because of the very absence of rules, domination which originates in the market or other interest

---

[62] As Allen Wood puts it, "Hegel wants to have it both ways: a free market system for the full blossoming of subjective freedom, and a corporate organization of civil society for ethical existence and determinate particularity. Hegel even *needs* to have it both ways, since both subjective freedom and ethical existence are equally indispensable if the modern self is to actualize its freedom through the institution of civil society. If Hegel's account of civil society turns out to be utopian, then perhaps it is only through an illusion that people continue to believe that a market-based civil society offers the possibility of subjective freedom": Allen W. Wood, *Hegel's Ethical Thought* (New York: Cambridge University Press, 1990), pp. 242–3 (original emphasis).

[63] Karl Marx, *The German Ideology* (1845), in Robert C. Tucker, ed., *The Marx/Engels Reader*, trans. S. Ryazanskaya (2nd ed., New York: W. W. Norton, 1978), p. 199; Karl Marx and Friedrich Engels, *Manifesto of the Communist Party* (1848), ibid., p. 491; Marx, *German Ideology*, pp. 197–8, 164 (original emphasis).

constellations may be felt to be much more oppressive than an authority in which the duties of obedience are set out clearly and expressly,"[64] and he insists, like Marx, that "[i]t is quite ridiculous to attribute to today's high capitalism...any 'elective affinity' with 'democracy' or indeed 'freedom' (in *any* sense of the word)." However, Weber does not share Marx's confidence in capitalism's demise, famously describing it as an "iron cage" from which there is no apparent escape: "[A]ny sober observer," he concludes, "would be bound to conclude that all *economic* auguries point in the direction of a growing *loss* of freedom."[65] This pessimism about the prospects of freedom in the modern world reached a kind of apotheosis in the middle of the 20th century with the writings of the so-called Frankfurt School, which argued that the material conditions of industrial production and the ideological apparatus that it generates have made it all but impossible to imagine or even to desire alternatives to the status quo. Thus Max Horkheimer writes of "the continual coercion that modern social conditions put upon everyone," an "accretion of freedom [which] has brought about a change in the character of freedom." "Our spontaneity has been replaced," he argues, "by a frame of mind which compels us to discard every emotion or idea that might impair our alertness to the impersonal demands assailing us." Herbert Marcuse puts the point more succinctly, arguing that "[t]he distinguishing feature of advanced industrial society is its effective suffocation of those needs which demand liberation." "The slaves of developed industrial civilization are sublimated slaves," he concludes, "but they are slaves."[66]

---

64 Max Weber, "Domination and Legitimacy," in idem, *Economy and Society: An Outline of Interpretive Sociology*, ed. Guenther Roth and Claus Wittich (Berkeley: University of California Press, 1978 [1922]), p. 946. Weber nevertheless insists that for methodological purposes the term "domination" should be reserved for "authoritarian power of command," thereby "exclud[ing] from its scope those situations in which power has its source in a formally free interplay of interested parties such as occurs especially in the market": ibid. (emphasis removed).

65 Weber, "On the Situation of Constitutional [*Bürgerliche*] Democracy in Russia" (1906), in idem, *Political Writings*, ed. Peter Lassman and Ronald Speirs (New York: Cambridge University Press, 1994), p. 69 (original emphasis). The "iron cage" metaphor is drawn from Talcott Parsons's translation of Weber's *The Protestant Ethic and the Spirit of Capitalism* (New York: Charles Scribner's Sons, 1958), p. 181. The German phrase is *stahlhartes Gehäuse*, which a recent translation renders more precisely, if less memorably, as a "shell as hard as steel": *The Protestant Ethic and the Spirit of Capitalism and Other Writings*, trans. Peter Baehr and Gordon C. Wells (New York: Penguin Press, 2002), p. 121; cf. the translators' discussion at pp. lxx-lxxi.

66 Max Horkheimer, *Eclipse of Reason* (New York: Continuum Books, 2004 [1947]), p. 67; Herbert Marcuse, *One-Dimensional Man: Studies in the Ideology of Advanced Industrial Society* (Boston: Beacon Press, 1964), pp. 7, 32.

However, the influence of the idea of positive liberty was not limited to the precincts of Marxian or pseudo-Marxian critical theory. Indeed, in the English-speaking world the appeal to positive liberty was used by thinkers such as Green, Hobhouse, and John Dewey to promote liberal and reformist rather than radical and revolutionary ends. The roots of this way of thinking lie in Mill, who, although he held that laissez-faire "should be the general practice" and that "every departure from it, unless required by some great good, is a certain evil," was nevertheless skeptical about the association of freedom with a private property regime. For Mill, economic questions must be strictly subordinated to questions of individual well-being, and so he argues in *On Liberty* that "the principle of individual liberty is not involved in the doctrine of Free Trade," because "restraints [on trade] affect only that part of conduct which society is competent to restrain, and are wrong solely because they do not really produce the results which it is desired to produce." Indeed, the limited range of choices that are available to the average worker led him to suggest that "[t]he restraints of Communism would be freedom in comparison with the present condition of the majority of the human race" – though he goes on to ask, rather presciently, whether in a "Communistic" society "the absolute dependence of each on all, and surveillance of each by all, would...grind all down into a tame uniformity of thoughts, feelings, and actions."[67]

This appeal to human flourishing as the proper end of human freedom, and to the regulation of economic activity as a necessary means for achieving that end, proved to be enormously influential in the decades following Mill's death. Thus Green argued in 1881 that "[w]hen we measure the progress of a society by its growth in freedom, we measure it by the increasing development and exercise *on the whole* of those powers of contributing to social good with which we believe the members of society

---

[67] Mill, *Principles of Political Economy*, p. 945 (book 5, chapter 11); *On Liberty*, p. 293 (chapter 5); *Principles of Political Economy*, p. 209 (book 2, chapter 1). Mill argues in particular that "[t]he generality of labourers...have as little choice of occupation or freedom of locomotion, are practically as dependent on fixed rules and on the will of others, as they could be on any system short of actual slavery": ibid. Statements like this led Mises to blame Mill for "the thoughtless confounding of liberal and socialist ideas that led to the decline of English liberalism" and to add, rather strikingly, that "[i]n comparison with Mill all other socialist writers – even Marx, Engels, and Lassalle – are scarcely of any importance": *Liberalism*, pp. 153–4. Mill, for his part, remarked in a letter to the journalist John Plummer that "Spencer, in his *Social Statics*, carries his hostility to government agency beyond reasonable bounds": letter to John Plummer, October 3, 1863, *Collected Works*, vol. 15, p. 888.

to be endowed; in short, by the greater power on the part of the citizens as a body to make the most and best of themselves." "[I]t is the business of the state," he suggests, "not indeed directly to promote moral goodness, but to maintain the conditions without which a free exercise of the human faculties is impossible," and "the true and the only justification of the rights of property" is that they "contribut[e] to that equal development of the faculties of all which is the highest good for all." Green is even more skeptical than Mill that the "rights of property" go very far in this respect: "Could the enlightened self-interest or benevolence of individuals, working under a system of unlimited freedom of contract, have ever brought them into a state compatible with the free development of the human faculties? No one," he insists, "can have any doubt as to the answer," and "[n]o one has a right to do what he will with his own in such a way as to contravene this end."[68]

Hobhouse, in his own influential statement of liberal principles, agrees with Green in thinking that "[t]he foundation of liberty is the idea of growth," and that the ideal society is one "which lives and flourishes by the harmonious growth of its parts, each of which in developing on its own lines and in accordance with its own nature tends on the whole to further the development of others." Because it is "the function of the State...to secure conditions upon which its citizens are able to win by their own efforts all that is necessary to a full civic efficiency," and because "[t]he opportunities of work and the remuneration for work are determined by a complex mass of social forces which no individual, certainly no individual workman, can shape," he concludes that "[t]he 'right to work' and the right to a 'living wage' are just as valid as the rights of person or property." He therefore insists that "every citizen should have full means of earning by socially useful labour so much material support as experience proves to be the necessary basis of a healthy, civilized existence," and that "if...the means are not in actual fact sufficiently available he is held to have a claim not as of charity but as of right on the national resources to make good of the deficiency."[69] Dewey, who Hayek once described as "the leading philosopher of American left-wingism," argues more bluntly that "the demand for liberty is a demand for power" and urges "those who are struggling to replace the present economic system by a cooperative one" to "remember that in struggling for a new system of social restraints and controls they are also struggling for a more

---

[68] Green, "Liberal Legislation," pp. 199, 202, 200, 203, 200 (original emphasis).
[69] Hobhouse, *Liberalism*, pp. 59, 65, 76, 79, 89–90 (chapters 5–6).

equal and equitable balance of powers that will enhance and multiply the effective liberties of the mass of individuals."[70]

This "social" brand of liberalism proved so popular that by mid-century Mises, Hayek, Milton Friedman, and the other defenders of market freedom found it necessary to remind their readers of the "classical" meaning of the word.[71] Moreover, by associating freedom with self-realization, and by making self-realization depend among other things on the proper design of political institutions, the social liberals came closer than either the radical defenders or the radical critics of capitalism to embracing a genuinely republican conception of freedom. However they, like the defenders of market freedom, endorse the republican position in a rather one-sided way. Rather than associate freedom with the absence of arbitrary power, the social liberals seek to identify the conditions under which "true consent" could be given to a particular set of economic and political arrangements. The validity of their position, like that of their juristic predecessors, therefore hinges on the question of the proper meaning of individual choice: Are we free insofar as we are able to enter into whatever contracts we choose, or must we choose in such a way that we advance our genuine interests as human beings? This question offers a choice between the competing values of negative and positive liberty, not between one or the other of these values and republican freedom itself. Indeed, when the question is posed in this way, it becomes difficult to conceive of republican freedom as an independent political value.

At the heart of republican political thought is the claim that the control of arbitrary power is a necessary condition for the practice of virtue. The enjoyment of republican freedom is therefore bound up with the exercise of collective control over the institutions – especially, but not only, the political institutions – by which we are governed. It follows that republican freedom can only be enjoyed in the company and through the cooperation of other people – it is, in this sense, a "relational" good. For

[70] John Dewey, "Liberty and Social Control" (1935), in Jo Ann Boydston, ed., *The Later Works of John Dewey* (Carbondale: Southern Illinois University Press, 1981–91), vol. 11, pp. 360, 362. For Hayek's criticism of Dewey, see *Road to Serfdom*, p. 30n, and *Constitution of Liberty*, pp. 17 and 424.

[71] See, for example, Mises's preface to the English-language edition of *Liberalism* (1962); chapters 1–2 of Hayek's *Road to Serfdom* and his essay "Why I Am Not a Conservative," included as a "postscript" to the *Constitution of Liberty*; and Friedman's *Capitalism and Freedom* (Chicago: University of Chicago Press), pp. 5–6. Bettina Bien Grieves reports that Mises's book, which was published in German in 1927 under the title *Liberalismus*, first appeared in English as *The Free and Prosperous Commonwealth* because the original title was deemed "too confusing" for English-speaking readers: *Liberalism*, p. ix.

republicans the aim is neither to depersonalize power nor to transcend it, nor even to ensure that it is distributed equally, whatever that might mean in practice. Rather, republicans seek to ensure that the exercise of power is guided and checked by those who are subject to it in such a way that it is made to serve the common good. Freedom so understood is a property of states (or polities) as well as of the individuals who live in them, and so it follows that we cannot enjoy republican freedom without making collective judgments about what kinds of relationships and forms of behavior are worthy of a free people. By combining a concern for individual independence with a concern for the cultivation and practice of virtue, and by connecting each of these concerns to the realm of political action, this conception of freedom brings together aspects of negative and positive liberty without being reducible to either of them. Nevertheless, we have seen that when republican ideas were invoked over the course of the 19th and 20th centuries, they were increasingly tied to one or the other of these distinctively modern ways of thinking. As a result, whereas republicans had once been criticized for valuing freedom at the expense of political values such as peace, security, and justice, now they were criticized for providing a muddled defense of a more coherent conception of freedom – or for defending a value that is not really freedom at all.

Conclusion

Markets and the New Republicanism

> A movement whose main promise is the relief from responsibility cannot but be antimoral in its effect, however lofty the ideals to which it owes its birth.
>
> Friedrich Hayek, *The Road to Serfdom*

I began this book by pointing out that the close association in modern political thought between freedom and the market is both historically anomalous and, in some respects, morally troubling. To the extent that the defenders of market freedom are able to monopolize the language of freedom in public life, they are able to skew the terms of debate in a way that tends to exaggerate the merits of market-based solutions to matters of public concern. When we ask whether governments should use fiscal and monetary policy to try to stimulate the economy, or whether certain businesses are "too big to fail," or whether individuals should be shielded from the consequences of bad economic decisions or bad economic conditions, or whether those who suffer at the hands of the market – the unemployed, the uninsured, the unlucky, the poor – should receive public assistance, there is a folk intuition that says that in a truly free society none of these things would happen: that economic growth would be promoted by private rather than public means, failing businesses would be allowed to fail, people would have to live with the consequences of their bad decisions or bad luck, those in need would be left to their own devices, and so on. The contrary policies can be defended only by appealing to some other value or set of values: justice, solidarity, prosperity, stability, sustainability, or charity, for example. Yet the idea that freedom means *market* freedom – freedom to do what you want with what is yours and to enjoy the rewards or suffer the consequences – profoundly shapes debates about public policy even when other values prevail in a given case. In short, the very language that we use to talk about questions of political economy – the language of the "free" market – predisposes us to respond to those questions in a certain way, even when there is reason to think that this may not be the best response either in economic or in human terms.

I also suggested at the beginning of this book that the best way to challenge the hegemony of this market-centered conception of freedom is by learning to see it as something that was invented at a particular time and place, in response to specific practical demands and in order to serve specific ideological purposes. We have now seen that the association of freedom with the market resulted from the contingent fact that the early modern Europeans inherited their conception of political freedom from the self-governing republics of classical antiquity, and that the threat that the rise of modern commercial societies posed to established beliefs and ways of life – that markets are ungovernable, and that participation in markets is incompatible with the cultivation of civic and martial virtue – appeared as a threat to freedom in this republican sense. However, the republican association of freedom with the control of arbitrary power and the practice of virtue proved to be ambiguous and flexible enough that it could be used to defend as well as to criticize the rise of commerce. The resulting debate laid bare the tensions that had always been contained in the republican conception of freedom, exposing ideological vulnerabilities in both the pro- and the anti-commercial understandings of republican freedom. The commercial republicans responded by weaving the republican association of commerce with peace, prosperity, and the absence of dependence together with the juristic appeal to consent as the foundation of legitimate political rule, and the resulting ideological synthesis gave rise to the market conception of freedom with which we are now familiar.

My aim in pursuing this line of inquiry has not been to demonstrate the superiority of republican to market freedom (or vice versa), or to show that all questions about the meaning and value of freedom can be answered by appealing to one or the other of these views. As I said at the outset, our aim in theorizing about freedom should not be to construct a conceptual framework that captures all of its possible meanings, still less to arrive at a single "best" understanding of the term. Rather, we should design our inquiry in a way that helps us to respond to the practical challenges of a given time and place, and I believe that a framework that centers around the contrast between republican and market freedom speaks more directly to the practical challenges of our own time and place than the leading alternatives. My aim, then, has been to make intelligible to the contemporary reader the idea that freedom is something that can be realized in – and not simply threatened by – political action, while doing justice to the more recent and undeniably powerful claims of the market and its apologists. Such an effort faces two related challenges. First, it must show that there is a distinctively republican conception of freedom that can neither be collapsed into nor divided without remainder between the negative and positive conceptions of liberty that succeeded it. Second and more importantly, it must show that this republican conception of freedom provides a viable alternative not only to the negative and positive liberty traditions, but to market freedom itself. I believe, and now wish to argue, that it is only when we bring the internal complexity of the republican position into the foreground that the nature of the contrast between republican and market freedom, and the significance of a theory of freedom that is built around the distinction between them, becomes clear. I also believe that the recent revival of scholarly interest in republican thought, as rich and fruitful as it has been, has not been entirely successful on these grounds.

Scholarly interest in modern republicanism can be traced back to the 1960s, when a group of intellectual historians, most notable among them Bernard Bailyn, J. G. A. Pocock, Quentin Skinner, and Gordon Wood, began to call into question the idea that American political thought, and early modern political thought more generally, was as monolithically liberal as scholars at the time generally supposed.[1] These scholars objected in particular to the claim that a straight line could be drawn from the governing ideology of the 20th-century capitalist democracies back to the political thought of the 17th and 18th centuries, a claim that both liberals and Marxists were concerned, each for their own purposes, to promote.[2] By attending to the classical and Renaissance roots of early

---

[1] See in particular Bernard Bailyn, *The Ideological Origins of the American Revolution* (Cambridge, MA: Harvard University Press, 1967); Gordon S. Wood, *The Creation of the American Republic, 1776–1787* (New York: W. W. Norton, 1969); J. G. A. Pocock, *The Machiavellian Moment: Florentine Political Thought and the Atlantic Republican Tradition* (Princeton, NJ: Princeton University Press, 1975); Quentin Skinner, *The Foundations of Modern Political Thought* (New York: Cambridge University Press, 1978), vol. 1.

[2] The liberal reading of 18th-century political thought, and of American political thought more generally, was influentially set out in Louis Hartz's *The Liberal Tradition in America: An Interpretation of American Political Thought Since the Revolution* (New York: Harcourt, Brace, 1955). C. B. Macpherson offers an influential Marxian

modern ideas, they called attention to the central role that the language of self-government, virtue, and the common good – and of tyranny, corruption, and faction – played in the early modern period, and they showed how this language fit within a larger tradition of thought that had its own logic and coherence. They were engaged, in other words, in a project of historical recovery, an effort to restore a forgotten intellectual heritage to its rightful place in early modern political history, and (here opinions were more mixed) to defend it as an ideal worth pursuing in the present. Even Skinner, despite his well-known aversion to the trans-historical use of political concepts, has recently described himself as "a kind of archaeologist, bringing buried intellectual treasure back to the surface, dusting it down and enabling us to reconsider what we think of it."[3]

However, as we might expect in light of the discussion so far, the republican historians disagreed among themselves about what exactly it was that they were recovering and what exactly was valuable about it, and these disagreements were – and remain – especially sharp with regard to the question of the meaning and value of republican freedom. The immediate challenge was to fit the republican view into the negative-positive liberty framework that had risen to dominance in the early decades of the 20th century and received its canonical statement in Isaiah Berlin's "Two Concepts of Liberty," first published in 1958. For Pocock, "[t]he republican vocabulary...articulate[s] the positive conception of liberty.... [I]t is the freedom *to* speak, *to* act, *to* associate, *to* enter upon relations with one's equals, *to* take decisions, *to* affirm what one's city and one's self shall be; to be – in short – the political creature it is said one is, and ought to be, by nature. It is less a freedom to do than to be; less an assertion of right than an exercise of virtue." Because positive liberty in this "civic humanist" sense is embedded in the open-ended possibilities of the *vivere civile* rather than in the closed structures of natural law, Pocock sees in its recovery an opportunity to transform our understanding of the history of political thought, a history that has, he argues, "from the beginning, and for good reasons, been conceived as an interplay between the languages of philosophy, theology and jurisprudence" and has therefore had "an inbuilt bias in favour of a negative concept of liberty." Indeed, he suggests

reading of 17th-century political thought in his *The Political Theory of Possessive Individualism: Hobbes to Locke* (New York: Oxford University Press, 1962).

[3] Quentin Skinner, *Liberty before Liberalism* (New York: Cambridge University Press, 1998), p. 112. Skinner's methodological essays have been revised and collected in his *Visions of Politics*, vol. 1: *Regarding Method* (New York: Cambridge University Press, 2002).

that because "the intensely rhetorical, historical and Roman language of
republican citizenship does not fit easily into this framework," historians
have hitherto been guided by "an impulse not to rewrite the history of
civic humanism, but to write it out of history as far as possible."[4]

Although Pocock and Skinner have each emphasized that they are
working along similar lines in their efforts to recover the republican
tradition,[5] the analysis of republican freedom that Skinner worked out
over the course of the 1980s came to exactly the opposite conclusion: As
we saw in Chapter 1, Skinner argues that republicans hold a negative
conception of liberty, differing from their liberal successors only in the
claim that freedom so understood is best secured through the practice
of civic virtue rather than through the granting of individual rights by
the state. He makes the rather daring inference that Machiavelli, who he
takes to be representative of republican thinking on this question, "has
no quarrel with the Hobbesian assumption that the capacity to pursue
[our] ends without obstruction is what the term 'liberty' properly signifieth" but "merely argues that the performance of public services, and
the cultivation of the virtues needed to perform them" are "instrumentally necessary to the avoidance of coercion and servitude" and are thus
"necessary conditions of assuring any degree of personal liberty in the
ordinary Hobbesian sense of the term." Indeed, Skinner goes so far as
to argue, in direct opposition to Pocock, that "the republican writers...
never appeal to a 'positive' view of social freedom. They never argue, that
is, that we are moral beings with certain determinate purposes, and thus
that we are only in the fullest sense in possession of our liberty when
these purposes are realised."[6]

---

4 Pocock, "Virtues, Rights, and Manners: A Model for Historians of Political Thought"
   (1981), reprinted in idem, *Virtue, Commerce, and History: Essays on Political Thought
   and History* (New York: Cambridge University Press, 1985), p. 40; "Foundations and
   Moments," in Annabel Brett and James Tully, eds., *Rethinking the Foundations of Modern
   Political Thought* (New York: Cambridge University Press, 2006), pp. 43–4 (original
   emphasis); see also the "Afterword" to the 2003 edition of *The Machiavellian Moment*,
   esp. pp. 558–62, 572–3.
5 See, for example, Pocock, "Virtue, Rights, and Manners," pp. 38–9, 46–7; "Afterword" to
   Machiavellian Moment, pp. 553–62; "Foundations and Moments," passim. Skinner has
   likewise acknowledged that Pocock's *Machiavellian Moment* "exercised a profound influence" on his work and has characterized his debt to Pocock, among a handful of others,
   as "immense, enormous, vast, stonking and meta": "Surveying *The Foundations*: A
   Retrospect and Reassessment," in Brett and Tully, eds., *op. cit.*, p. 240; *Visions of Politics*,
   vol. 1, p. xi (cf. vol. 2, p. xiv and vol. 3, p. xii).
6 Skinner, "The Idea of Negative Liberty," in Richard Rorty, Jerome B. Schneewind, and
   Quentin Skinner, eds., *Philosophy in History: Essays on the Historiography of Philosophy*

The republican tradition began to attract the attention of political theorists in the 1980s and 1990s as thinkers such as Michael Sandel and Charles Taylor drew on republican ideas in working out what became known as the "communitarian" critique of liberalism, and thinkers who were more sympathetic toward liberalism, including Richard Dagger and Cass Sunstein, argued in response that republican and liberal ideas do not contradict but rather complement one another. Despite this important point of disagreement, the communitarian and liberal republicans each agree with Pocock in associating republican freedom with self-government and the cultivation of civic virtue. For Sandel, "[t]he republican conception of freedom...requires a formative politics"; it "does not take people's existing preferences, whatever they may be, and try to satisfy them" but "seeks instead to cultivate in citizens the qualities of character necessary to the common good of self-government." Sunstein agrees that republican government is "not a scheme in which people impress...their private preferences on the government," but rather "a system in which the selection of governing values [is] the object of the governmental process," adding that the chief threat to such a government is "the elimination of civic virtue and the pursuit of self-interest by political actors." Taylor finds that the republican tradition "defines participation in self-rule as the essence of freedom," and Dagger's "republican liberalism" aims to cultivate the "ability or capacity to lead a self-governed life," by "combin[ing] a respect for the rights and liberties of the individual as a citizen...with a recognition of the need for active, public-spirited citizenship."[7]

What is missing from these accounts is an appreciation of the republican concern with the control of arbitrary power and thus with the proper design of political institutions: Even Sunstein, the most institutionally minded of the thinkers just mentioned, holds that "[e]ducation and prevailing morality...provide the principal lines of defense against the

(New York: Cambridge University Press, 1984), p. 217; "The Paradoxes of Political Liberty," *Tanner Lectures on Human Values* 7 (1986), p. 247 (emphasis added).

7 Michael J. Sandel, *Democracy's Discontent: America in Search of a Public Philosophy* (Cambridge, MA: Harvard University Press, 1996), pp. 6, 25; Cass R. Sunstein, "The Enduring Legacy of Republicanism," in Stephen L. Elkin and Karol Edward Soltan, eds., *A New Constitutionalism: Designing Political Institutions for a Good Society* (Chicago: University of Chicago Press, 1993), pp. 175–6; Charles Taylor, "Cross-Purposes: The Liberal-Communitarian Debate," in Nancy Rosenblum, ed., *Liberalism and the Moral Life* (Cambridge, MA: Harvard University Press, 1989), p. 179; Richard Dagger, *Civic Virtues: Rights, Citizenship, and Republican Liberalism* (New York: Oxford University Press, 1997), pp. 38, 104.

dangers of faction."[8] The political philosopher Philip Pettit was the first contemporary scholar to give sustained attention to the central role that the absence of arbitrary power – what he calls "non-domination" – plays in defining the republican conception of freedom. "Domination" for Pettit means "having to live at the mercy of another, having to live in a manner that leaves you vulnerable to some ill that the other is in a position arbitrarily to impose." We are unfree on this view even if the dominating agent never takes advantage of his or her position, because we can never be sure if and when such interference will come. Although Pettit agrees with his classical forebears in finding the paradigmatic case of domination in the relationship between master and slave, he also calls attention to its presence or potential presence in relationships that the classical republicans regarded as being non- or extra-political in nature, such as those between men and women, between employers and employees, between different cultures, and even between human beings and the natural world. In each of these cases, non-domination is to be desired because it "goes with being able to look the other in the eye"; it means that "you...do not have to live either in fear of [the] other...or in deference to them.... You are a somebody in relation to them, not a nobody. You are a person in your own legal and social right."[9]

If Pocock's view of republican freedom is participatory, Pettit's is juridical: He takes self-government to be valuable only insofar as "it is necessary for promoting the enjoyment of freedom as non-domination...not because freedom, as a positive conception would suggest, is nothing more or less than the right of democratic participation." Indeed, Pettit agrees with the classical republicans – and with Tocqueville and Mill – in thinking that "direct democracy may often be a very bad thing, since it may ensure the ultimate form of arbitrariness: the tyranny of a majority."[10] Thus where Sandel, Taylor, Sunstein, and Dagger follow Pocock in associating republican freedom with positive liberty in the sense of active citizenship and political self-rule, Pettit agrees with Skinner in associating republican freedom with the idea of negative liberty: Indeed, he

---

[8] Sunstein, "Enduring Legacy of Republicanism," p. 176. Dagger agrees in thinking that "[t]he best hope [for preventing corruption] lies in 'the education of desire' or, more optimistically, in an appeal to 'the compulsion of duty'": *Civic Virtues*, p. 16.

[9] Philip Pettit, *Republicanism: A Theory of Freedom and Government* (2nd ed., New York: Oxford University Press, 1999 [1997]), quoted at pp. 4–5, 71. For an illuminating discussion of the kinds of relationships in which we should be concerned about the presence of arbitrary power see, ibid., chapter 5.

[10] Ibid., p. 8.

originally portrayed republican freedom as a *kind* of negative liberty, differing from its liberal rival only in its greater "resilience."[11] Pettit has argued more recently that Berlin's negative-positive liberty dichotomy "has served us ill" by obscuring the republican alternative, and Skinner, who has revised his own "negative" interpretation of republican freedom to bring it more closely in line with Pettit's view, now refers to republican freedom as a "third concept of liberty."[12] Pocock nevertheless complains that this "neo-Roman" view seems "oddly incomplete when set beside the Aristotelian definition of liberty as equality," where equality is understood as "an actual and positive relationship; a friendship or fraternity... which is to be enjoyed for its own sake and, when converted into decision, becomes a necessary way of asserting one's humanity." "To have no master," he argues, "is a means or prerequisite of equality" in this sense, "not the end for which one has it," and "when put forward as an alternative to the positive freedom of the citizen, it begins to look like a diminution of the latter."[13]

Thus if Pocock and his followers focus on the cultivation of virtue to the neglect of the control of arbitrary power, then Pettit and Skinner focus by contrast on the control of arbitrary power to the neglect of the cultivation of virtue. Both sides are vulnerable, in other words, to the difficulty that we identified at the end of Chapter 5: that once we lose sight of the internal complexity of republican freedom – the claim that the cultivation and practice of virtue *depends* on the control of arbitrary power, and vice versa – then the republican position threatens to collapse into either the negative or the positive liberty view.[14] Nevertheless, we can

---

[11] See, for example, Pettit, "Negative Liberty, Liberal and Republican," *European Journal of Philosophy* 1 (1993), pp. 15–38; "Liberalism and Republicanism," *Australian Journal of Political Science* 28 (1993), pp. 162–89; and "A Definition of Negative Liberty," *Ratio* 2 (1989), pp. 153–68.

[12] Pettit, *Republicanism*, p. 18; Skinner, "A Third Concept of Liberty," *Proceedings of the British Academy* 117 (2002), pp. 237–68. Skinner has recently written that "[i]t was only with the help of Philip Pettit's path-finding work that I eventually managed to clarify to my own satisfaction the defining characteristics of the theory I had [previously] sketched": "Surveying *The Foundations*," p. 257. For Skinner's presentation of the idea of freedom as non-domination, see *Liberty before Liberalism*, pp. 68–75; on the remaining disagreements between Skinner and Pettit, see ibid., pp. 82–5 and Pettit, "Keeping Republican Freedom Simple: On a Difference with Quentin Skinner," *Political Theory* 30 (2002), pp. 339–56; cf. *Republicanism*, pp. 300–3.

[13] Pocock, "Foundations and Moments," pp. 46–7.

[14] Ian Carter has argued, for example, that Skinner and Pettit's brand of republican freedom must be understood either as a "resilient" form of negative liberty, or in positive terms as "a conception of freedom as collective self-mastery or self-determination": *A Measure of Freedom* (New York: Oxford University Press, 1999), pp. 237–45, quoted at

find support for the more complex position in the writings of the contemporary republicans if we know to look for it. We have seen, for example, that Pocock thinks of virtue not as a fixed or "natural" quality, but rather as one that is realized, if at all, in the open field of political action. It follows that the cultivation and practice of virtue so understood is only possible so long as the field remains open, that is, so long as no individual or faction within the polity has the power to impose its will unilaterally on the whole. We have also seen that for Pettit the value of non-domination consists above all in the fact that it prevents individuals from being "demeaned by their vulnerability...forced to fawn or toady or flatter in the attempt to ingratiate themselves."[15] Skinner calls these pathologies by their proper name, emphasizing that for the early modern republicans, as for their classical forebears, "slavery inevitably breeds slavishness," and that "those condemned to a life of servitude will find themselves obliged to cultivate the habits of servility."[16] Despite their differences, then, contemporary republicans agree with their predecessors in thinking that our character is fundamentally shaped by the social and political context in which we find ourselves, and that we are only free insofar as we are able to shape that context in turn.

The shared, if sometimes only tacit, allegiance of contemporary republicans to this more complex understanding of republican freedom is brought out most clearly in their defense of deliberative forms of civic engagement. Here again contemporary republicans hold on the one hand that in order to be free we have to play an active role as citizens in shaping the social and political forces by which we are in turn shaped, and

---

pp. 244–5. See also Robert E. Goodin, "Folie Républicaine," *Annual Review of Political Science* 6 (2003), pp. 60–1.

[15] Pettit, *Republicanism*, p. 5; cf. pp. 22, 25, 60–1, 132. Pettit devotes the final chapter of his *Republicanism* to a discussion of the need for civic virtue – or, as he prefers to say, "civility" – to sustain a republican polity, though he places greater emphasis on law-abidingness than on active citizenship.

[16] Quentin Skinner and Martin van Gelderen, "Introduction" to idem, eds., *Republicanism: A Shared European Heritage* (New York: Cambridge University Press, 2002), p. 2. Skinner therefore seems to me to err by suggesting, in response to prodding by Pocock, that "the crown's opponents in early Stuart England" had "almost nothing [to say] about the need for the body of the people to cultivate the civic virtues" ("Surveying *The Foundations*," p. 260). As Skinner himself has observed, thinkers such as James Harrington, John Milton, and Algernon Sidney were obsessed with the idea that absolute monarchy breeds corruption, precisely because the king can command, as Sidney puts it, "a most obsequious respect, or a pretended affection for his person, together with a servile obedience to his commands," so that "all application to virtuous actions will cease": *Discourses Concerning Government* (1683/1698), chapter 2 §28, quoted in Skinner, *Liberty before Liberalism*, p. 93; see more generally ibid., pp. 87–96 passim.

on the other hand that the presence of arbitrary power poses a threat to our freedom precisely because it has a corrupting effect on our character. The aim of a republican politics is therefore to ensure that the field of relations with which our beliefs and preferences are formed is designed in such a way that our virtue is cultivated and the common good is served. Institutionally speaking, this requires that we register our preferences about matters of public concern in a visible and politically salient context so that we are obliged to defend them in other-regarding terms. Morally speaking it requires not only that the political community be responsive to our interests as individuals, but that we be responsive as citizens to the interests of the political community. In short, the proper content of our interests, and the extent to which it is up to the political community to help us realize them, is an issue that we have to work out together in public life. As Sunstein puts it, "through discussion people can, in their capacities as citizens, escape private interests and engage in pursuit of the public good" – an aim that is, he points out, "closely allied with the republican beliefs that the motivating force of political behavior should not be self-interest, narrowly-defined, and that civic virtue should play a role in political life."[17]

Republicans are of course hardly alone among contemporary political theorists in criticizing the "pluralistic" conception of democracy as a mechanism for the mere aggregation of individual preferences.[18] The republican version of this line of argument is distinctive in that it associates a deliberative politics with the enjoyment of *freedom*, in the double-barreled republican sense that to act according to our selfish preferences is to act unvirtuously, and that to be subject to a political will formed out of the aggregation of such preferences is to be subject to the

---

[17] Sunstein, "Enduring Legacy of Republicanism," p. 176; "Beyond the Republican Revival," *Yale Law Journal* 97 (1988), p. 1550. Sunstein is careful to add that "[t]he republican position is not that *every* issue is subject to political resolution; it is instead that *some* questions can yield general agreement through deliberation": ibid., p. 1555 (emphasis added); cf. Pettit, *Republicanism*, p. 190.

[18] See, among many possible examples, Jon Elster, "The Market and the Forum: Three Varieties of Political Theory" in Jon Elster and Aanund Hylland, eds., *Foundations of Social Choice Theory* (New York: Cambridge University Press, 1986), pp. 103–32; Bernard Manin, "On Legitimacy and Political Deliberation," trans. Elly Stein and Jane Mansbridge, *Political Theory* 15 (1987), pp. 338–68; Joshua Cohen, "Deliberation and Democratic Legitimacy," in Alan Hamlin and Philip Pettit, eds., *The Good Polity: Normative Analysis of the State* (New York: Basil Blackwell, 1989), pp. 17–34; Jürgen Habermas, "Three Normative Models of Democracy," in Seyla Benhabib, ed., *Democracy and Difference: Contesting the Boundaries of the Political* (Princeton, NJ: Princeton University Press, 1996), pp. 21–30.

arbitrary will of the most powerful faction or factions. In other words, contemporary republicans go beyond other deliberative democrats in offering a fundamental criticism not only of "aggregative" democracy, but of the market-centered conception of freedom on which it rests. Pettit holds, for example, that "interest-group pluralism . . . is inherently inimical to the goal of promoting freedom as non-domination" and concludes that republicans are therefore "bound to hold out against the way in which such pluralism wants to have self-seeking or 'naked' preferences become the motor of political life."[19] Sunstein agrees that for republicans "politics has a deliberative or transformative dimension" whose "function is to select values, to implement 'preferences about preferences,' or to provide opportunities for preference formation rather than simply to implement existing desires. . . . In this respect," he argues, "political ordering [of preferences] is distinct from market ordering."[20] Dagger puts the point more succinctly, pointing out that "the so-called consumer-citizen is, in traditional republican terms, a corruption of what a citizen should be."[21]

The obvious objection to this line of argument, and the one that is most often advanced by the defenders of market freedom, is that it is both misleading and dangerous to associate freedom with the pursuit of an end as fundamentally ambiguous and contested as the "common" good. Not only does such a view threaten to countenance the kind of paternalism that so worried Berlin, it also threatens to elide the paradoxes that go along with any effort to associate individual liberty with a project of collective will formation – the kinds of paradoxes that Rousseau explores so brilliantly and inconclusively. The defenders of market freedom emphasize that politics is a matter of trading values off against each other, and that it is only in a competitive market economy that individuals are allowed to decide for themselves how these tradeoffs are made. As Milton Friedman puts it, "[e]very extension of the range of issues for which explicit agreement is sought strains further the delicate threads that hold society together," whereas "[t]he wider the range of

---

[19] Pettit, *Republicanism*, p. 205; cf. ibid., pp. 187–90 and 202–5 passim. The term "naked preferences" is Sunstein's; see his *The Partial Constitution* (Cambridge, MA: Harvard University Press, 1993), esp. pp. 25–37.

[20] Sunstein, "Beyond the Republican Revival," pp. 1545, 1550; "Enduring Legacy of Republicanism," p. 176; see more generally his "Preferences and Politics," *Philosophy and Public Affairs* 20 (1991), pp. 3–34.

[21] Dagger, "Neo-Republicanism and the Civic Economy," *Politics, Philosophy and Economics* 5 (2006), p. 159; cf. *Civic Virtues*, pp. 104–8.

activities covered by the market, the fewer are the issues on which explicitly political decisions are required and hence on which it is necessary to
achieve agreement." The market is, in this sense, "a system of proportional representation." Friedman concludes, like Hayek, Mises, Spencer,
and Sumner before him, that state interference with individual choice
is a bad thing in itself, not necessarily a bad to be avoided absolutely,
but nevertheless a cost that should be weighed against whatever benefits
might be expected to result. "[G]overnment may enable us at times," he
concedes, "to accomplish jointly what we would find it more difficult or
expensive to accomplish severally," but "any such use of government is
fraught with danger. We should not and cannot avoid using government
in this way. But there should be a clear and large balance of advantages
before we do."[22]

From this point of view, it is political decision making and not the
pursuit of individual interests that is the "arbitrary" factor in social life.
The defenders of market freedom do not argue, of course, that market
actors are entirely autonomous, as if we could somehow free ourselves
from social pressures once and for all. Friedman admits, for example, that "[t]he participant in a competitive market has no appreciable
power to alter the terms of exchange" and indeed "is hardly visible as
a separate entity."[23] Nevertheless, as we saw in Chapter 5, it is possible
to believe that individuals are not entirely responsible for the economic
circumstances that they face and still believe that there are good reasons
to treat them as if they were. As Hayek puts it, we must choose between
"submission to the impersonal and seemingly irrational forces of the
market" and "submission to an equally uncontrollable and therefore
arbitrary power of other men."[24] Rather than associate freedom either
causally or constitutively with the display of civic virtue and the deliberative formation of a public will, the defenders of market freedom argue
that we should carve out a sphere within which everyone can do as they
please and allow the common good, in the only sense worthy of the
name, to emerge as the unintended by-product of those self-regarding
actions. Institutionally speaking, this line of argument treats the market

---

[22] Milton Friedman, with the assistance of Rose D. Friedman, *Capitalism and Freedom*
(Chicago: University of Chicago Press, 1962), pp. 23–4, 15.
[23] Ibid., p. 120.
[24] Friedrich Hayek, *The Road to Serfdom* (Chicago: University of Chicago Press, 1944),
p. 224; cf. idem, *The Constitution of Liberty* (Chicago: University of Chicago Press,
1960), pp. 82–3.

and the democratic state more or less interchangeably as sites of preference aggregation, and the citizen more or less interchangeably as a consumer and a voter.[25] Morally speaking, it requires that we absolve individuals of direct responsibility for the social consequences of their own (legal) actions – or, in other words, that we no longer treat individual virtue as a matter of public concern.

The latter claim is softened, of course, by the further claim that the unregulated pursuit of self-interest will on balance lead, regardless of the intentions of the individuals concerned, to collectively optimal social outcomes. As we saw in Chapter 4, however, the defenders of market freedom are not always consistent in adhering to this consequentialist line. Consider, for example, the line of argument that Friedman lays out in his influential book, *Capitalism and Freedom* (1962), a book that continues to set the agenda for the market-based approach to public policy. Friedman offers familiar economic arguments against minimum-wage laws, agricultural subsidies, tariffs, and similar policies – and against the myopia of the electorates that support and enact them – on the grounds that their market-distorting effects impose diffuse costs on society in the form of higher unemployment, higher prices, losses in economic productivity, and so on that outweigh whatever particular benefits they provide.[26] He does not deny, however, that there are cases in which governments can act directly to improve the material well-being of their citizens; he merely argues that in such cases the value of economic efficiency is trumped by the value of individual liberty. For example, he objects to the provision of in-kind assistance (such as housing, food, and health-care subsidies) to the poor and to mandatory state retirement programs such as Social Security, not because such programs do not achieve their desired ends, but rather because they are paternalistic and therefore unacceptable from the standpoint of market freedom: "If a man knowingly prefers to live for today," he asks, then "by what right do we prevent him from doing so? We may argue with him, seek to persuade him that he is wrong, but are we entitled to use coercion to prevent him from doing

---

[25] For two classic statements of this position, see part 4 of Joseph A. Schumpeter's *Capitalism, Socialism and Democracy* (New York: Harper & Row, 1942) and Anthony Downs, *An Economic Theory of Democracy* (New York: Harper Collins, 1957). For a more recent statement, see Adam Przeworski, "Minimalist Conception of Democracy: A Defense," in Ian Shapiro and Casiano Hacker-Cordón, eds., *Democracy's Value* (New York: Cambridge University Press, 1999), pp. 23–55.

[26] Friedman, *Capitalism and Freedom*, e.g., pp. 35–6, 180–2.

what he chooses to do? Is there not always the possibility that he is right and that we are wrong?"[27]

The implications of Friedman's commitment to anti-paternalism are most dramatically illustrated in his discussion of racial segregation and discrimination – an example of state interference in the "private" sphere that most people today are likely to regard as having been both justified and largely successful. Friedman argues that racial prejudice expresses a "taste," no different in kind from a taste for opera or (as he says) for attractive housekeepers. The only difference between racial and other forms of discrimination, he suggests, is that "we" share the taste in one case and not in the other. He emphasizes that he personally objects to the practice of racial discrimination, on the grounds that "a man should be judged by what he is and what he does and not by these external characteristics." He nevertheless insists that it is not up to the state to decide which criteria of discrimination are admissible and which inadmissible: "[I]n a society based on free discussion," he argues, "the appropriate recourse is for me to seek to persuade [racists] that their tastes are bad and that they should change their views and their behavior, not to use coercive power to enforce my tastes and my attitudes on others." He concludes that anti-discrimination laws are an unjustifiable imposition on the individual's freedom to act according to his tastes, "similar in principle" to the Nuremberg laws and Jim Crow.[28] Whatever we think of the merits of this line of argument, it provides an especially clear illustration of the fact that the appeals to consequentialism and anti-paternalism in market ideology are often at odds with one another, so that proponents of market freedom can lean first on one foot and then the other in defending their position.

The appeal of this way of thinking, whether it is applied to the poor and the elderly or to racial minorities, does not lie in the freedom that it offers to the vulnerable parties concerned but rather in the freedom that

[27] Ibid., p. 188; on public housing assistance and mandatory retirement programs see pp. 178–80 and 182–9, respectively; in the former case Friedman conflates the public subsidization of housing costs with the construction of public housing projects. Elsewhere he concedes that "the number of citizens who regard compulsory old age insurance as a deprivation of freedom may be few" but insists that "the believer in freedom has never counted noses": ibid., p. 9.

[28] Ibid., pp. 108–15, quoted at pp. 111, 113. Friedman admits that even racially unbiased whites were not free to hire or to openly serve blacks in the segregated South, but he does not draw the inference that the aggregate effects of individual behavior can themselves pose a threat to individual liberty. In this sense, his position is more superficial than Hayek's.

it offers to those who would otherwise be obliged to act on their behalf. As we saw in Chapter 5, the promise of market freedom is the promise of a world in which poverty, racial discrimination, and a host of other social problems will simply go away without our having to take explicit action to solve them; indeed, we are told that because markets provide the most efficient means of distributing scarce resources, any deliberate action that we might take outside a market framework would only be likely to make matters worse. Thus although it is often said that markets promote "personal responsibility," we can see that in a market society the framework within which we act is one in which we are *absolved* of responsibility for the larger social consequences of our actions: We become, morally speaking, invisible to other people, and what could be more liberating than that? In such a society, as Karl Polanyi puts it, "[a]ny decent individual could imagine himself free from all responsibility for acts of compulsion on the part of a state which he, personally, rejected; or for economic suffering in society from which he, personally, had not benefited. He was 'paying his way,' was 'in nobody's debt,' and was unentangled in the evil of power and economic value. His lack of responsibility for them seemed so evident that he denied their reality in the name of his freedom." Friedman puts the point more bluntly, pointing out that "it is difficult to argue that [the market actor] has any 'social responsibility' except that which is shared by all citizens to obey the law of the land and to live according to his lights."[29]

Can republican and market freedom be enjoyed in the same social world? We have already seen that the republican association of freedom with the absence of arbitrary power raises doubts about the compatibility of republican and market *institutions*. After all, it is a cardinal principle of market theory that economic efficiency requires that people be made systematically vulnerable to sudden and adverse changes of economic fortune.[30] Republicans therefore have reason to worry not only that inegalitarian market *outcomes* might create opportunities for the exercise of arbitrary power, but that the market as a mechanism for *generating*

---

[29] Karl Polanyi, *The Great Transformation: The Political and Economic Origins of Our Time* (Boston: Beacon Press, 1944), p. 266; Friedman, *Capitalism and Freedom*, p. 120.

[30] Hayek distinguishes, for example, between "the security which can be provided for all outside of and supplementary to the market system and the security which can be provided only for some and only by controlling or abolishing the market," and he argues that although a prosperous society should provide "the certainty of a given minimum of sustenance for all," it should not try to "protect individuals or groups...against losses imposing severe hardships having no moral justification yet inseparable from the competitive system": *Road to Serfdom*, pp. 133, 135.

those outcomes might function as an arbitrary power in the lives of those who are subject to it. Nevertheless, as we saw in Chapter 3, it is possible to mount a republican defense of a market economy on the grounds that it provides an efficient means of generating wealth and a useful mechanism for checking the arbitrary power of the state. Thus Pettit argues that "the republican tradition can join with the liberal and libertarian traditions in hailing the market for what it achieves" in expanding the realm of economic choice, even as he emphasizes that the republican conception of freedom provides grounds "for redistributing property or restricting the powers associated with absolute or relative wealth, so that inequality in non-domination is minimized." Sunstein argues along similar lines that "markets are mere instruments to be evaluated by their effects," reminding his readers that they can "produce economic inefficiency and (worse) a great deal of injustice." Dagger agrees that republicans can properly "attach instrumental value to markets within the proper sphere" as long as they do not "spill into, and corrupt, other parts of life."[31]

The question for contemporary republicans, as for the commercial republicans of the 18th century, is not whether markets are incompatible with republican freedom, but rather what kind of justification for markets a commitment to republican freedom can yield.[32] If their commitment to virtue gives republicans reason to be suspicious of a politics that treats individual preferences as givens in public life, their concern with arbitrary power gives them reason to be equally suspicious of a politics that seeks to place as wide a range of social outcomes as possible in the hands of the market. A republican world is one in which citizens have to make collective decisions, fallible but binding, not only about matters of economic policy, but also about matters of public concern more generally speaking. In such a world, morally dubious preferences – whether racist, sexist, or merely selfish – are not treated simply as "tastes" but must be publicly defended and subjected to the evaluation and judgment of the political community. As Albert Hirschman has observed, "[a] taste is

---

[31] Pettit, "Freedom in the Market," *Politics, Philosophy and Economics* 5 (2006), pp. 134, 141 (cf. *Republicanism*, p. 205); Sunstein, *Free Markets and Social Justice* (New York: Oxford University Press, 1997), pp. 9, 4; Dagger, "Neo-Republicanism and the Civic Economy," p. 158.

[32] Thus although Gerald Gaus is correct to point out that republicans are skeptical about the moral legitimacy of many market transactions, he "goes too far," as Dagger puts it, in arguing that from a republican point of view "the market is almost totally delegitimized": "Backwards into the Future: Neorepublicanism as a Postsocialist Critique of Market Society," *Social Philosophy and Policy* 20 (2003), p. 68; cf. Dagger, "Neo-Republicanism and the Civic Economy," p. 157.

almost defined as a preference about which you do not argue – *de gustibus non est disputandum*," but "[a] taste about which you argue, with others or yourself, ceases ipso facto being a taste – it turns into a *value*" – and "*de valoribus est disputandum*."[33] Similarly, in such a world, the negative externalities of economic behavior – poverty, unemployment, economic vulnerability, ecological degradation – are treated not as regrettable but unavoidable by-products of life in a "free" society to be handled as far as possible by non-political means, but rather as matters of direct public concern.

Thus institutionally speaking, we have on the one hand a view that says that social outcomes should be determined for better or worse by the consciously expressed will of the political community, and on the other hand a view that says that social outcomes should be determined as far as possible by the anonymous and impersonal mechanism of the market. Morally speaking, we have on the one hand a view that says that freedom consists in a willingness to take responsibility for the larger social consequences of one's actions, and on the other hand a view that says that freedom consists in the renunciation of such responsibility and of the moral imperatives that go along with it. According to the former view, the pursuit of freedom requires that when power is exercised over us, we have a say in determining how it is exercised, or at least that we can be reasonably confident that its exercise will advance our interests and those of society as a whole. According to the latter, the pursuit of freedom requires that we carve out a space within which individuals can do as they please with what belongs to them. A theory that focuses on the contrast between republican and market freedom presents us, in other words, with a choice between *responsibility* and *irresponsibility* as models of human freedom – a choice that is easier to grasp than Pettit's distinction between non-domination and non-interference, of more obvious practical import than Pocock's distinction between civic humanistic and juristic discourses of freedom, and crisper than Berlin's distinction between negative and positive liberty.[34]

[33] Albert O. Hirschman, "Against Parsimony: Three Easy Ways of Complicating Some Categories of Economic Discourse," in idem, *Rival Views of Market Society and Other Recent Essays* (New York: Viking, 1986), pp. 145, 147 (original emphasis).
[34] There is some precedent for linking freedom and responsibility: David Miller has argued, for example, that "the appropriate condition for regarding an obstacle as a constraint on freedom is that some other person or persons can be held morally responsible for its existence," and Philip Pettit has written an entire book based on the premise that freedom consists in "fitness to be held responsible" for the consequences of one's actions. See David Miller, "Constraints on Freedom," *Ethics* 94 (1983), quoted at p. 72, and Pettit, *A*

Each of these positions captures an important set of intuitions: The defenders of republican freedom remind us that we are free only if and insofar as the powers to which we are subject are carefully supervised, and the defenders of market freedom remind us that there is a fine line between enabling the collective supervision of power and enabling the power of collective supervision. Just as there is a plain sense in which freedom means assuming the burdens of self-government, so also is there a plain sense in which freedom means being released from those burdens or not being asked to take them up at all. The question, again, is not which of these views is superior to the other, but rather what their proper sphere of application might be and whether they can be made to work together fruitfully. The key to answering this question – and I will end on this note – is to keep firmly in view the fact that the pursuit of either conception of freedom imposes substantial costs on certain people – on the vulnerable in particular. Despite the unintentional nature of markets themselves, the decision to allow a given range of social outcomes to be determined in this way rather than another is itself one that either has been or could be intentionally made. Despite the best intentions of virtuous citizens, even well-ordered political processes yield decisions that many people have reason to regard as arbitrary. We therefore cannot entirely deny responsibility for the public consequences of our private actions, any more than we can entirely prevent the public from behaving irresponsibly. In each case, the language of freedom is used to justify or encourage forms of behavior that are considered socially desirable on other grounds, not to identify a "real" property of the individuals or institutions concerned. By exploring the origins and limitations of republican and market freedom, and by fleshing out the ethical and practical implications of each view, I hope to have made it less likely that we will fall into this particular ideological fallacy.

Theory of Freedom: From the Psychology to the Politics of Agency (New York: Oxford University Press, 2001), and cf. chapter 5 of Hayek's *Constitution of Liberty*. It is less common to see freedom explicitly associated with irresponsibility, although I take it that this is the intuition to which Berlin appeals when he defines negative liberty in terms of "the area within which the subject...is or should be left to do or be what he is able to do or be, without interference by other persons": "Two Concepts of Liberty," in idem, *Liberty*, ed. Henry Hardy (New York: Oxford University Press, 2002 [1969]), p. 169.

Index